keep on running the story of island records

Edited by Chris Salewicz

I never expected Island Records to grow into the international phenomenon it became. When I was starting out making my first record with Lance Hayward in 1959, all I wanted to do was to get that one album released. Even in Britain when at first I was only releasing Jamaican singles, I felt I was in a different business entirely from the world of EMI and Decca – they controlled 95 per cent of the UK pop business but that wasn't my world.

When the 'underground rock' thing started to happen, I could see a big change was taking place. Everything was starting to break down. The whole thing became more jazz and more loose. Which fit in with what I was about: my roots were Jamaica and jazz. I was in the right place at the right time.

I was looking for a label for popular material because Island was so identifiable as a label just doing Jamaican music. Then I realised I couldn't get rid of the name Island, because it was the overall name of the company. So that's when I came up with the idea of the pink Island label, because I thought it was so far away from Jamaican music that people wouldn't make the connection. Later, when we had such success with Bob Marley, it was as though the Jamaican connection had come full circle: when U2 would come down to Jamaica to visit, it felt like an expansion of that.

I was always very interested in artwork. If you felt that the artwork was intriguing then there must be something going on inside. There's some thought, there's some creativity. Artwork was very important to Island's life. You can see in this book how Island's artwork developed and transformed itself, always seeming a reflection of the larger world.

I was very fortunate to connect with some great individuals along the way: songwriters, artists, designers, producers, film-makers, recording engineers, video directors and many, many talented people who proudly worked at Island over the years to introduce and promote their work.

Chris Blackwell

Chris Blackwell with Junior Marvin (left), Bob Marley and Jacob Miller on a 1980 trip to Brazil. Photo taken by Nathalie Delon.

Chris Blackwell with Countryman (centre) and
Dickie Jobson on the set of the film *Countryman*
in Jamaica. Picture by Nathalie Delon.

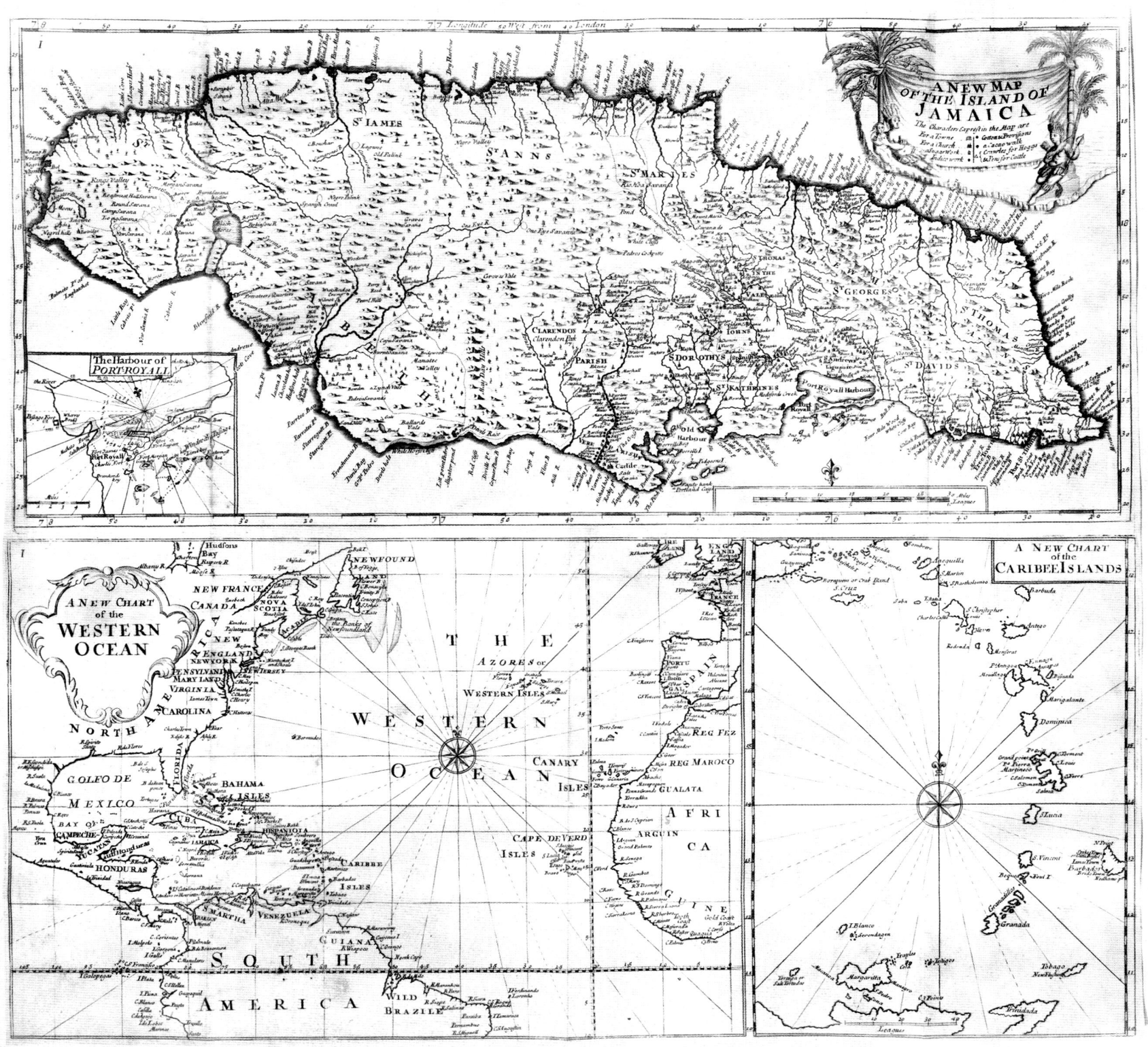

out of jamaica
the pink label
season of the witch
glitterball
roots-rock reggae
singular voices
the tuff gong
globalisation
from africa and beyond
re-birth of the cool
the new millennium

out of jamaica

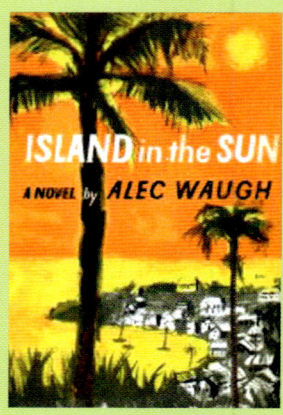

Lance Hayward (bottom left), the first act released on Island Records, performing in Kingston.

The book cover for Alec Waugh's *Island in the Sun*, Chris Blackwell's inspiration for the name of his label.

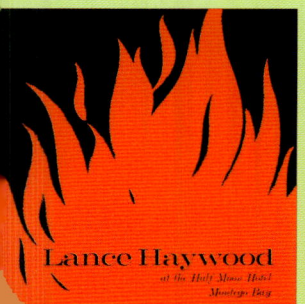

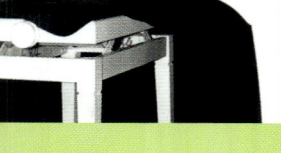

By Chris Salewicz

Jamaicans in the mid-1950s were familiar with whom they should stay away from. Specifically, that strange tribe of outcasts known as Rastafarians: even the downtown ghetto-dwellers knew that these eccentric-appearing individuals – known at the time on the island as 'beardmen' – carried pieces of dead bodies in the bags they all bore.

Such a view had been inculcated into the mind of a young man called Chris Blackwell who, when he was 19, went with a couple of friends on a motorboat ride from the former pirate haven of Port Royal along the south coast of the island. When the boat became stranded in a swamp on a completely isolated part of the coastline, however, he struck out for the shore. After about four hours of struggling through the swamps he came upon a beach. By this time he was completely exhausted. He felt like he was dying from thirst. Hearing a voice, he looked up: a Rastafarian, his dreadlocks tumbling about him like Iliana vines, stood over him. The dread led the young Chris Blackwell to a nearby encampment, where he gave him some water. Chris collapsed asleep.

When he awoke it was to the sound of voices reading from the Bible and reasoning. As the Bible continued to be read, he was fed ital food. Chris Blackwell would never be the same again.

Not long after, in 1958, Chris Blackwell, who had been teaching water-skiing at the Half Moon Hotel in Montego Bay, decided to record the young, blind jazz pianist who was playing with his band at the hotel. He was called Lance Hayward. His first recording, an LP of jazz standards released in 1959, was the relatively inauspicious birth of an independent record label destined to have a vast influence on global popular music – Island Records. Soon after, Blackwell had his first hit with a local artist called Laurel Aitken and the tune 'Boogie In My Bones'; the record made the Cuban-born Aitken the biggest star in Jamaica in 1960. With the proceeds Chris Blackwell set up shop in a small office on South Odeon Avenue in uptown Kingston's thronging commercial suburb of Half Way Tree.

In 1961 the first James Bond movie, *Dr No*, was filmed on location in Jamaica. Drawing on his local expertise, producer Harry Saltzman made Blackwell his production assistant. When the film, destined to be enormously successful, wrapped, Saltzman offered him a more permanent position. Torn between the two paths diverging before him, Chris Blackwell took advice from a local seer, a Lebanese woman. His future was clear to her: he should stick with the record business, she said.

Her prediction was soon proved accurate: in 1962 Blackwell moved his operation to the UK, acquiring the rights to the recordings of the Jamaican sound system giants Sir Coxson

10 | Keep On Running

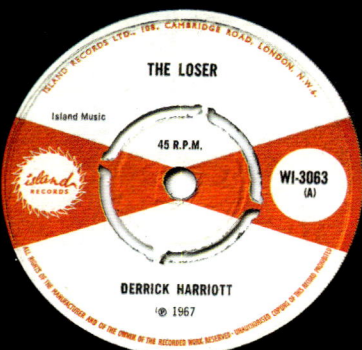

Chris Blackwell on the set of *Dr No* in 1961 (left); to his right is the actress Ursula Andress; behind her is Sean Connery, the first James Bond.

Dodd, Duke Reid and King Edwards among others, selling them to Jamaican immigrants. So began Island Records in Britain. There were four original partners – Blackwell, Graham Goodall, an Australian music engineer living in Jamaica, the Chinese-Jamaican record producer Leslie Kong, and Kong's brother. In May, 1962, the four of them invested a total of £4,000 in Island Records Ltd - only £2,700 of this was used. Goodall was later to leave the consortium and start his own label

Chris Blackwell would personally deliver the records to the shops in the West Indian communities of London, Birmingham and Manchester, driving up and down the just completed M1 motorway in his blue Mini-Cooper. Records like Jimmy Cliff's 'Miss Jamaica' and Derrick Morgan's 'Forward March' moved quickly, such approval justifying Blackwell's decision to move to Britain: a strong title would sell between twenty and thirty thousand copies.

With the intention 'that you could compete with yourself on the record shops' shelves,' Chris Blackwell introduced additional brand labels under Island's umbrella title: Black Swan, for example, which released Jamaican ska stars; and the Jump Up label, which featured the best Trinidadian calypsoes, like those of the celebrated Lord Kitchener. The idiosyncratic thinking of the citizens of the Caribbean islands was obliged to be taken into consideration: Jamaican artists coming to the UK might sign deals with both Chris Blackwell and, for example, Emil Shallett's Melodisc label – accordingly, to avoid contractual problems, the Maytals initially recorded for Island as The Mighty Vikings.

Island's album releases were less target-marketed, more pragmatic. For example, one of the first LPs issued by Island, under the Surprise Records label, was *Music to Strip By* – it came packaged with a G-string. Another big seller was based on the greatest political scandal to rock post-war Britain: *That Affair*, which celebrated the Profumo case, in which the combined sexual intrigues of goodtime girl Christine Keeler, Tory Minister of Defence John Profumo, a Russian diplomat and a Jamaican immigrant called Lucky Gordon unwittingly brought down the Conservative government; on the record Blackwell himself played the part of Gordon.

Meanwhile, Island's Jamaican 'pre-release' 45s had hit a chord not merely with the immigrant population. This was the era when the most powerful underground force in Britain was its mass tribal group of Mods. Hipper than the rest, the Mods took

> At first Chris Blackwell would personally deliver Island's Jamaican sounds to shops in the West Indian communities of London, Birmingham and Manchester, driving up and down the recently opened M1 motorway in his blue-and-white Mini-Cooper.

to Jamaican music and styles, adopting the immigrants' love of mohair suits and pork-pie hats. In clubs such as the RamJam in Brixton, blacks and whites, both wearing the same uniforms, danced side-by-side to the same sounds. This cultural shift might only have been taking place at one of society's extreme margins, but it was still revolutionary, reflecting a worldwide shift in thinking that had its most public expression in the Freedom marches of the United States.

The sound of Britain was also changing. Britain's North Sea ship-based pirate radio stations beamed out a previously unimaginable succession of pop music, based on American Top 40 radio. With great suddenness, the desperate greyness of the 1950s was dissolved irrevocably. The first of these pirate stations was run by an Irishman called Ronan O'Rahilly. He had already founded The Scene, London's top Mod club by virtue of its never-ending source of the best American black music, courtesy of Guy Stevens, its DJ. Stevens was believed to have the best collection of R&B in Britain; groups like the Rolling Stones and the Who would go to visit him to discover new songs for their repertoire. Chris Blackwell offered Stevens the chance to run Sue, a label releasing the hottest American R&B whose first hit was Inez & Charlie Foxx's 'Mockingbird'.

In 1963, Blackwell had set up a production company called BPR with promotion man Chris Peers and producer Harry Robinson: the idea was to find artists, produce them and lease the tapes to major record companies. The second tune was a hit – The Caravelles' breathy 'You Don't Have To Be A Baby To Cry'. The same year Roy and Millie's ska tune 'We'll Meet' had been a big-selling record for Island – Roy was Roy Patton and Millie was Millie Small, who was just fourteen years old. From Clarendon in the centre of Jamaica, Millie had been given a break by Coxson Dodd, the Jamaican sound system and record company entrepreneur, and had begun to record for his Studio One label, for thirty shillings a side. 'We'll Meet' was a tune that had been recorded for Dodd, such an obvious hit that Dodd paid both her and Roy £5 a side. This song and particularly Millie's voice was the most popular of all the records amongst Chris Blackwell's friends: so he decided to bring Millie over to England and try and produce a pop hit with her.

Five years previously, in New York, Blackwell had bought a copy of the original 'My Boy Lollipop' by the American singer Barbie Gaye and sold it to one of the sound system guys in Jamaica – first making a tape copy for himself. Going through various ideas while looking for material for Millie to record now that she was in England he discovered the tape: it was given a ska arrangement by the great Jamaican jazz guitarist and arranger Ernest Ranglin. 'It came out exactly as I heard it in my head – it seemed to be a hit,' said Blackwell. The tune, licensed to the Philips' Fontana label, sold six million copies and Millie toured worldwide.

Millie with then Jamaican Prime Minister Edward Seaga at the St Peter's Square offices of Island Records in 1987; Seaga was being presented with Marcus Garvey's Rod of Correction: a relative of an Island employee had been in the next hospital bed when the great Jamaican prophet of black consciousness had died in Hammersmith in 1940.

Island itself, however, was in financial distress. At the urging of Tim Clark, another refugee from Britain's colonies (Kenya, in his particular case), the album *Rugby Songs* was released on the Surprise label. The record, a collection of bawdy bar-room ballads, cost hardly anything to make, and sold over quarter of a million copies, Island's biggest LP success up to then. *Rugby Songs II* was equally successful.

Meeting Edward Seaga at the 1964 World Fair in New York, Blackwell was introduced to a young Jamaican singer called Jimmy Cliff - he had already released a few 45s by the artist but they had never met. The pair clicked, and Blackwell suggested that he come and build his career in the UK.

Taking Millie up to appear on the influential and important ATV pop show, *Thank Your Lucky Stars*, Blackwell checked out a local act called The Spencer Davis Group. The singer, he said, 'sounded like Ray Charles on helium as his voice was so high-pitched.' This singer's name was Steve Winwood, and like Millie he was also only fourteen years old. Looking for a hit for the group - their first three records, licensed to Fontana, had made the top 50 - Blackwell checked another of his artists, the songwriter Jackie Edwards. Edwards had just written a perfect song for the group, 'Keep On Running'. The hit was followed by even larger successes – 'Somebody Help Me', 'Gimme Some Lovin'', and 'I'm a Man'. These successes caused Island to move on up, to new offices at 155 Oxford Street in London's West End.

The licensing of Jamaican records, however, remained the mainstay of Island's operation, although Guy Stevens continued to lead his forays into American R&B with the Sue label. But a major cultural shift was underway. Marijuana and LSD opened up the heads of the hip elite and their followers. Artists and audiences alike began to perceive the artistic worth and potential longevity of the 'youth craze' of pop music. 'Underground rock' was born, a form that shifted the balance from the three minute single to one in which the album artist dominated the culture. It also caused old alliances to dissolve.

The splintering asunder of The Spencer Davis Group created Steve Winwood's Traffic, released on Island Records, which through a combination of synchronicity and serendipity, now launched itself anew, as the quintessential 'underground' rock label. Traffic perfectly captured the spirit and mood of the time, as did its label. As the dream of the Sixties was realised, in all its liberated, day-glo colours, in the last three years of the decade, so the most creative musical artists of the period clamoured to record for Island.

The sound of Britain was also changing. From Britain's North Sea, ship-based pirate radio stations beamed out a previously unimaginable succession of pop music, based on American Top 40 radio.

Keep On Running | 15

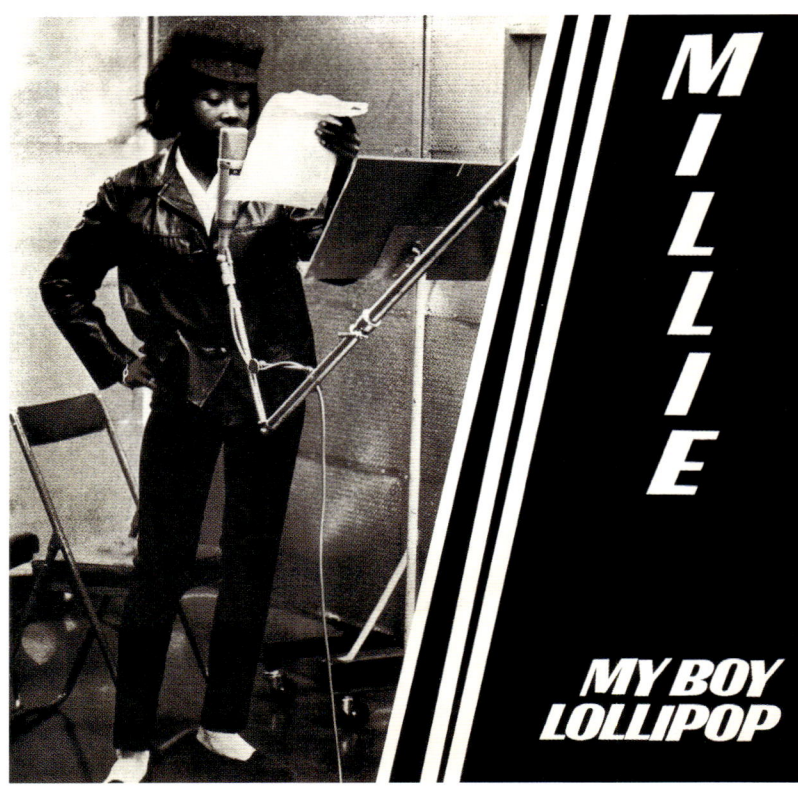

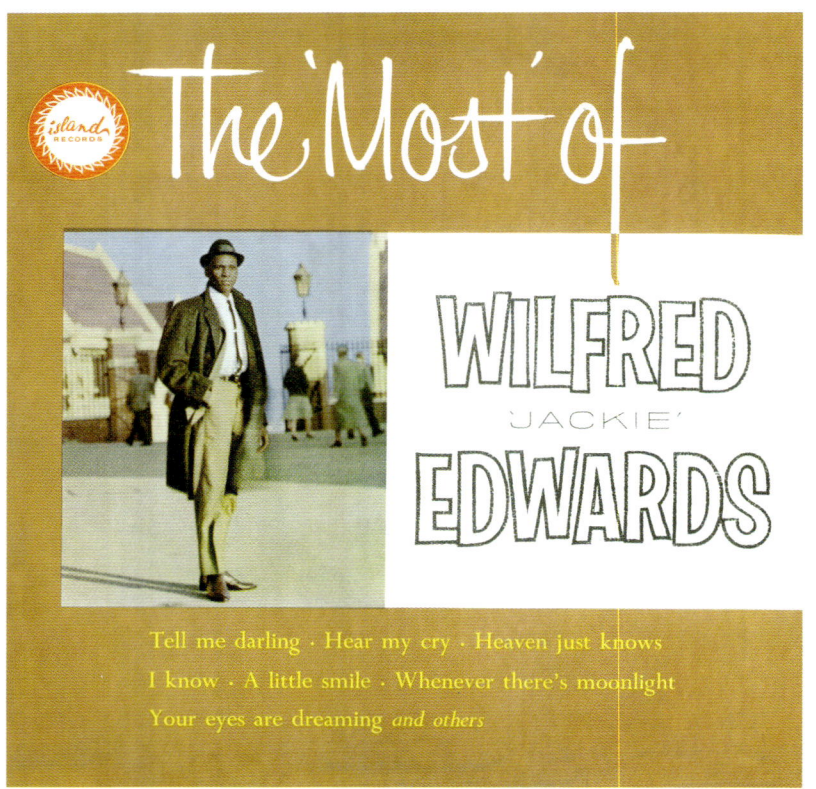

Jamaica's seminal Eric Dean Orchestra (above), featuring a young Ernest Ranglin on guitar and Don Drummond on trombone.

Although never on Island Records, The Spencer Davis Group contributed indubitably to the future of the company. At first known in their native Birmingham as The Rhythm and Blues Quartette, the renowned residency at the Golden Eagle pub's R&B nights of guitarist Davis, keyboards-player Steve Winwood, bass-player Muff Winwood, and drummer Pete York brought them to the attention of Chris Blackwell. He signed them to Phillips Records' Fontana label, and the four-piece then became one of the hardest gigging groups in Britain. It was not until 'Keep On Running', released in November 1965, that The Spencer Davis Group really broke through: this Jackie Edwards-penned tune reached number one – as did its successor, 'Somebody Help Me', also written by Edwards, in conjunction with the multi-talented Steve Winwood. But by the time 'I'm a Man' was released in January 1967 the group was almost over. Steve Winwood was about to go off with three other Midlands musicians – Jim Capaldi, Dave Mason, and Chris Wood – and form Traffic, who would record for the new form of Island Records. Muff Winwood, meanwhile, went to work as an A&R man for Island.

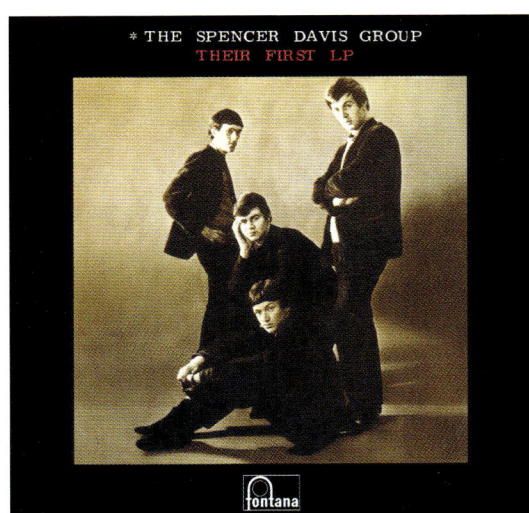

MONO IWP 3

TREAT HER RIGHT
ROY HEAD

DADDY ROLLIN' STONE
DEREK MARTIN

LITTLE LATIN LUPE LU
THE RIGHTEOUS BROTHERS

SO FAR AWAY
HANK JACOBS

HARLEM SHUFFLE
BOB AND EARL

OH! BABY
BARBARA LYNN

YOU CAN'T SIT DOWN
PHIL UPCHURCH COMBO

WATCH YOUR STEP
BOBBY PARKER

BONY MARONIE
LARRY WILLIAMS

THE LAST MINUTE
JIMMY McGRIFF

BAREFOOTIN'
ROBERT PARKER

LET THE GOOD TIMES ROLL
SHIRLEY & LEE

INCENSE
THE ANGLOS

SHOTGUN WEDDING
ROY 'C'

Part of the myth of the celebrated Guy Stevens (far left) was that when Pye Records released their first Chuck Berry singles, the record label pressed the copies directly from American Berry imports owned by him. Renowned for having the largest collection of American R&B in Britain, Stevens was regularly consulted by the likes of the Rolling Stones and the Who as to the best songs for them to cover.

Guy Stevens was the DJ at The Scene, a small basement club in Ham Yard, a cul-de-sac off Great Windmill Street in London's Soho. The Scene, a top Mod club visited regularly by The Beatles, was renowned for the finest, purest R&B tunes played there.

In April 1964 Chris Blackwell asked Stevens to run his new label, Sue Records, whose first release – and minor hit – was Charlie and Inez Foxx's 'Mockingbird'; Chris Blackwell had first heard the tune in Jamaica the previous July, and had offered Juggy Murray, the US producer who had released the song in America, to set up a UK version of his Sue Records. Subsequent Sue releases came from not only the American Sue label, but from all manner of tiny American independent record companies. Although Sue scored a memorable hit for Roy C with his 'Shotgun Wedding' title, the label, presided over by Guy Stevens, had scores of other chart entries for tunes such as Bob and Earl's 'Harlem Shuffle', James Brown's 'Night Train', Chris Kenner's 'Land of 100 Dances', Donnie Elbert's 'A Little Piece of Leather', Bobby Parker's 'Watch Your Step', and The Philip Upchurch Combo's 'You Can't Sit Down'. Under Guy Stevens, Sue Records also introduced British ears to the likes of such blues artists as Elmore James and Sonny Boy Williamson, releasing LPs by these stalwarts.

Busted for drugs, Guy Stevens received a short prison sentence, during which his entire record collection was stolen from his home, severely traumatizing him when he was released. However, he bounced back, discovering, naming, and producing Mott the Hoople, as well as Spooky Tooth and Free.

In 1979 Guy Stevens produced The Clash's *London Calling* album, later named Rolling Stone's Album of the Decade. Less than two years after that record's release, however, Guy Stevens died: he had overdosed on drugs prescribed to wean him from a debilitating alcohol habit.

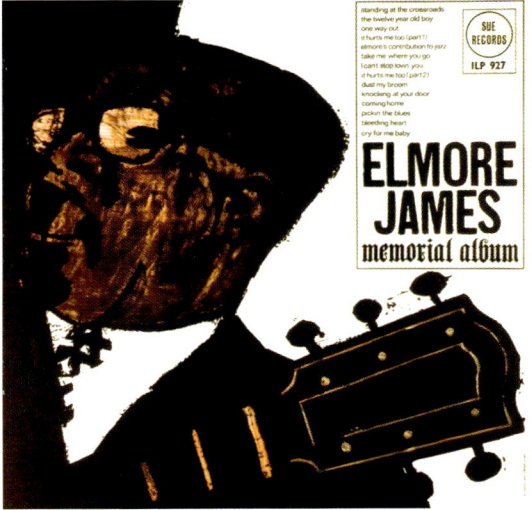

Keep On Running | 21

The original Traffic line-up, from the cover of their second LP: (left-to-right) Jim Capaldi (drummer), Chris Wood (multi-instrumentalist), Steve Winwood (keyboards), Dave Mason (guitar). Traffic fired Island's move into 'underground rock'.

the pink label

The Hipgnosis cover image says it all: a group of twenty-six scruffy musicians dressed in the style of the period and set against a wintry backdrop. It's a recognisably English landscape – green, manicured, with old oaks – and the faces are pinched with cold, hard scrabbling youth and, perhaps, dim memories of rationing past.

by Jon Savage

Except for the one black face – Rebop Anthony Kwaku Baah, then of Wynder K. Frog, later to join Traffic – and the one female, Sandy Denny, moving out of shot on the right front, all the musicians sport long hair: some have sideburns, even beards. Greatcoats and scarves abound, a bit of fur and leather.

It's just like a school-photo: Island Records, Class of Early 1969. You can see members of Traffic, Fairport Convention, Spooky Tooth, Clouds, Wynder K.Frog, Nirvana – Patrick Campbell–Lyons' moon-face is a dead-ringer for Oscar Wilde, Free (serious students) and Jethro Tull (making silly faces at the back).

Titled *You Can All Join In*, this was a perfect piece of image casting. The musicians look human, approachable. There are enough of them to please every palate, offer enough models for identification. For that is the point: inclusiveness. This is a label with a strong identity, and you too can be part of the Island family. All you have to do is fork out 14/6d.

The late sixties were the golden age of the sampler: the trend had started in 1968 with CBS UK's *The Rock Machine Turns You On* – fourteen tracks for the price of under two singles. In a period of rapid musical expansion and heavily restricted pop TV and radio, these cheap and cheerful albums were a marketing godsend.

Several of them, including *You Can All Join In*, sold well enough to make the LP top twenty. For many people of a certain generation, samplers were the first albums they could afford, assuming an importance way beyond their original intention. They were a window into another, expansive world.

On the rear sleeve of *You Can All Join In* are pictures of eight Island albums by the featured artists, including *Traffic*,

Keep On Running | 23

> 'Paper Sun' had the requisite 1967 flourishes – the tablas, the sitar – but it also had a relaxed and spacious feel that belied the bitter La Dolce Vita lyric.

All of Us, What We Did On Our Holidays, This Was – groundbreaking records all. It was perfect timing: for Spring 1969 saw the emergence of Island Records as a major musical force.

The tracks on *You Can All Join In* and *Nice Enough To Eat* – the second Island sampler of 1969 – have become etched into a whole generation's DNA: 'A Song For Jeffrey', 'Meet On the Ledge', 'Rainbow Chaser', 'Better By You, Better Than Me', 'At the Crossroads', 'Woman'.

You Can All Join In was the album that established pink Island – so-called because of the label on the records, with its distinctive colour and elaborate logos, a design which changed twice in 1969, from an orange/black 'eye' design to a more elaborate black block and finally a large lower case 'I'. And with this pink label, during this period of a few years, Island came to define British rock.

Island's move into rock music did not happen overnight. Chris Blackwell had encountered The Spencer Davis Group during an early 1964 tour with Millie (then high in the charts with 'My Boy Lollipop') and guided their move into fully-fledged pop stars: four top tens and two number ones from 1965 through until early 1967.

The team that he gathered around the SPG was the future Pink Island in embryo. Much of the obscure black material that the group covered was sourced by Blackwell's associate, Guy Stevens, a brilliant DJ and music obsessive then running the Scene Club and heading the Island-backed Sue label – which had a deservedly high reputation for their issues of blues and soul material.

The SPG's hit songs were provided by Jamaican writer and singer Jackie Edwards, who would release several pink Island 45's during 1967. And from late '66, the American producer Jimmy Miller began working with the group, remixing 'Gimme Some Lovin'' and adding extra percussion on the storming 'I'm A Man'.

Miller had already worked with SPG singer Stevie Winwood on the early 1966 45, 'Incense', released on Fontana. The Anglos were supposed to be a New York band but were in fact Winwood and Miller with a back up group: the single was a brilliant, intense piece of blue-eyed soul.

Other rock 45s released on the white and red Island during 1966 came from a brief but fertile link-up with Kim Fowley. There was his slice of acid agitprop, 'The Trip', and two storming freakbeat singles with Them remnants the Belfast Gypsies: 'Gloria's Dream' and (as the Belfast Gypsies) 'People Let's Freak Out'.

24 | Keep On Running

Pink Island was launched in early spring 1967 with Owen Grey's tough version of Ray Sharpe's 'Help Me', backed with another version of 'Incense'. But it was the third single that really put the label on the map: 'Paper Sun', the first 45 by Traffic, which reached the top five in high summer 1967.

This was not just a big hit, but the harbinger of a new musical mood. Formed by Stevie Winwood and refugees from other Birmingham beat/R&B bands – Dave Mason, Chris Wood and Jim Capaldi – Traffic were determined not to be caught on the relentless mid-sixties' musical treadmill.

'Paper Sun' had the requisite 1967 flourishes – the tablas, the sitar – but it also had a relaxed and spacious feel that belied the bitter La Dolce Vita lyric. This was not teen pop or functional club music but something different: a new form that could encompass Indian drones, R&B basslines, and jazz improvisation.

Throughout the summer and autumn of 1967, Island continued to release a string of 45s. Nirvana's 'Tiny Goddess' and 'Pentecost Hotel' were both pirate radio favourites: beautifully produced orchestral pieces that hoped to catch some of the baroque pop feel initiated by Procul Harum's 'Whiter Shade of Pale'.

From Carlisle, The V.I.P.'s second single for Blackwell was a late mod stomper, 'Straight Down To the Bottom' – written and produced by Jimmy Miller. Fourteen Island singles later, they had become Art, and produced a pounding cover of Buffalo Springfield's 'For What It's Worth' ('What's That Sound').

But Traffic were the label's signature group. 1967 saw two further top ten hits – the delightfully whimsical 'Hole In My Shoe' and 'Here We Go Round the Mulberry Bush' – but the real news was the release of their first album, *Mr. Fantasy*: a top ten record and the real start of Island as a rock label.

The Beatles' *Sergeant Pepper's Lonely Hearts Club Band* had set the standard, and, like many 1967 albums, *Mr. Fantasy* was a total package: of artwork and music that broadcast the existence of an alternative world. With its increased cover space and improved sound, the album became the favoured format for cutting-edge groups.

From the beginning, Traffic were presented as different. Stories in the pop press remarked upon the fact that they had fled the city in favour of communal life in a remote cottage, while in their Island biog 'Stephen' Winwood wrote: 'I live on the Berkshire Downs, and my only influence is my environment and past mistakes'.

The *Mr. Fantasy* record cover shows Traffic being entertained by a sacrificial, hieratic puppet figure in their sparse Berkshire cottage while a fire blazes in the open range. Elsewhere there are pictures of the quite obviously stoned group members in various rural settings, with dry ice and esoteric props.

Traffic were supposed to be a 'feel' band, and they were encouraged to be so by their producer, Jimmy Miller. Recording at Olympic Studios in Barnes, Miller's function was, as engineer (and, later, Jimi Hendrix producer) Eddie Kramer told mixonline.com in 2003, 'a terrific catalyst'. 'He had a great sense of humor. And he was unstoppable in the sense that his energy

From the beginning Traffic were presented as different. Stories in the pop press remarked upon the fact that they had fled the city in favour of communal life in a remote cottage.

CEREMONY.
An Electronic Mass.
Written by Pierre Henry and Gary Wright.
Performed by
SPOOKY TOOTH/PIERRE HENRY.

level was always up. He really, really dug the music; he was always so into the band: "How can I get you guys to feel this track the way I'm feeling it?" He would sing parts. He was like a master of ceremonies.' Kramer remembered when they were cutting *Mr. Fantasy*: 'we were in the middle of a take and there's a part where the tempo changes – it jumps – and I look around and Jimmy Miller's not in the control room. The next thing I see out of the corner of my eye is Jimmy hauling ass across the room, running full-tilt. He jumps up on the riser, picks up a pair of maracas and gets them to double the tempo! That, to me, was the most remarkable piece of production assistance I'd ever seen. They were shocked to see him out there, exhorting them to double the tempo. Their eyes kind of lit up. It was amazing. That was Jimmy!'

The musical content on *Mr. Fantasy* oscillated between these spirited live band performances and Dave Mason's Toy-town psych studio creations. This was indicative of a deeper split in the band, exacerbated by the huge success of Mason's 'Hole In My Shoe' in the autumn. Having hits had not been part of the plan.

The result was that, almost as soon as *Mr. Fantasy* was released, Mason had left the band for the first time. In the short term, he would produce Family's first album *Music In a Doll's House* – a high water mark of UK psych – and release the droning, medieval sounding solo single 'Little Women'.

Other rock long players released by Pink Island during 1967 and early 1968 included the first by Nirvana, *The Story of Simon Simopath* – a concept album enlivened by the "Pentecost Hotel" 45 – and two transitional records by the former V.I.P.'s: *Supernatural Fairy Tales* as Art, and *It's All About* as Spooky Tooth. Like many musicians from the mid-sixties, the members of Spooky Tooth had passed through Mod, R&B and psychedelia. Adding American Gary Wright on organ and vocals, they began specialising in doomy, heavy rock – of which their first 45 as Spooky Tooth, 'Sunshine Help Me', was an excellent example.

Throughout this period Island continued to issue singles and albums in a variety of styles, including Soul, Ska, Rock Steady, Southern Soul, Blues and – in summer 1968 – Guy Stevens' own Testament of Rock'n'Roll: a collection of old Sue 45s reissued in a psychedelic cover to catch the brief Rock'n'Roll revival.

It wasn't until autumn 1968 that Rock Island flourished. Released in October, Traffic's second LP – simply entitled *Traffic* – went top ten. Dave Mason was, briefly, back in the fold,

contributing the funky 'Feelin' Alright' and the album-opener of 'You Can All Join In' (briefly released as a 45).

This was quickly followed by the first album from a group who had come up through the British Blues Boom. Jethro Tull's *This Was* also went top ten. It was a live snapshot: a mixture of Roland Kirk-style noodling, blues improvisations and taut, exciting riff rockers like the single 'A Song For Jeffrey'.

The cover was extraordinary: the four members of the group were made up to look twice, or three times their age – in a rustic studio set. Live, they were dominated by the antics of front-man Ian Anderson: a threatening presence with his long greatcoat, straggly beard, one-legged flute-playing and manic stare.

Around this time Island released the second and best record by the group who by autumn 1968 almost seemed like an anomaly, the ghosts of psychedelia past. With lush orchestrations by Syd Dale, Nirvana's *All Of Us* contained the classic singles 'Tiny Goddess' and the Top 40 'Rainbow Chaser' – with its phased strings.

It also featured Island's single most disturbing record cover: a severe, grey upon grey still from a Leni Riefenstahl propaganda film showing various victorious generals – including Napoleon – progressing triumphantly through the serried bodies of the vanquished: not an image that reflected the baroque pop within.

The organically shifting Traffic line-up kept you on your toes: who would be in them next? This Brian Cooke shot of the group for the *Welcome to the Canteen* album artwork was shot at Mike's Café in Blenheim Crescent in London's Notting Hill – convenient for the Island headquarters in nearby Basing Street – in July 1971. (left-to-right) Ric Grech (bass), 'Reebop' Kwaku Baah (congas, timbalas & bongos), Jim Capaldi (vocals, tambourine, percussion), Steve Winwood (vocals, organ, electric piano, guitar), Chris Wood (saxophones, flute, electric piano, organ), Dave Mason (vocals, lead guitar, acoustic guitar), Jim Gordon (drums).

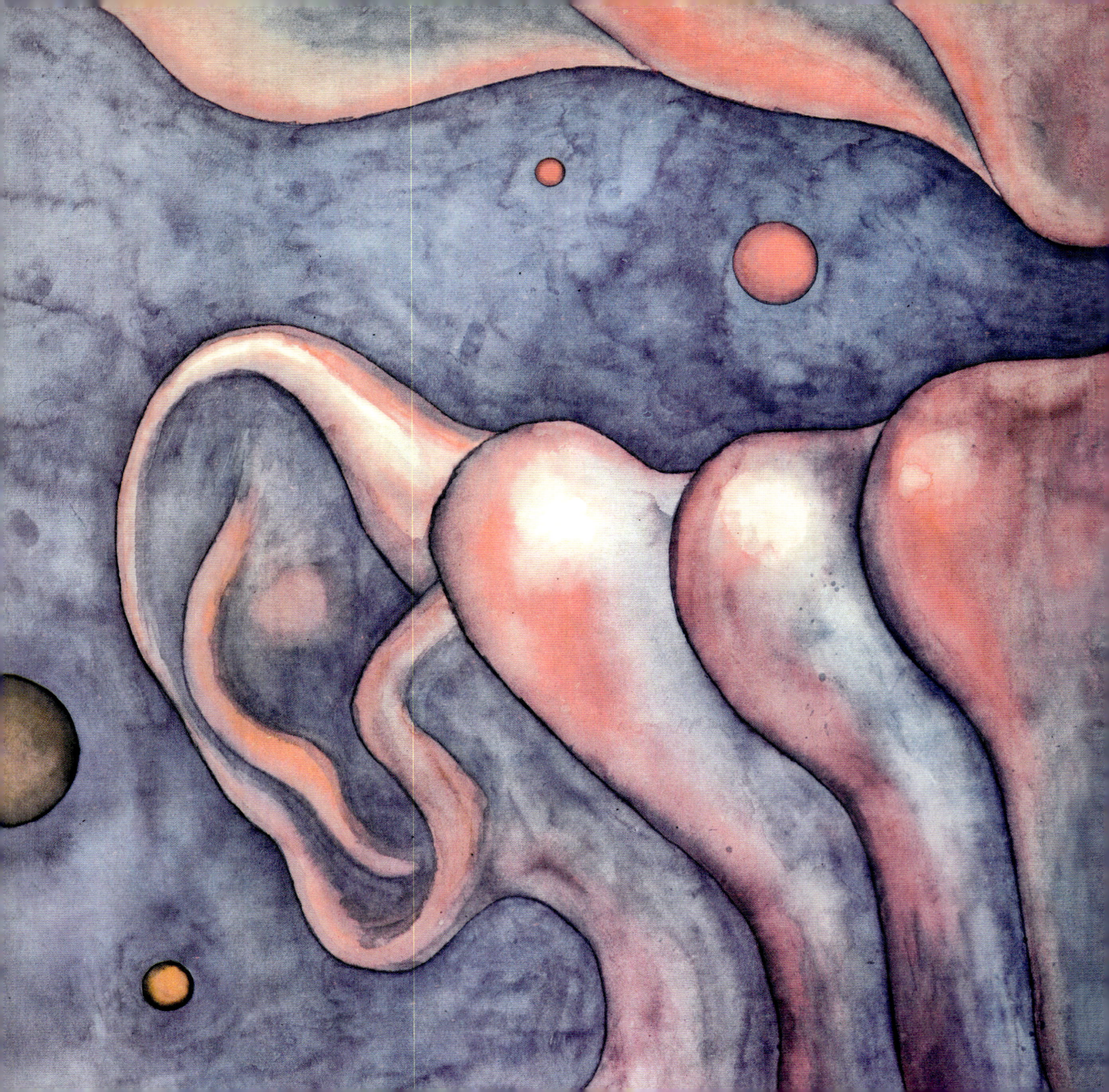

Island also released the first album by Free in late 1968, *Tons of Sobs*. This teenage Blues group had only been playing for a few months before they were signed by Chris Blackwell: he remembered them as 'an unbelievable band. They were all very young, but great players, with one of the all-time best singers in rock.'

Despite their ages – ranging between 20 and 16 – Free arrived as if fully formed: sporting a gatefold sleeve with an allusive photo by Mike Sida, *Tons of Sobs* was a winning mixture of braggadocio and depression, with tough blues covers rubbing against depressive lyrics and slow, almost Gregorian chants.

1969 was the year that Island really took off, with key albums by Fairport Convention and White Noise – a groundbreaking electronic effort by David Vorhaus and Brian Hodgson and Delia Derbyshire from the BBC Radiophonic Workshop. The next major record was Spooky Tooth's second, *Spooky Two*.

Issued in five different coloured sleeves, with an inside photo depicting the band communing with nature, this remains a storming rock record: full of funky breaks – the much-sampled drum pattern on 'Waiting On The Wind' – depressive chants, and monstrous riff-rockers, like the infamous 'Better By You, Better Than Me'.

In the summer, the label had its first number one album with Jethro Tull's *Stand Up* – a more focussed effort with an infamous gimmick: a pop-up inner sleeve. Both *Stand Up* and the top three single 'Living in the Past' showed the group moving away from strict blues into their own barbed medieval style.

That was the last Tull record for Island proper, as manager Terry Ellis went off to form Chrysalis with spin-off band Blodwyn Pig, whose one album for Island – which sported a memo-rable front cover image of a pig wearing shades and phones, smoking a spliff – was also released that spring. (Chris Blackwell had promised Terry Ellis that if he had ten Top 20 hits he would give him his own label; after Ellis had had nine of those hits, Blackwell let him start up the Chrysalis label.)

By now there was a recognisable Island patch, building on the label's soul tradition and extending it into funky rock, with lavish, eye-catching sleeves. Free's second, eponymously-titled album was the perfect example, with another arresting Mike Sida cover – of yes, a naked woman etched out in stars against a background of sun and clouds.

Produced by Chris Blackwell, Free toned down the heavy blues in favour of measured, almost pastoral pieces like 'Lying in the Sunshine' and 'Mouthful of Grass'. They were not afraid to do slow, with all the four musicians – Paul Rodgers, Andy Fraser, Paul Kossoff and Simon Kirke – working in perfect, exquisite counterpoint.

Guy Stevens, meanwhile, was busy with new protégés Mott The Hoople. Christened by Stevens after a Willard Manus novel that he had read during a brief period in prison, Mott were designed to match Dylan vocals with the Procul Harum sound – with organ and piano up in the mix – and a heavy rhythm section. With its M.C. Escher cover, Mott The Hoople was a perfect 1969 product: with tough rockers – like the US single 'Rock'n Roll Queen' – rubbing up against a Dylan-esque version of Sonny's 'Laugh At Me' (originally a Protest pastiche) and the eleven minute long 'Half Moon Bay' – an extended piano-led drone.

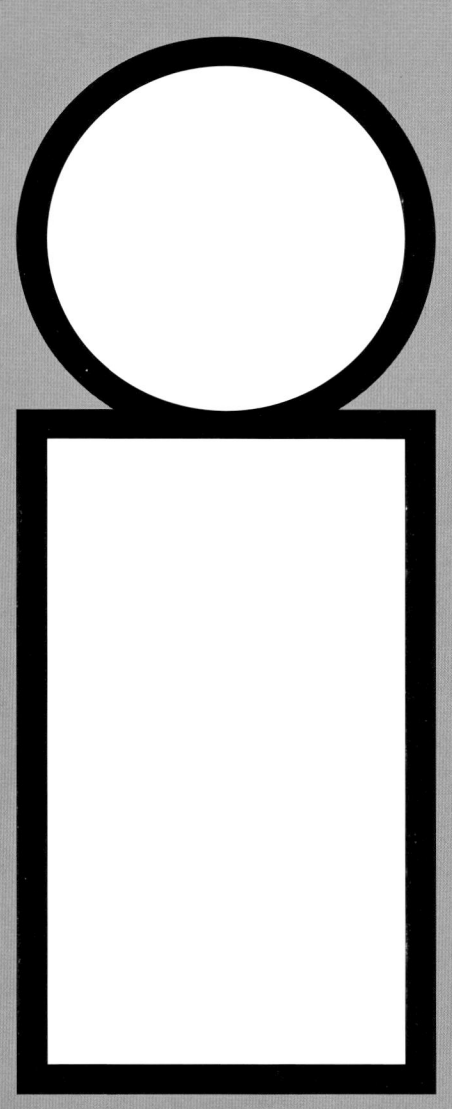

This was the era of lavish 12" sleeves, and the next two Island albums outdid the rest. Quintessence was formed out of a Ladbroke Grove commune who eschewed excessive drug use in favour of meditation and community activism – aims celebrated on their best known track, 'Notting Hill Gate'.

In Blissful Company was a convincing fusion of rock and Indian music, with an extraordinary 12 page gatefold sleeve designed by the late Barney Bubbles. There were plentiful photos of the group mixed in with Indian graphics and cut-out optical illusions: a complete guide to their life and beliefs.

In contrast, the cover of King Crimson's *In the Court of the Crimson King* relied on a single, indelible image: a close-up of a man in extremis, all in red, blue and purple, with his nostrils and gaping mouth and haunted eyes heavily accented. Inside was a smiling, shamanic face, with gesturing hands and pointed teeth.

It was Barry Godber's only cover – he died of a heart attack in early 1970 – but it perfectly reflected the music within: as Robert Fripp later stated, 'The face on the outside is the Schizoid Man, and on the inside it's the Crimson King. If you cover the smiling face, the eyes reveal an incredible sadness.'

In the Court of the Crimson King was one of the very first progressive albums, with varied time signatures and textures, a heavy use of mellotrons, allusive, complex lyrics and no track under 5 minutes. It veered from neo-Psych to meditative electronic textures to the harsh, claustrophobic nightmare of '21st Century Schizoid Man'.

This was the state of play when Island released their second sampler of 1969: *Nice Enough To Eat*. With tracks from all the big hitters – and the one-off single by hoax-turned-real-band Heavy Jelly: the Guy Stevens' produced 'I Keep Singing That Same Old Song' – it was an even more attractive proposition.

The next year was transitional for Island: some of its first wave artists – like Spooky Tooth – began to run out of steam, while the A&R policy changed to reflect the mood of the times. The psychedelic era was almost over, and in its place came singer-songwriters, hard rock bands and progressive groups.

One of the year's first releases was a one-off by Renaissance, the group put together by ex-Yardbirds Keith Relf and Jim McCarty. Relying heavily on the classical piano of John Hawken (a refugee from the Nashville Teens), it represents a joyous celebration of the freedom that musicians were given at the time, in contrast to the high-sixties pop treadmill.

That freedom was epitomised by Traffic's fourth album, *John Barleycorn Must Die*. There was another side to Island during this period, personified by artists like Fairport Convention and John and Beverley Martyn: the convincing marriage of traditional English folk music with West Coast or American rock.

With its rustic, worn sleeve, *John Barleycorn Must Die* was relaxed and mature: Traffic's finest hour. Its six long songs – two derived from an aborted Steve Winwood solo album –

> With its rustic, worn sleeve, John Barleycorn Must Die was relaxed and mature: Traffic's finest hour. Its six long songs – two derived from an aborted Steve Winwood solo album – mashed up rock, soul, jazz and, in the stunning title track, traditional British folk.

FREE

mashed up rock, soul, jazz and, in the stunning title track, traditional British folk. Naturally, the group split almost as soon as it was released.

The next highpoint was Free's breakthrough long-player, *Fire and Water*, released hot on the heels of their number one single, 'All Right Now'. Apart from the elongated version of the hit single, highlights included the glacially slow 'Oh I Wept' and the punk protest of 'Mr Big', complete with manically popping bass solo.

Another significant 1970 release was the first album by Emerson Lake and Palmer, a prog supergroup put together from members of the Nice, Atomic Rooster and King Crimson. Although the group would become notoriously excessive, *Emerson Lake and Palmer* was restrained and, in places, showed their mod/soul roots.

Despite these successes, there was a sense that, by the time of the third Island sampler, *Bumpers*, the heyday of Pink Island was beginning to wane. There were good records by Bronco and Crimson off-shoot McDonald & Giles, but label stalwarts like Quintessence, Mott The Hoople and even Free were treading water.

There was a move into jazz-rock and country rock, neither of which dispelled the feeling that the musicians who had come up through the sixties – clubland and psychedelia – had hit the wall. As if to mark the end of this era, in late 1970 Island changed the Pink 'i' label for the long-lasting 'palm tree' logo.

That's not to say that none of them produced any good music after then. Free combined and recombined several times over the next few years – to great effective on storming 45s like 'Wishing Well' – before fragmenting into Sharks (Andy Fraser) and the much more successful Bad Company (Rodgers and Kirke).

Traffic continued their erratic course over another five albums – including *The Low Spark of High Heeled Boys*, *Shoot Out at the Fantasy Factory* and *On the Road* – before calling it quits with 1974's *When the Eagle Flies*. Jim Capaldi quickly re-leased two solo records, including 1975's fine *Short Cut Draw Blood*.

By then, Island had long reconfigured itself. Key moments were the release of *Roxy Music* in summer 1972, and *Catch a Fire*, the first rock-marketed Bob Marley and Wailers album in April 1973. For a brief period, the label went glam and then continued to deep-mine the music that was Chris Blackwell's speciality and passion: reggae.

For two to three years at the end of the sixties, however, Island Records defined the state of British Rock. Under the aegis of Blackwell, Jimmy Miller – who became the Rolling Stones' producer during their long, second wind – and Guy Stevens, Island gave musicians space and time to create what they wanted.

What they got was a new kind of music: exploratory, eclectic rock grounded in soul, R&B and pop. Then it was superbly packaged, with eye-catching and imaginative sleeves by photographers and designers like Hipgnosis, Keith Morris, Jimmy Grashow and Tony Wright. This house style – soulful, funky, loose but considered – was perfectly tailored for the times.

Pink Island albums were a total package that embodied the late sixties requirement that music should be more than just an industrial product, that it should offer another way of perceiving the world. They reflect a moment of creativity and optimism in their first-time freshness and excitement.

Pink Island albums were a total package that embodied the late sixties requirement that music should be more than just an industrial product, that it should offer another way of perceiving the world. They reflect a moment of creativity and optimism in their first-time freshness and excitement.

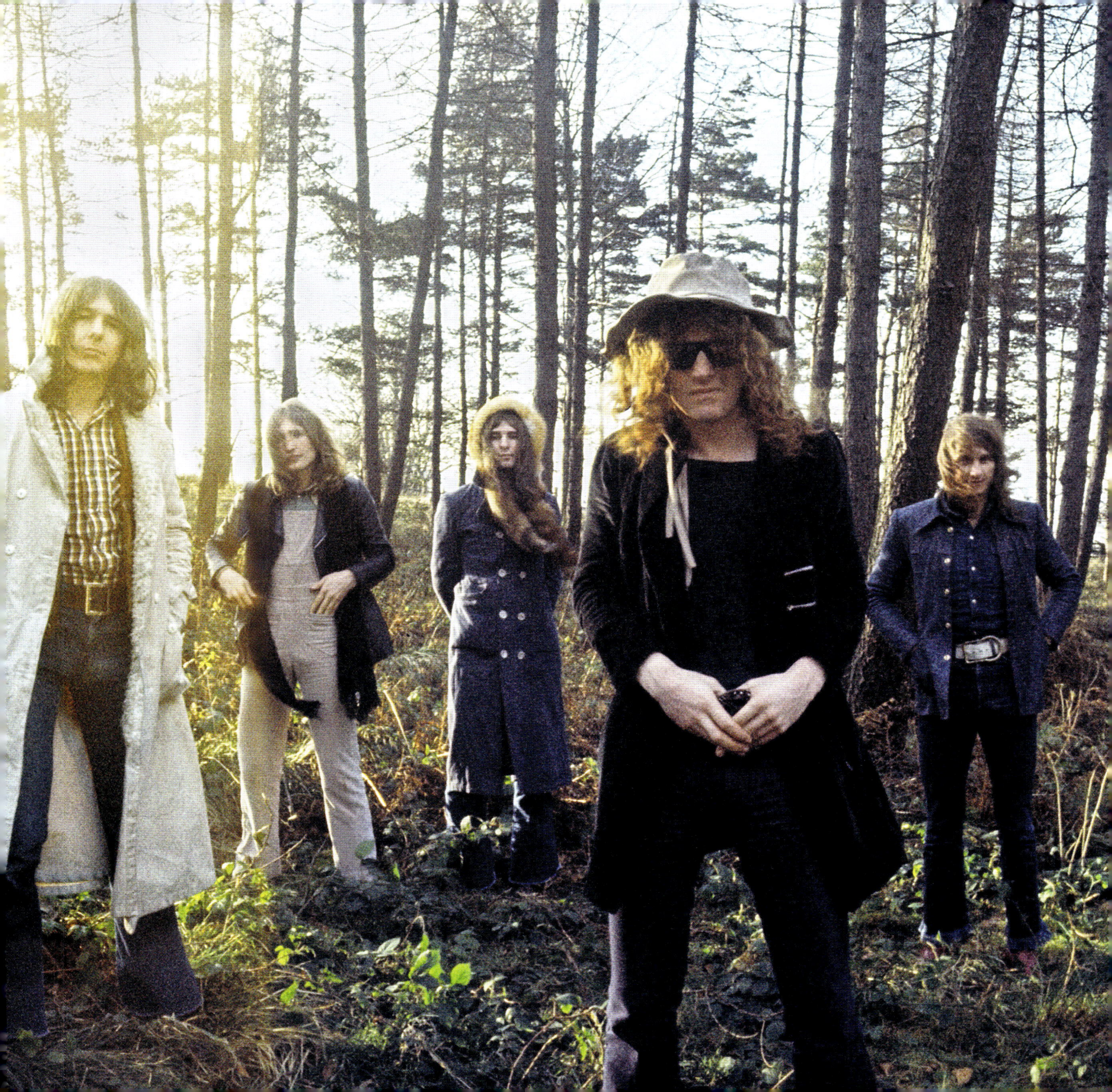

JETHRO TULL
STAND UP

Supernatural Fairy Tales

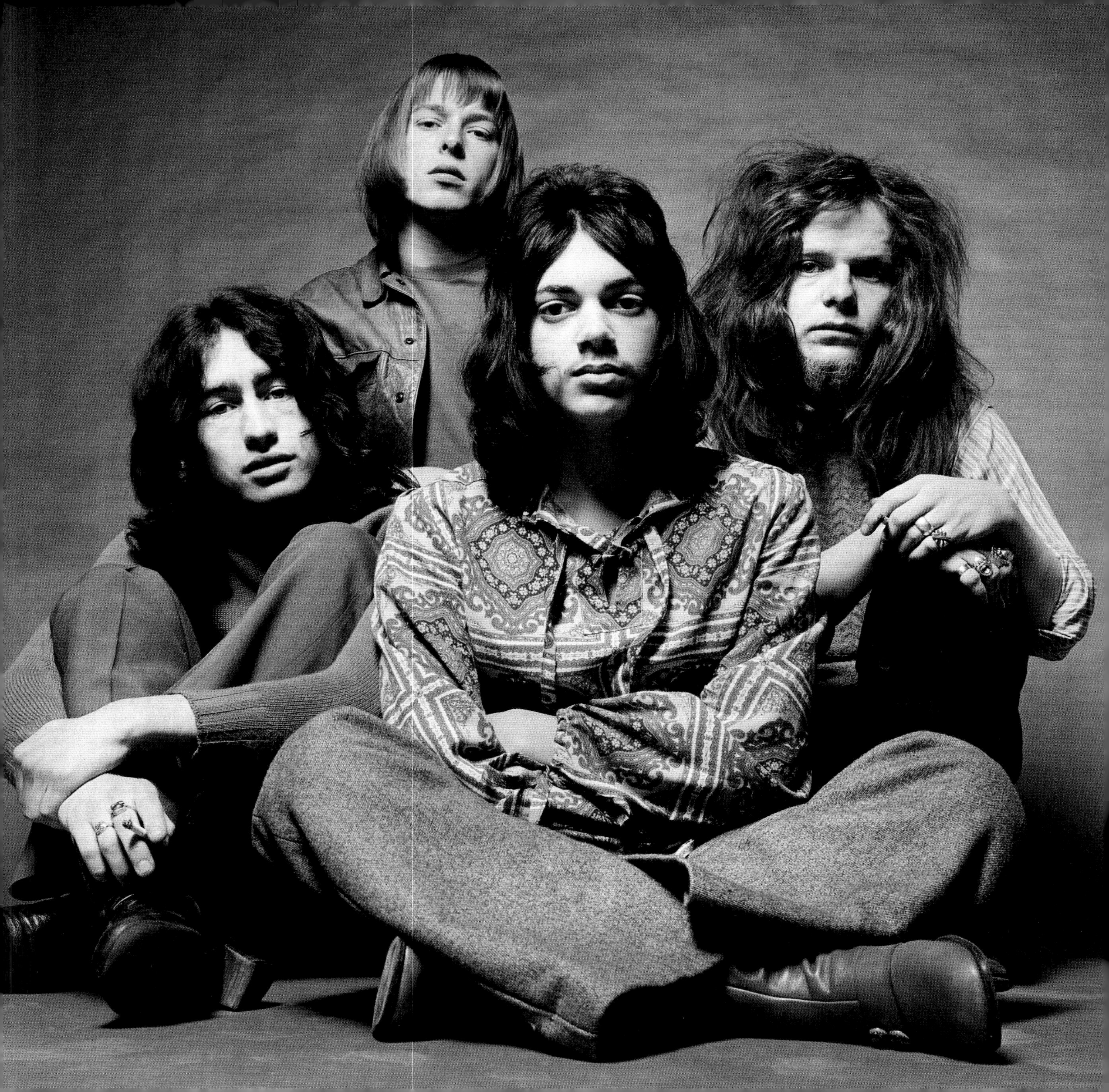

Keep On Running | 43

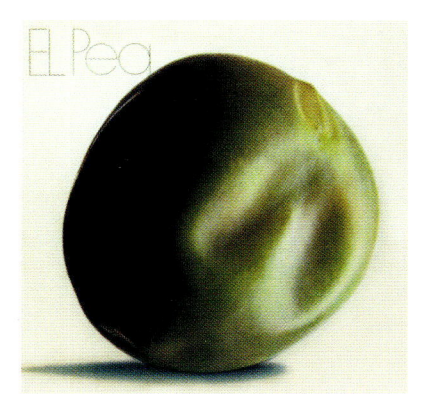

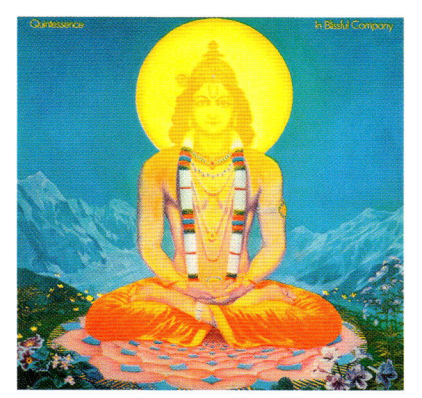

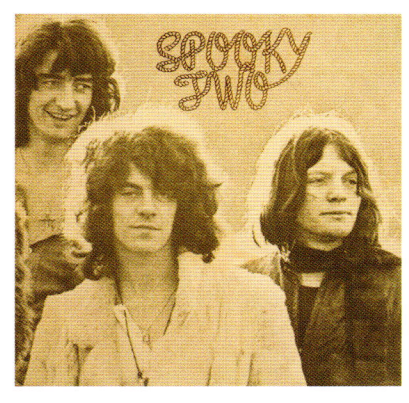

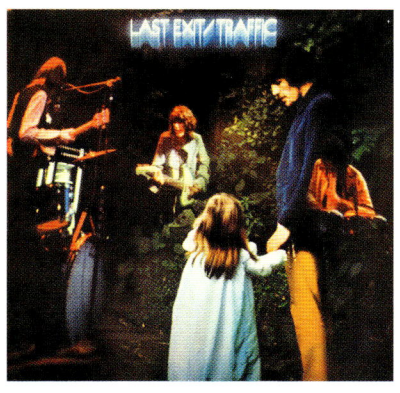

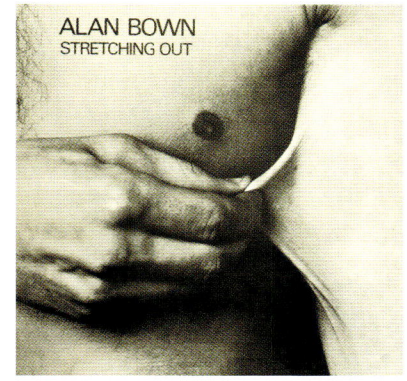

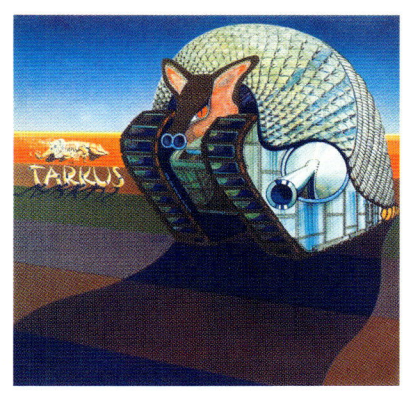

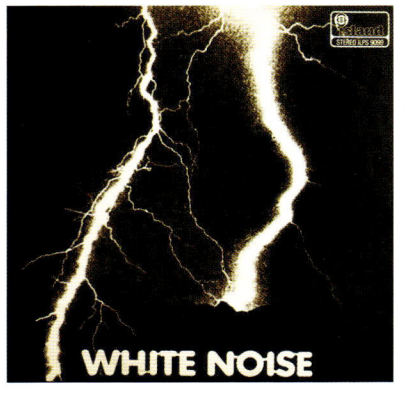

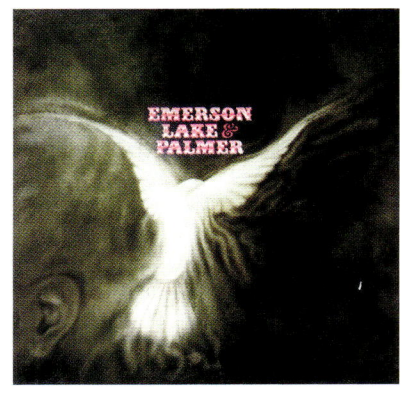

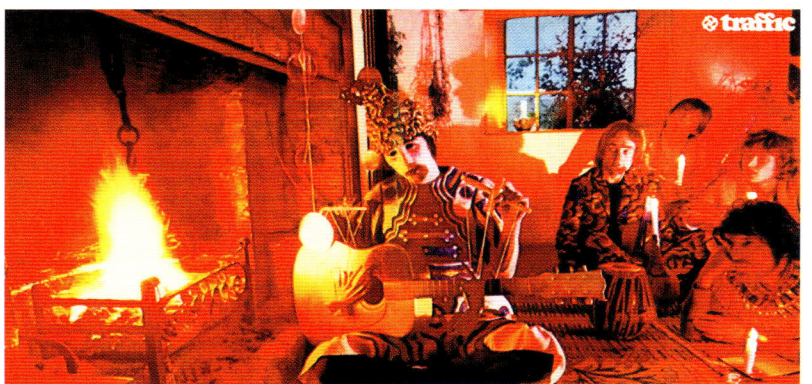

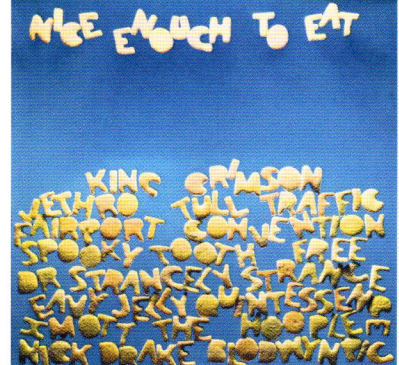

season of the witch

by Joe Boyd

Folk-rock in the late 1960s was part of a game of cultural tag between Britain and America. Island Records and my production company, Witchseason, played a central role during those years. Applying what I learned in one country across the Atlantic in the other was central to all the work I did during that era.

In the late '50s I was a blues-obsessed kid growing up in East Coast America and Britain was a promised land. The best blues and jazz reissues that turned up at Injun Joe's Jazz Record Center in New York City came from England. My first visit, in 1964, as tour manager for the Blues and Gospel Caravan – which starred Muddy Waters – proved that English blues audiences were way ahead of America, particularly in their appreciation of urban R&B, which American fans found too close to 'commercial' rock'n'roll.

A month or so after the end of the tour, I was taken to a Birmingham pub where Stevie Winwood and the Spencer Davis Group (managed by Chris Blackwell) were playing. I was astounded: they were playing 'beat group' (no one used the word 'rock' in those days) versions of folk songs, Leadbelly blues and Jamaican blue beat. I knew plenty of American musicians with equally eclectic tastes, but they played acoustic instruments. The Spencer Davis Group were the original 'folk-rock'!

When I returned to New York in the winter of '64-'65, I told producer Paul Rothchild from Elektra Records about Spencer Davis and suggested we try to start a folk-rock group from among the ambitious folkies in Greenwich Village. Some, like Richie Havens and Fred Neil, were ahead of us, performing with bongos and electric bass at local coffee houses. Members of the group we tried to form ended up as the core of the Lovin' Spoonful, but by then the Brill Building sharks from Kama Sutra Records smelled Top 10 blood and the innocent Elektra folkies were left behind.

By 1967, when I was an independent producer in London looking for new artists for my Witchseason production company, folk-rock was very much an American phenomenon. Bob Dylan, Lovin' Spoonful, Buffalo Springfield, the Byrds… that was how the term was defined. Imagine my surprise when I went to a small club in Chinatown's Gerrard St to audition a group from North London who wanted to play at UFO; they were called Fairport Convention and their repertoire consisted of covers of Dylan, Phil Ochs, Eric Anderson and other American singer-songwriters. Their style was an attempt to mimic West Coast

NICK DRAKE
PINK MOON

CAT STEVENS
Mona Bone Jakon

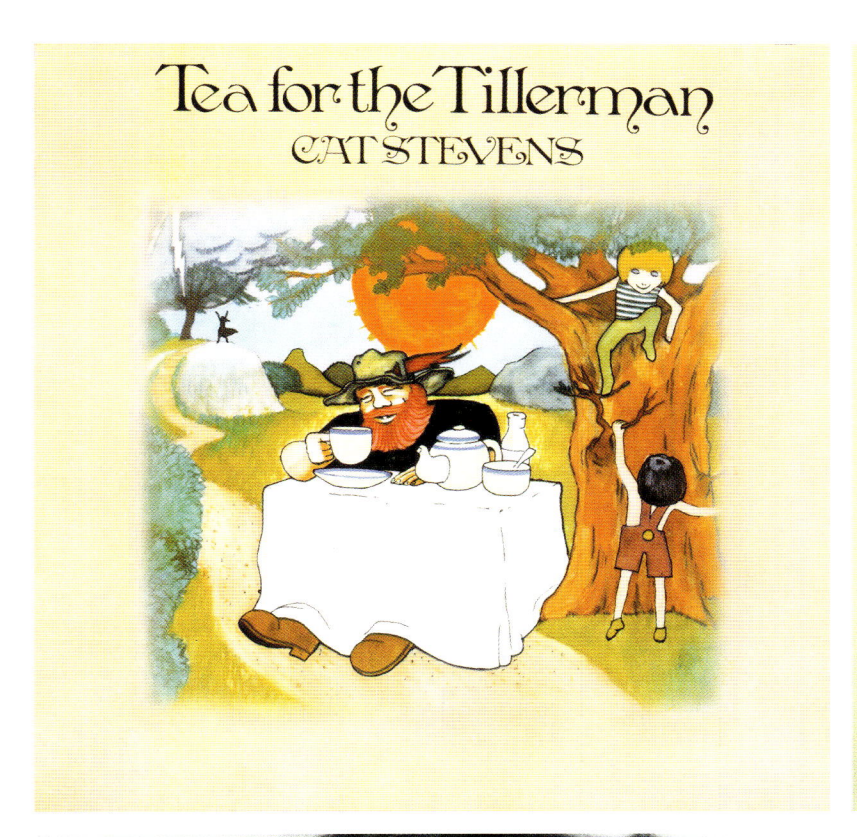

CAT STEVENS

The death and rebirth experienced by Cat Stevens in 1968 utterly altered his life. A hit teen star by the end of 1966, a bout of tuberculosis two years later turned him introspective. Writing over 40 songs during the period when he was hospitalized and recuperating, he was preparing himself for a new course. Armed with this new material, and a bearded, more grown-up persona, Cat Stevens signed to Island Records in 1970, releasing his *Mona Bone Jakon* album, replete with its dustbin image cover-art: the 'Lady D'Arbanville' single off the album reached number 8. But it was the next album, *Tea for the Tillerman*, that broke Cat Stevens around the world, including the United States, where it was a Top 10 record, eventually selling over three million copies. *Teaser and the Firecat* and *Catch Bull at Four*, its successors, easily emulated such sales. Cat Stevens was one of the biggest musical stars in the world, and certainly at the time the leading act on Island Records.

Keep On Running | 47

FAIRPORT CONVENTION

What we did on our holiday

folk-rockers, but like the best emulations, failed in the most interesting manner. The lead guitarist was 17-year old Richard Thompson and his playing was as stunning then as it is today.

In 1967, Polydor Records, the pop division of German classical giants Deutsche Grammophone, was the hip new place to be for adventurous producers. Within a year of opening their doors – and launching their British catalogue with a series of LPs by James Last (!) – they had signed Cream, Jimi Hendrix, The Who and The Bee Gees. One of their early hits was 'This Wheel's On Fire' by the Brian Auger Trinity featuring Julie Driscoll. That was a Bob Dylan song and suddenly there was a rash of UK covers from His Bobness's demo of songs performed with The Band – 'Mighty Quinn' by Manfred Mann and later 'I'll Keep It With Mine' and 'Si Tu Dois Partir (If You Gotta Go, Go Now)' by Fairport.

Polydor released the first Fairport LP, but I was unhappy: the people I originally dealt with had left the company and I felt stranded with an unsympathetic team. As I was mixing Fairport's second LP at Morgan Studios in Willesdon, North London, I ran into Chris Blackwell. He told me how much he liked the first Fairport LP and about the new, more-than-just-bluebeat Island label. Within a month, I had left Polydor; Fairport Convention and my new discovery Nick Drake became Island artists.

Fairport by then had a new lead singer. Sandy Denny had been a 'name' on the folk club circuit since 1965. She had a big voice that carried to the back of the pub function rooms and sang a mixture of British traditional songs and folk songwriter originals. I was a bit allergic to the American singer-songwriter model, so hadn't been that interested. But in the summer of 1967 she gave me a test pressing of an LP she recorded in Copenhagen with the Strawbs on which she performed 'Who Knows Where the Time Goes?' I thought she sounded great on record and the song was tremendous, but Fairport already had a lead singer in Judy Dyble and besides, I was afraid Sandy might be too stroppy and powerful a personality for the mild-mannered Fairport lads from Muswell Hill.

But when Dyble left in 1968, Sandy accepted an offer to join earlier recruit, Iain Matthews, at the vocal mic. Being backed up by Richard Thompson and the superb Fairport rhythm section was a dream come true and she couldn't have been more docile. *What We Did On Our Holidays* was followed in May 1969 by *Unhalfbricking*; the latter album is a mature work by

Led by the enthusiasm of bassist Ashley Hutchings and the experience of Denny, they decided to devote themselves to the invention of a folk-rock as English as *Big Pink* was American.

a very confident group. It included a couple of Dylan songs, one rendered into Cajun French (their first and only hit single) plus new compositions by Richard and Sandy. Most striking was 'A Sailor's Life', a sea-faring ballad that Sandy had taught the group during one of their long van rides. We invited ace fiddler Dave Swarbrick to join them for the session and his and Richard's solos laid down a marker for how a rock band could approach a British traditional folk song. Suddenly, folk-rock was not just about American roots and shoots.

By the time *Unhalfbricking* was released, however, tragedy had struck the group: their van came off the road late at night on the way back from a Midlands gig, killing drummer Martin Lamble and Richard's girlfriend Jeannie Taylor. When they re-formed, with Swarbrick and new drummer Dave Mattacks, the trans-Atlantic influence would take an entirely new form. Vowing not to return to the repertoire they performed with

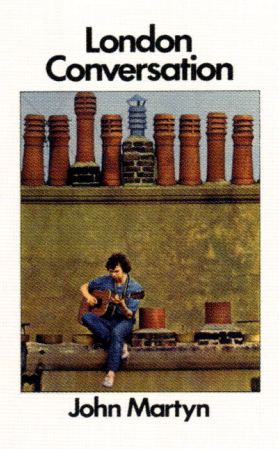

One of the first signings to Island Records, John Martyn was a consummate artist with a staggering breadth of material. Blessed with great good looks, he had the whole world in his pocket – and indulged himself accordingly. Tony Wright's cover of his *One World* album (opposite page) was a stunning tour de force.

Lamble, Fairport were searching for a new identity. The record everyone in the music business was listening to that spring, Fairport included, was *Music From Big Pink* by The Band. All were in awe of this celebration of American roots music, albeit by a group composed largely of Canadians. It was such a marvellous statement that it warned Fairport off any return to their earlier Dylanesque American folk-rock. How could you compete with *Big Pink*? 'A Sailor's Life' provided the answer. Led by the enthusiasm of bassist Ashley Hutchings and the experience of Denny, they decided to devote themselves to the invention of a folk-rock as English as *Big Pink* was American.

When *Liege and Lief* was released, it immediately became Fairport's best selling and most highly acclaimed album. In 2007, it was voted Britain's most influential folk album of all time. But the group that created it was never able to enjoy the fruits of their labours. Sandy and Ashley both left before the end of the year to form new bands, Fotheringay and Steeleye Span, while the all-male Fairport had just 15 glorious months of worldwide touring that made their name and established the brand and reputation that endures to this day. Ashley's replacement, Dave Pegg, joined new drummer Mattacks and rhythm guitarist Simon Nicol to become one of the era's great rhythm sections, performing peerlessly on countless sessions for me and many other producers.

Steeleye signed with another label, but Island (and our American licensees A&M) were not about to let Sandy escape. A&M, Chris Blackwell and I agreed that a solo LP by Sandy would be a huge success. But Sandy was determined to form a democratic group, *Fotheringay*, with her Australian boyfriend, singer Trevor Lucas. The economics never added up, however, so the group only lived to produce one LP. In the spring of 1971, after my own departure for Warner Brothers in Los Angeles, Richard Thompson left Fairport to start a solo career. Who would have predicted that within little more than a year of the release of *Liege and Lief*, its creators would be scattered to the winds?

But there was more to Island's folk-rock arsenal than Fairport and its offshoots. In 1967, before Witchseason's deal with Island, Chris Blackwell had signed the Glaswegian singer-songwriter and virtuoso guitarist John Martyn. His first two solo albums, *London Conversation* and *The Tumbler* were well-received but sold modestly. When he moved in with Beverley Cutner, former lead singer of a Birmingham jug band whom Witchseason had signed for her husky voice and clever romantic songs, everyone thought we had the perfect pairing for success. We rented them a house in the folk-rock bosom of Woodstock, NY, where they hung out with members of The Band and other luminaries. The album that resulted, *Stormbringer*, had a luscious cover photo and Warner Brothers snapped up the US

Keep On Running

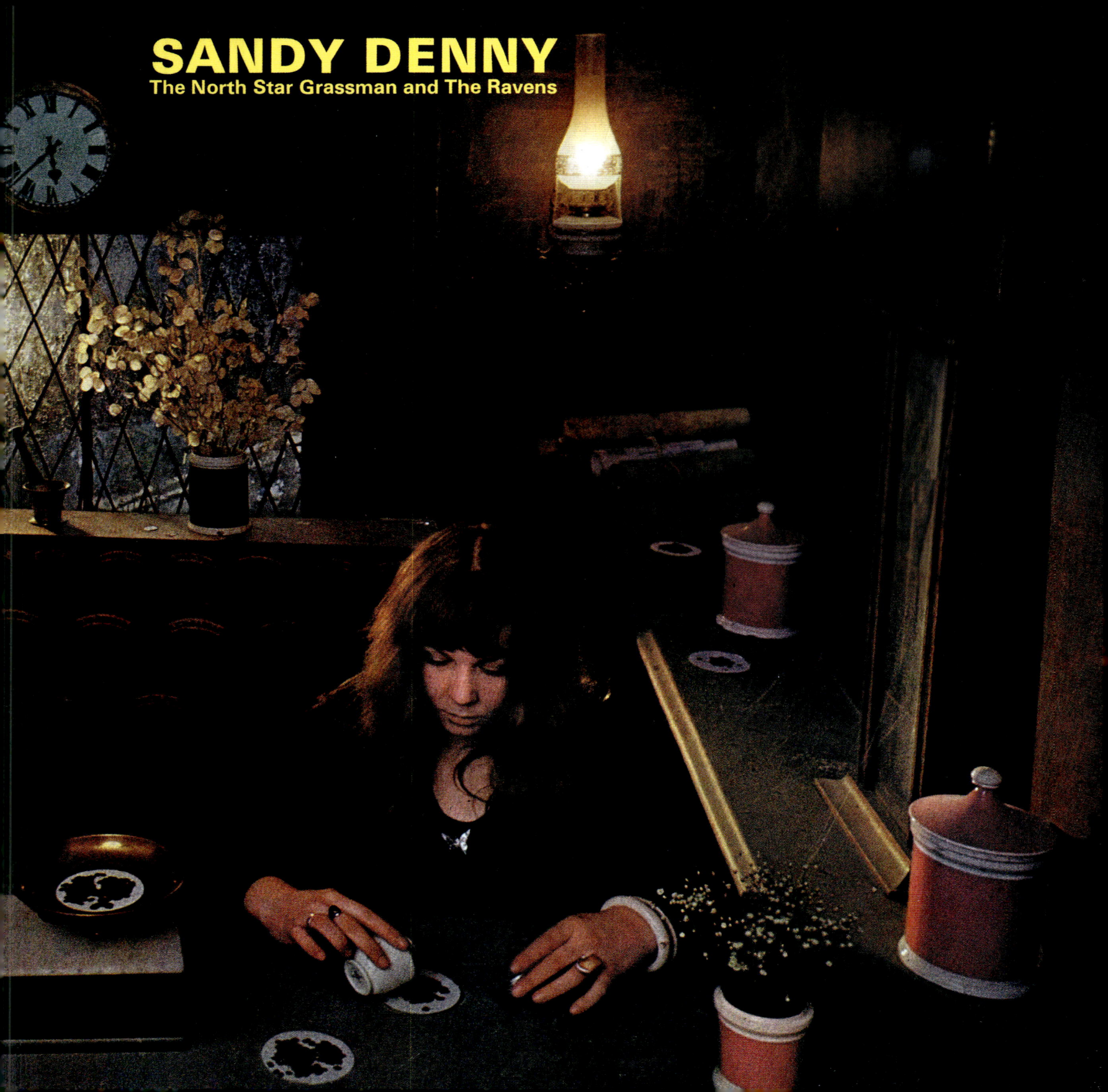

SANDY DENNY
The North Star Grassman and The Ravens

rights, but it never took off. Beverley found being a mother of two too time consuming to spend much time touring, and John resumed his solo career.

Record sales were never a problem for one of Beverley's former label-mates at Decca's Deram label. Steve Georgiou recorded his first hit for them under the name of Cat Stevens and the Deram exodus led him to Island, where he had hit after hit, creating his own melodic brand of folk-rock for a mass audience.

And of course Island's in-house stars Traffic spent so much time in the Berkshire countryside they eventually drank the folk-rock Kool Aid, bringing out *John Barleycorn* in 1969.

Among these various hits and misses lurked a singer-songwriter whose recordings failed dismally at their time of release but who may now be the most famous of them all: Nick Drake. Nick was an upper-middle class boy who prepared for Cambridge at Marlborough School where he starred on the running track and learned the guitar. He spent the summer of 1967 busking on the streets of Aix-en-Provence where he evolved from a pleasant singer of blues and Dylan songs into a songwriter and guitarist of quiet brilliance.

He played a few songs at a Vietnam protest concert at London's Roundhouse where Fairport were one of the headliners. Despite the understated delivery, Ashley Hutchings was sufficiently intrigued to ask for his telephone number: 'He's kind of interesting,' Ashley told me. I was stunned by the songs and his guitar playing, signed him up and from 1968 to 1970 we made two of the most rewarding albums I ever produced. They were released to thundering indifference, not helped by the fact that Nick was a shy and diffident live performer who took ages to achieve his complex guitar tunings and had no jokes to tell as he did so. The one time an audience sat quietly and just listened – when Nick opened for Fairport at the Festival Hall – he got a huge ovation. But most of the time, impatient audience chatter was louder than Nick's singing.

The indifference of record buyers and critics was certainly not matched by his fellow musicians. Those who played on his recording sessions adored Nick and worked tirelessly to give him what he wanted and what the songs deserved. Sound Techniques Studio engineer John Wood and I learned very quickly that we needn't listen much to Nick during a session; better to focus on the sidemen and make sure they weren't making mistakes since Nick's performances were always flawless. Listeners still comment on the remarkable sound of that long-lost studio off the Kings Road in Chelsea; Nick's recordings are classic examples of old-fashioned live recording in a high-ceilinged room.

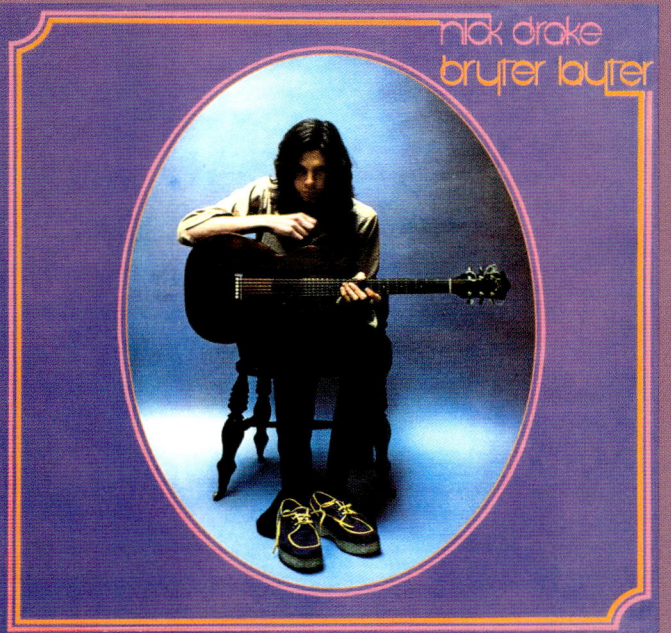

In January 1971 I left London and Witchseason to take up a position at Warner Brothers Films in Los Angeles. John Martyn was probably glad to see the back of me; he celebrated my departure with *Bless the Weather*, his most successful album. Sandy Denny made a series of solo albums and even re-joined Fairport at one point, building a legacy of brilliant songs and performances but never quite delivering the great album that would have made her the international star she deserved to be.

Nick Drake, now ranked among the most influential English singer-songwriters of the last 50 years, released his debut album *Five Leaves Left*, filled with brooding, autumnal songs, in 1969. By 1972, he had recorded a further two albums, although none sold more than five thousand copies in their initial releases. Nick Drake's legend was cemented by his 1974 death; when Volkswagen featured his song 'Pink Moon' in a television advertisement, within one month Drake had sold more records than he had in the previous thirty years.

> Sandy Denny made a series of solo albums and even re-joined Fairport at one point, building a legacy of brilliant songs and performances.

Keep On Running | 53

HOKEY POKEY

RICHARD THOMPSON — Guitar, Mandolin, Electric Dulcimer, Hammer Dulcimer, Piano, Vocals

LINDA THOMPSON — Vocals

Side 1
1. Hokey Pokey (The Ice Cream Song)
2. I'll Regret It All In The Morning
3. Smiffy's Glass Eye
4. The Egypt Room
5. Never Again

Side 2
1. Georgie On A Spree
2. Old Man Inside A Young Man
3. The Sun Never Shines On The Poor
4. A Heart Needs A Home
5. Mole In A Hole

Engineered by JOHN WOOD, recorded at Sound Techniques, London

Produced by JOHN WOOD and SIMON NICOL

SIMON NICOL — Guitar, Piano, Organ, Electric 12 String Guitar, Vocals
JOHN KIRKPATRICK — Accordion
TIMI DONALD — Drums, Percussion
IAN WHITEMAN — Piano, Flute, Organ (Heart Needs A Home)
PAT DONALDSON — Bass
ALY BAIN — Fiddle
SIDONIE GOOSSENS — Harp

Thanks to a select few from the C.W.S. Manchester Silver Band

Sleeve design & painting by Sort Sleeve Studio

ILPS 9305

> Few dare describe themselves or others with the dreaded words 'folk-rock'. But the influence is there for all to hear. And the most ubiquitous sound of all is the breathy close-mic voice, arpeggio guitar and introspective lyrics of the legions of Nick Drake followers.

Fairport confounded those who expected them to collapse after Richard's departure not only by making the highly successful *John Babbacombe Lee* album, but by holding festivals every August since to celebrate their undying life as a group for whom no two albums ever have the same personnel. Former Fairport singer Iain Matthews may have had the biggest success of all the Witchseason folk rockers with his rendition of Joni Mitchell's 'Woodstock' in 1970.

In 1972 Richard Thompson released *Henry the Human Fly*, a marvellously eccentric record that contains some of his best songs, then married Linda Peters and made six classic recordings between 1973 and 1982 that virtually define the best of that bastard genre, 'folk-rock'.

Cyberspace and the few record store shelves left are full these days with all kinds of acoustic pop music, new folk, freak-folk, alt-country, neo-trad and roots music of every sort. Few dare describe themselves or others with the dreaded words 'folk-rock'. But the influence is there for all to hear. And the most ubiquitous sound of all is the breathy close-mic voice, arpeggio guitar and introspective lyrics of the legions of Nick Drake followers. Nick sat - mostly ignored - in the corner during the 'folk-rock' years. Somewhere, his ghost is wryly laughing.

Joe Boyd (left) with his protégées, The Incredible String Band.

STEREO ILPS 9102

Formed in 1970 by singer Sandy Denny upon her departure from Fairport Convention, the folk rock group Fotheringay took its name from Fotheringhay Castle, where Mary Queen of Scots was imprisoned in England. That medieval edifice was also the inspiration for the song 'Fotheringay', included by Fairport Convention on their 1969 album *What We Did On Our Holidays*, when Denny was still with the group. Trevor Lucas and Gerry Conway, two former members of the fashionable group Eclection, and two former members of Poet and the One Man Band, Jerry Donahue and Pat Donaldson, completed the Fotheringay line-up. But the quintet released only one album before the group dissolved. A kind of follow-up was released 38 years later.

FOTHERINGAY

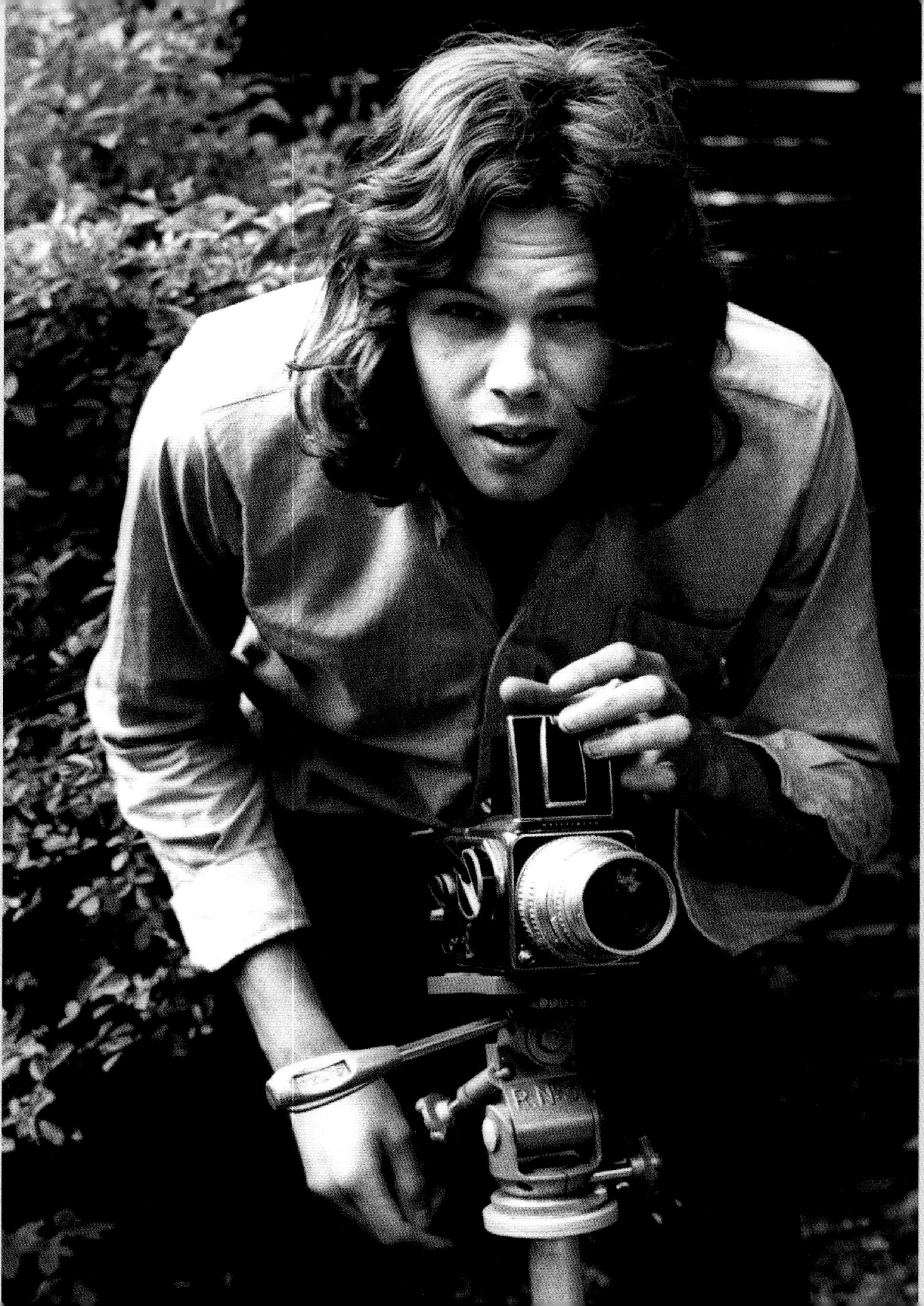

RICHARD THOMPSON
HENRY THE HUMAN FLY!

Liege
& Lief
Fairport
Convention

JADE WARRIOR
WAVES

FOLK ROUTES

FAIRPORT CONVENTION

ALBION COUNTRY BAND
BATTLE OF THE FIELD

The Incredible String Band
Liquid acrobat as regards the air

FAIRPORT CONVENTION
FULL HOUSE

I WANT TO SEE
THE BRIGHT LIGHTS
TONIGHT
RICHARD AND LINDA
THOMPSON

Claire
Hamill

Nick Drake
FIVE LEAVES LEFT

SANDY

JOHN MARTYN
INSIDE OUT

MYRRH

STORMBRINGER!

JOHN MARTYN solid air

RICHARD & LINDA THOMPSON
Pour Down Like Silver

Night Comes In
Jet Plane in a Rocking Chair
Hard Luck Stories
For Shame of Doing Wrong
Streets of Paradise
The Poor Boy is Taken Away
Beat The Retreat

THE HISTORY OF FAIRPORT CONVENTION

FAIRPORT CONVENTION 1 — Nov 1967 – May 1968
Fairport played its first gig in the spring of 1967. On drums was Shaun Frater, his only Fairport gig. Throughout the summer played at U.F.O. & Middle Earth etc. as a five piece. Ian Macdonald joined in Nov. Made a single for Track & an album for Polydor.

JUDY DYBLE	ASHLEY HUTCHINGS	RICHARD THOMPSON	SIMON NICOL	MARTIN LAMBLE	IAN MATTHEWS
vocals, autoharp, piano & recorder. Leaves May '68	(ex Dr. K's Blues Band & Ethnic Shuffle Orchestra) vocals/bass	guitar/vocals	guitar/vocals	(ex capt. Rugeley's blues band) drums	(ex Bradford F.C. & the Pyramid) vocals

Giles Giles & Fripp. Later forms Trader Horne.

Ian Matthews — changes name from Macdonald.

FAIRPORT CONVENTION 2 — MAY 1968 – JUNE 1969
Developed into a sort of Spoonfully country/American folk rock repertoire with large lumps of traditional British folk starting to creep in. Swarbrick guested on 'Unhalfbricking'.

SANDY DENNY	ASHLEY HUTCHINGS	RICHARD THOMPSON	SIMON NICOL	MARTIN LAMBLE	IAN MATTHEWS
(ex solo folksinger, ex Strawbs) vocals/guitar, joins May 68	bass	guitar/vocals	guitar/vocals	drums, died in a motorway accident June 1969	vocals, leaves Jan 69

Ian Matthews forms Matthews Southern Comfort, with whom he stays for a couple of years (and 3 albums) before going solo, making 2 albums and then forming Plainsong with Andy Roberts in 1972.

FAIRPORT CONVENTION 3 — SEP 1969 – NOV 1969
Recuperated & re-formed after road accident. Swarbrick arrives and brings along his vast traditional repertoire & influence. Band is now playing 90% British traditional folk-rock.

SANDY DENNY	ASHLEY HUTCHINGS	RICHARD THOMPSON	SIMON NICOL	DAVE MATTACKS	DAVE SWARBRICK
vocals, leaves Dec 69	bass, leaves Nov 69	guitar/vocals	guitar/vocals	drums, joins Aug 69	violin/mandolin/vocals, joins July 69

DAVE SWARBRICK joins after many years of professional folk playing – with the Ian Campbell Group, Martin Carthy, etc.
DAVE MATTACKS joins after gigs with the Pioneers!, Andy & the Marksmen!! and various dance bands!!!

Sandy Denny formed FOTHERINGAY in March 70 with Trevor Lucas: gtr/voc, Gerry Conway: drums, Pat Donaldson: bass, Jerry Donahue: gtr. Album: ILPS 9125. Fotheringay broke up in Jan 1971. Recorded a solo album 'The North Star Grassman & the Ravens' Sept. 1971 ILPS 9165.

Ashley Hutchings formed STEELEYE SPAN in Jan 1970 & did 1 album on RCA and 2 on B&C. Also produced an album by Shirley Collins on B&C. Left Steeleye Span Nov 1971.

FAIRPORT CONVENTION 4 — DEC 1969 – JAN 1971
Dave Pegg joins his oldmate Swarb (both from the Ian Campbell Folk Group), and the band continues to play electric traditional folk & their own material.

RICHARD THOMPSON	SIMON NICOL	DAVE MATTACKS	DAVE SWARBRICK	DAVE PEGG
guitar/vocals, leaves Jan 71	guitar/vocals	drums	viol/mand/vocals	bass/vocals, joins Dec 69

DAVE PEGG was previously with Roy Everett's Blueshounds, the Uglys, Exception, and the Ian Campbell Folk Group.

Richard Thompson does a few recording sessions and accompanies Sandy Denny on concert dates.

FAIRPORT CONVENTION 5 — JAN 1971 – DEC 1971
It is decided not to replace Richard Thompson and Simon Nicol takes over lead guitar. The group work on their Babbacombe Lee "opera".

SIMON NICOL	DAVE MATTACKS	DAVE SWARBRICK	DAVE PEGG
guitar/vocals, leaves Dec 71	drums/vocals	viol/mand/vocals	bass/vocals

THE BUNCH
Not a performing group – just a bunch of friends who got together to make 'Rock On' ILPS 9189. April 1972.

SANDY DENNY	ASHLEY HUTCHINGS	RICHARD THOMPSON	TREVOR LUCAS	DAVE MATTACKS	DAVE SWARBRICK	DAVE PEGG	ROGER HILL
vocals, back to solo work. New album: 'SANDY' ILPS 9207	bass/vocals	guitar/vocals	guitar/vocals	drums, leaves Feb 72	viol/mand/vocals	bass/vocals	guitar/vocals, joins Dec 71

FAIRPORT CONVENTION 6 — DEC 1971 – FEB 1972
Simon Nicol leaves to rejoin Ashley Hutchings, and is replaced by Roger Hill – one of Dave Pegg's Birmingham cohorts.

'MORRIS ON'
Another bunch of mates who just assembled to record 'Morris On' (June 1972) HELP 5.

BARRY DRANSFIELD	ASHLEY HUTCHINGS	RICHARD THOMPSON	JOHN KIRKPATRICK	DAVE MATTACKS
vocals/fiddle/gtr.	vocals/bass	vocals/guitar, recorded solo album June 1972 'Henry the Human Fly' ILPS 9197	vocals/accordian/concertina	drums/tamb

FAIRPORT CONVENTION 7 — FEB 1972
Dave Mattacks leaves to join the Hutchings/Nicol mob. He was replaced by Tom Farnell and the four gigged together before the current line up.

DAVE SWARBRICK	DAVE PEGG	TREVOR LUCAS	JERRY DONAHUE	TOM FARNELL
violin/vocals	bass/vocals/mandolin	guitar/vocals	guitar/vocals	drums

ALBION COUNTRY BAND
Formed in Spring 1972. First album currently being recorded – due out in the new year.

STEVE ASHLEY	ASHLEY HUTCHINGS	SUE DRAHEIM	ROYSTON WOOD	SIMON NICOL	DAVE MATTACKS
vocals/guitar	vocals/bass	fiddle	voc/concertina	guitar/dulcimer	drums/tamb

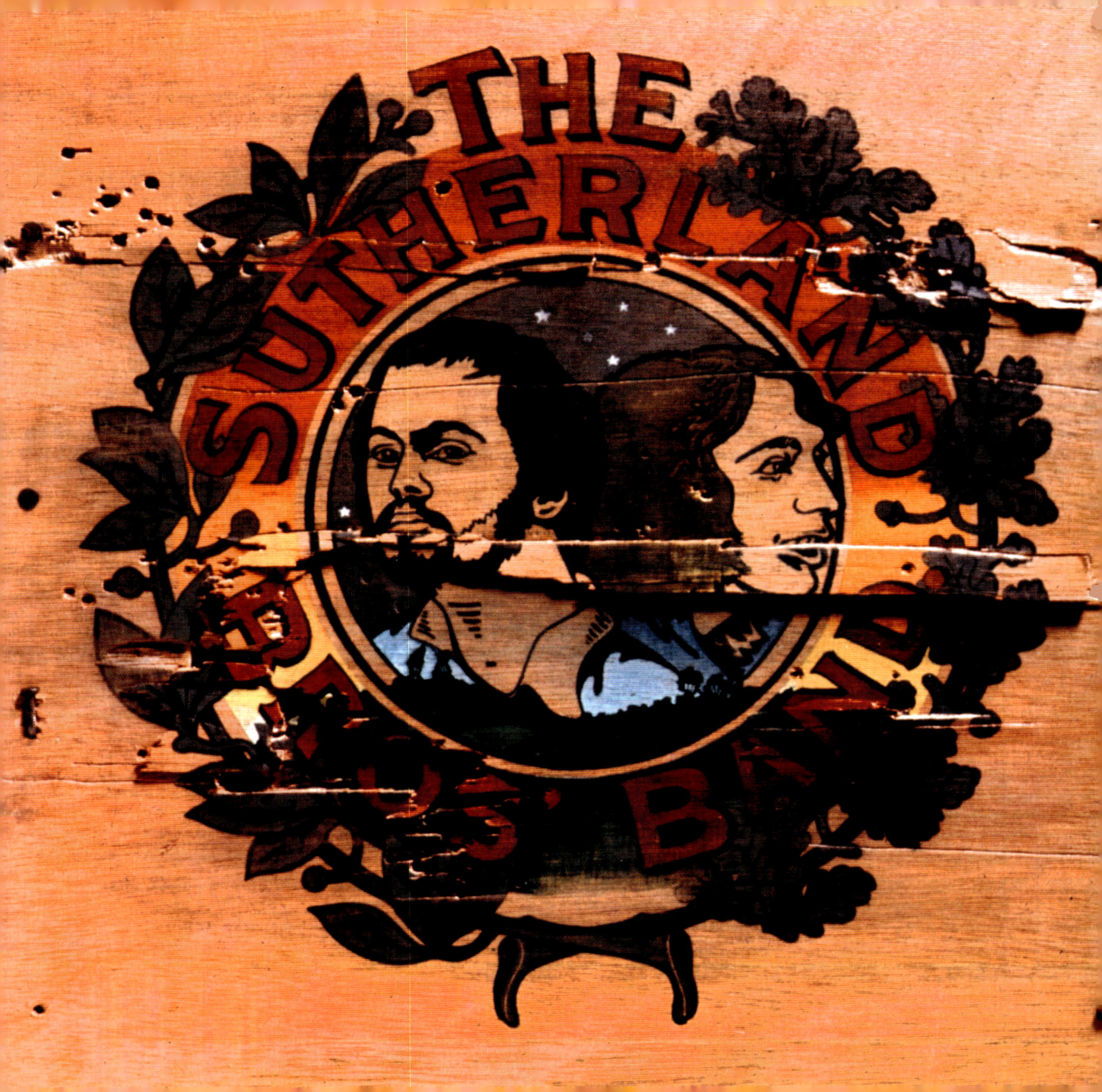

THE
SUTHERLAND
BROTHERS
BAND

glitterball

It was a sunny day in 1975 when the members of a band calling themselves Aswad – the Amarhaic word for "black", they said – walked into the West London headquarters of Island Records, carrying a cassette tape.

by Richard Williams

There were three of them, as I recall. They lived in Shepherds Bush, just down the road, and one of them, the drummer, was on his lunch break from school. They had no appointment, but not much was going on in the A&R office that particular lunchtime, so it seemed worth giving their tape a listen. While it played, they sat on the comfortable sofas in the basement room and explained that they'd had neither the time or the money to put down more than a handful of bass and drums tracks. The outline of the songs was barely discernible. They had no other evidence to show on behalf of their claim to a career as musicians: no manager, no gigs to which an A&R man could be invited. But the bass and drums were enough. Within a few days they were in the studio at the back of the building, fleshing those tracks out into demos. And a short time later they were returning to make their first album. Isn't that how the music business is supposed to be?

On good days, that indeed is how it is – or still was in the middle of the 1970s. It would take Aswad another ten years to get their number one hit, but in the meantime they had demonstrated, along with such contemporaries as Steel Pulse and Misty in Roots, that young British musicians could make something of the all-pervading inspiration of Bob Marley and The Wailers. Aswad were the first reggae outfit to break down barriers by going on the road with a punk band, and the first – even before Marley – to reproduce the radical techniques of dub live on stage. They backed the great Burning Spear, and their music was heard in the film *Babylon*, an accurate portrayal of the lives of young black Londoners.

Like many practitioners of reggae culture Aswad were always fond of big hats…Here (left-to-right) are Brinsley Forde, Angus 'Drummie Zeb' Gaye, and bass player Tony Gad.

It was the example of Marley, naturally, that had inspired them to make the short journey to Hammersmith. Island Records had been founded in the UK in 1962 by a Jamaican who had sold ska 45s out of the back of a Mini-Cooper, and ten years later the label was largely responsible for a surge of interest in reggae, thanks to its sponsorship of The Wailers, Jimmy Cliff, Burning

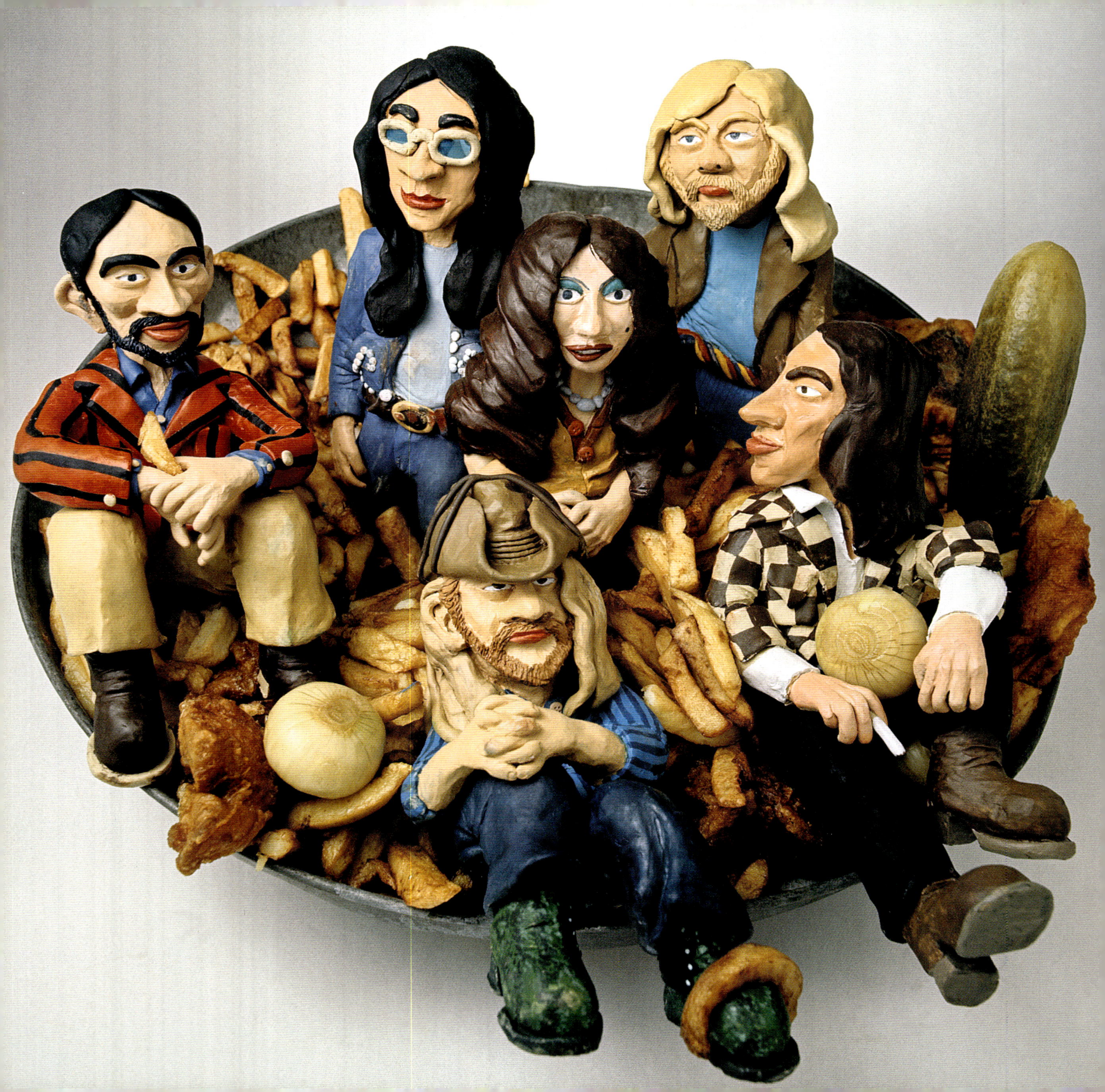

Spear and others, and its role in the making of *The Harder They Come*, a movie that played a pivotal role in turning the world on to the music coming from the slums of Kingston. By the time Aswad walked up the imposing front steps at 22 St Peter's Square, however, the company had taken on other dimensions, which were to define its future.

Island's move from Notting Hill to Hammersmith in 1973 had involved not just a change of location but a change of tone. After the funky informality of the office attached to a couple of recording studios in a converted church close to Portobello Road, the sumptuous new premises in one of St Peter's Square's stylish stucco town houses made an obvious statement about the company's growing stature. Having gone from Neasden to Notting Hill to one of London's most elegant squares in a matter of a decade, Island was growing and changing fast. It was taking on not just new artists but the production and distribution of records for other like-minded labels: an expanding sales force now also took orders for the releases on a list of other labels that included Terry Ellis's and Chris Wright's Chrysalis (Jethro Tull), Richard Branson's Virgin (Mike Oldfield, Henry Cow) and Gerry and Lillian Bron's Bronze (Uriah Heep). Eventually the company would even buy its own pressing plant.

It seemed significant, however, that Island's founder and presiding spirit, Chris Blackwell, chose to appropriate not one of the upper-storey rooms in the main house, with their fine views over the square, but the old laundry leading on to the alley at the back, where his office sat above a new studio and a rehearsal room: closer, in other words, to the business of making music than to the business of business. The choice also enabled him to float in and out of the company unannounced as he made his increasingly rare visits from his other bases in Jamaica and Los Angeles.

The changes were more than environmental. The music, too, was expanding to include styles that might once have been seen as conflicting with the Island ethos. To the old blend of West Indian music and hippie-era bands – the latter including Traffic, Spooky Tooth, Quintessence, Free, Fairport Convention – had been added genres that initially seemed at variance with the label's organic philosophy. The arrival of King Crimson in 1969 had introduced Island to the cutting-edge of progressive rock, with its classical borrowings and its overriding emphasis on technical sophistication, usually at the expense of real emotion. Three years later one of King Crimson's managers, David Enthoven, followed that success by offering the company their new band, Roxy Music, an ensemble of ideas as well as people.

Bred in artists' studios rather than sweaty clubs, Roxy Music chose a path that avoided the sort of dues-paying normally held to be essential for new bands. They also eschewed the wearing of denim, which had come to be seen as a sign of the authenticity much prized by young musicians. Instead they dressed up in an assortment of gear – space-cadet costumes, feather boas, tiger-skin leotards – that looked like the booty from a random raid on a theatrical costumier but actually formed an accurate visual representation of the range of their cultural concerns. The music, too, was a patchwork of retro (doo-wop, torch songs) and futurism (embodied by the sounds emerging from a primitive synthesiser played by a self-confessed non-musician), stitched together with a rough and ready approach worlds away from the increasing obsession with technical perfection displayed by orthodox rockers. They weren't funky, they weren't rootsy, they appeared to reject notions of authenticity; they had got it together not in a country cottage but at art colleges in Newcastle, Reading and Winchester, where their key members had studied. They were, in fact, the last band you'd expect to find on Island, where some employees recoiled in horror while others got the point straight away.

Initially cagey in his response to the enthusiasm shown by his senior executives, notably the managing director, David Betteridge, and the head of marketing, Tim Clark, Blackwell eventually consented to the signing. The appearance of Roxy Music's debut album, with a model in a 1950s swimsuit wrapped around the gatefold sleeve, reclining against satin sheets on which – with a deliberate sense of provocation – was propped a gold disc, created a sensation. The protests of appalled seekers after authenticity were drowned in the growing acclaim for Bryan Ferry, Brian Eno and their band, who – in parallel with David Bowie – were about to create a new appetite for glamour and hedonism among an audience tired of worthy

The album artwork for the first Vinegar Joe album, released in 1972.

> Interestingly, both Roxy Music and The Wailers made their first television appearances on BBC2's *The Old Grey Whistle Test*, usually a showcase for progressive rock, country rock and singer-songwriters.

drabness. Media attempts to link them with the Sweet, T Rex, Gary Glitter and David Essex as part of a glam-rock movement were soon overcome.

Within months Blackwell had reasserted the label's core values by launching Marley to global success. The Wailers' first Island album, *Catch a Fire*, brought reggae first to an initially sceptical rock audience, and then to the world. Interestingly, both Roxy Music and The Wailers made their first television appearances on BBC2's *The Old Grey Whistle Test*, usually a showcase for progressive-rock, country-rock and singer-songwriters. Both were brave bookings, in a sense: the presenter, Bob Harris, made plain his disapproval of Roxy Music's love of artifice, while a disdain for reggae could be assumed among the programme's regular audience. Both, however, made their mark. And by now Island was big enough for both of them, and more besides.

With Traffic usually on hiatus and the former Witchseason stable of folk-rockers mostly scattered to the winds, the enlarged Island had a hunger for new projects. Confirmation of its enhanced status came the year after the move to St Peter's Square when, amid strict secrecy and great excitement, David Geffen, the founder of Asylum Records, chose Island as the vehicle for the UK release in 1974 of *Planet Waves*, Bob Dylan's first album after his break from Columbia. Finding and developing Island's own talent, however, remained the absolute priority. On the reggae side, Blackwell created the Blue Mountain label for releases by Lorna Bennett ('Breakfast in Bed'), Zap-Pow ('This is Reggae Music') and others, while adding Burning Spear (Winston Rodney) to the main label's roster, alongside The Wailers. From the embers of the unsuccessful college-circuit band Vinegar Joe he plucked Robert Palmer, a Yorkshire-born singer with good looks, a smooth manner and a blue-eyed soul voice to die for.

Palmer was sent to America, where he recorded in New Orleans with the great pianist and composer Allen Toussaint and The Meters, and to Los Angeles, where he consorted – and, briefly, went on tour – with the members of the fashionable Little Feat. *Sneakin' Sally Through the Alley* and *Pressure Drop* were two of the most convincing albums ever made by a British soul singer, and the high-gloss finish applied to their artwork and

66 | Keep On Running

ROXY MUSIC

> Neither Cale nor Nico had a reputation for being particularly easy to handle, but that was one of the main elements of The Velvet Underground's appeal: they were outsider artists, and behaved as such.

After Traffic finally dissolved in 1975, Steve Winwood gradually eased into a solo career, beginning with 1977's Steve Winwood album. But it was his second solo record, 1980's Arc of a Diver, that was a true hit, reaching number 3 in the American charts. A clear marketing device, four separately coloured versions of the Tony Wright art-directed sleeve were released simultaneously.

marketing campaigns should have brought hits. But it was not until the 1980s, when the influence of punk and electronic disco music prompted Palmer to devise a crisper, more modern and original synthesis, that 'Johnny and Mary' and 'Addicted to Love' gave him the hits and the following that Blackwell had foreseen.

There were similar hopes for Jess Roden, a West Midlands contemporary of Palmer (both had sung with the soul band of the trumpeter Alan Bown, an Island artist in the late 60s) and an equally talented singer, but a series of impressive recordings – including one lovely album cut in New York with Joel Dorn – stubbornly refused to catch the public imagination. The modest, unassuming Roden toured frequently with a band that the company adored; if he lacked anything, it was the chutzpah that enabled Palmer to surround himself with model girls for the video accompanying 'Addicted to Love', an instant favourite of the programmers at the fledgling MTV.

The success of Roxy Music, however, had encouraged the faction of the company located at the front of 22 St Peter's Square in a wholehearted pursuit of artists whose work did not conform to the old palm-tree-and-spliff stereotypes, yet retained the integrity and credibility on which the company had been built. Some of these were engaging mavericks of the kind beloved by critics but easily ignored by the public.

Kevin Ayers had been a founder member of the Soft Machine, contemporaries of Pink Floyd in the days of UFO and the 14-Hour Technicolour Dream. The archetypal golden hippie in looks, songs and lifestyle, Ayers left an increasingly serious-minded band after a year or so and began a solo career with Harvest, EMI's progressive subsidiary, where a sequence of four albums earned critical plaudits but minimal sales. When Muff Winwood signed him in 1973 it was with half an eye on reproducing the sort of success that had turned Bryan Ferry, already enjoying success with his sideline solo albums, into a sort of modern matinee idol, but Ayers' Island debut, *The Confessions of Dr Dream and Other Stories*, replicated the response achieved by his previous label.

That year I arrived at St Peter's Square to take over as head of A&R. Muff would manage the Basing Street studios while still scouting new acts. Among my first signings were two artists formerly associated with The Velvet Underground: John Cale and Nico. The Velvets had been one of my enthusiasms since the release of their first album in 1967; six years later a tiny cult was beginning to mushroom, not least through the testimonials of Bowie, Ferry and Eno, each of whom readily acknowledged the role the New York band had played in their thinking – and, in Bowie's case, demonstrated in a Velvets-soundalike song called 'Queen Bitch'. Ayers' 'Stranger in Blue Suede Shoes' could also be seen as a homage. Their time seemed to be at hand.

Neither Cale nor Nico had a reputation for being particularly easy to handle, but that was one of the main elements of The Velvet Underground's appeal: they were outsider artists, and behaved as such. Signing Cale, however, was not a problem once the relevant authorities had listened to several of the lovely songs from *Paris 1919*, his 1973 solo album for Warner Brothers, a polished product made in Los Angeles with crack session musicians. Once he was in, I could add Nico almost as an afterthought, with Cale's encouragement – although it helped me to make my case that she was being managed by Jo Lustig,

Keep On Running | 69

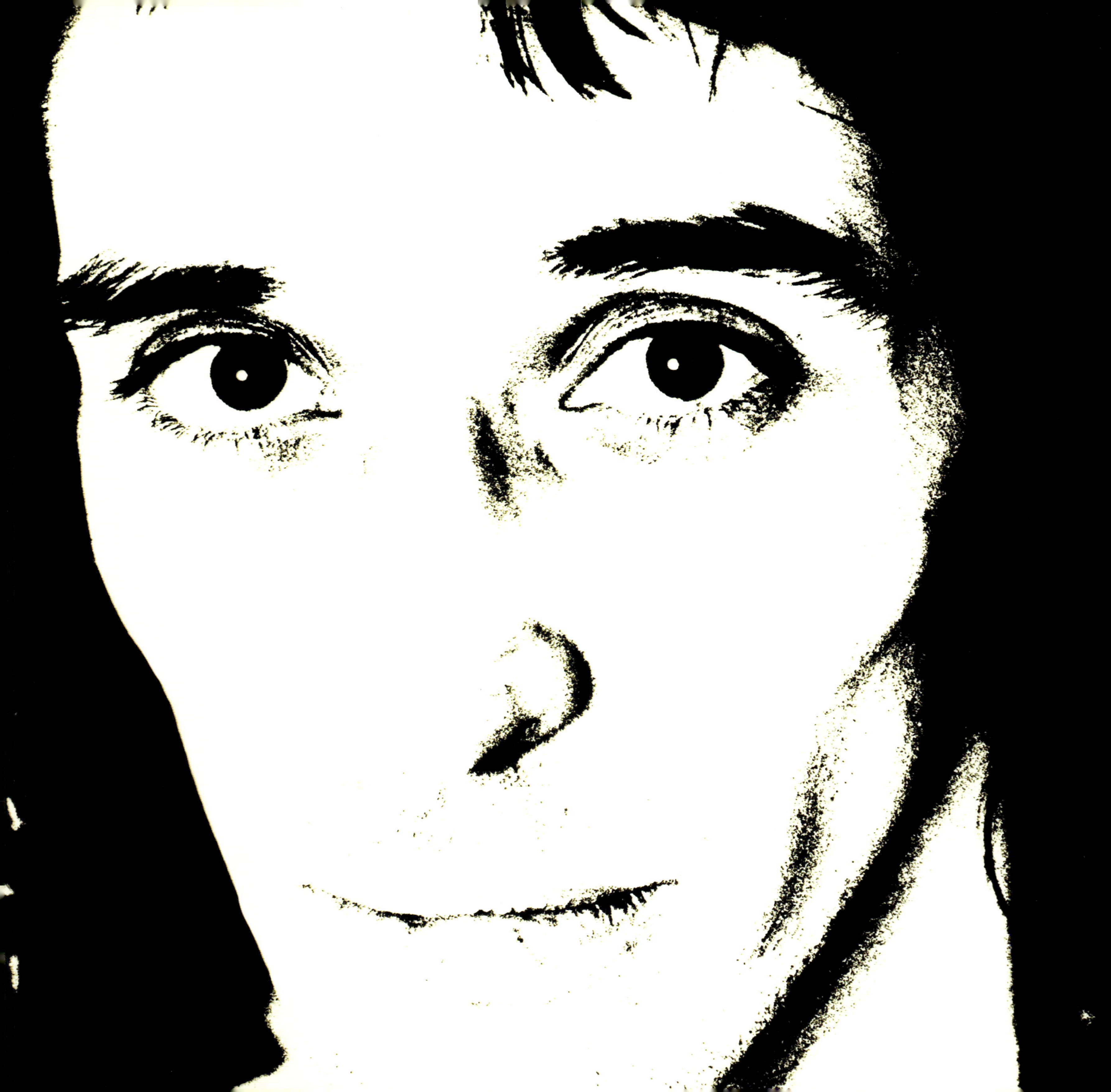

the pugnacious former Broadway press agent whose stable also included Steeleye Span and Richard and Linda Thompson. The interest of Eno, who had now been ejected from Roxy Music and was embarking on his own solo career, also helped, as did that of his former bandmate Phil Manzanera; both pledged themselves to give the newcomers a hand.

They helped Cale record *Fear*, his Island debut, whose vigorous harshness formed a contrast with the nostalgic languor of *Paris 1919*. They also participated in Nico's *The End*, arranged and produced by Cale as the belated final part of a trilogy begun by *The Marble Index* in 1969 and *Desertshore* the following year. Both albums lived up to my hopes and, as expected, they attracted critical attention. Not enough immediate commercial success, however, to fulfil the ambitions of a company that was now enjoying the sight of impressive sales graphs for other artists. In the optimistic, expansive, tolerant ambiance of the mid-70s, there seemed no good reason why these intriguing cult figures should not be transformed into major stars. And the same went for Kevin Ayers.

The idea for the Rainbow concert was advanced to Ayers, Cale and Eno at a lunch in an Italian restaurant off Kensington High Street in the spring of 1974. To put them together on stage, with Nico and perhaps a few others, might create a focus of attention, particularly among the music press, that would turn their cult followings into a large-scale audience. Each was an interesting performer: Ayers with his tousled loucheness, Cale with his ever-present undercurrent of violence, Nico with her imperturbable air of mystery, Eno the mascara'd boffin. It happened on June 1, 1974, in front of a full house in London's premier rock concert venue of the time, and it went off pretty much as planned. Eno rattled through a couple of songs from *Here Come the Warm Jets*, his first solo album, Cale stalked through his disturbing rewrite of 'Heartbreak Hotel', Nico paid tribute to Jim Morrison, her former lover, with a dramatic version of the Doors' 'The End', and Ayers performed a full set with a band including Mike Oldfield, already famous thanks to the success of *Tubular Bells*, and Robert Wyatt, an old Soft Machine colleague. Less than a month later, a live album was in the shops. There was another concert in Manchester shortly afterwards, and that October I took Cale, Nico and Eno to West Berlin, where they played in Mies Van Der Rohe's Neue Nationalgalerie and Nico's unexpurgated version of 'Das Lied Der Deutschen', better known as 'Deutschland Uber Alles', with Cale bashing mad arpeggios out of a grand piano and Eno evoking the drone of heavy bombers, provoked something close to a riot.

As you may have noticed, none of them became superstars. Ayers eventually retreated to the Mediterranean sunshine, emerging occasionally, his blonde hair more bleached than ever, for a low-key comeback. Cale pursued a career that included the production of Patti Smith's *Horses* and later reunions with Lou Reed and Eno, as well as an impressive output of solo recordings for a variety of labels. Nico lived for a while in Manchester, where she was adopted by the post-punk generation, and died in Ibiza in 1988. Eno went on to have the most varied and successful career imaginable, staying mostly beneath the radar as his invention of ambient music and generative music fed into his profoundly creative studio work with Bowie, Talking Heads, U2, Coldplay, Paul Simon and many others.

It was Muff who turned cult heroes into chart-toppers when he signed Sparks, the Los Angeles duo of Ron and Russell Mael. Like Roxy Music, they combined artiness – both brothers studied film-making at UCLA – with visual eccentricity and humour: the bubble-permed, baby-faced Russell might have looked the part of a heart-throb singer, but Ron, with his Hitler moustache and Chaplinesque air, was an unorthodox sight at the keyboard.

After failing to make much headway in the US, they decided to move to Britain, their spiritual home. An appearance on *The Old Grey Whistle Test* (once again to a less than ecstatic welcome from Bob Harris) led to the acquisition of an English manager and a coveted recording contract with Island. Muff helped them find a competent British rhythm section and produced their first album, *Kimono My House* (a typical title: a later effort was called *Gratuitous Sex and Senseless Violins*), from which a single, the wonderfully camp and melodramatically multi-faceted 'This Town Ain't Big Enough for Both of Us', went to No 2 in the chart, its progress boosted by a slot on *Top of the Pops*. For their second and third Island albums, *Propaganda* and *Indiscreet*, Muff handed them over to producer Tony Visconti. Later, having acquired a fanbase that included future members of New Order, The Smiths and Depeche Mode, they went back home to continue their unorthodox progress through the world of popular rhythm music.

I left the company in early 1976, just in time to avoid the tricky A&R decisions about whether to bid for The Sex Pistols, The Damned, The Clash, The Stranglers and Siouxsie and The Banshees. I'd enjoyed having a hand in the chart success of Pete Wingfield's 'Eighteen With a Bullet', a worldwide smash that failed to lay the foundation of a solo career for a man who was perfectly happy as a producer, songwriter and sessionman

made a couple of albums that I hoped would appeal to fans of Little Feat and Bonnie Raitt, but failed to connect. Nasty Pop, a five-piece Liverpool band with great songs and voices, turned out to be stranded in the hinterland between the beat boom and the new wave. Nor did I manage to persuade the company that the demos Eno and I had recorded with a New York band called Television, featuring the songs and guitar of Tom Verlaine, were worth following up. But I never regretted declining the invitations to saddle the label with such acts as City Boy, Bebop DeLuxe, Deaf School or The Babys.

> Eddie and The Hot Rods, who had a big hit with the irresistible 'Do Anything You Wanna Do' and were the band who went on tour with Aswad at a time when black and white were only starting to learn to unite.

de luxe. There had been the satisfaction of putting together, at Blackwell's behest, a couple of compilations of hot Latin music from Jerry Masucci's Fania label, leading to London's first salsa gigs – by Hector Lavoe at the Nashville Rooms and by the Fania All Stars, including Celia Cruz, Johnny Pacheco and Ray Barretto, at the Lyceum. My assistant, Howard Thompson, later to make his mark with Columbia and Elektra in New York, forced Island's toe into the waters of punk by signing Eddie and The Hot Rods, who had a big hit with the irresistible 'Do Anything You Wanna Do' and were the band who went on tour with Aswad at a time when black and white were only starting to learn to unite.

The personal failures included Peter Skellern, whose amiable, tuneful pop songs were probably more suited to Decca, who had given him a hit with 'Hold On to Love', than to Island, who managed not to make any impact whatsoever with a decent album called *Hard Times*. Bryn Haworth, a gifted slide guitarist,

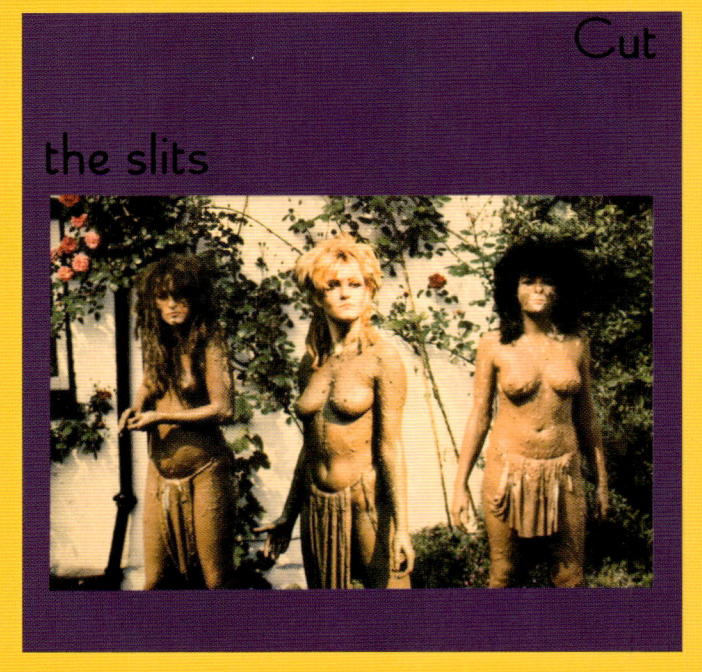

The most difficult – and last-to-be-signed – punk group, the all-girl Slits, with their Cut album produced by Dennis Bovell, significantly moved on the cause of female acts.

72 | Keep On Running

EDDIE·AND·THE·HOTRODS
TEENAGE DEPRESSION

the Chieftains 7

ENO

Ultravox! added the exclamation mark to their name as a reference to the krautrock group Neu! Signed to Island in 1976, they released their *Ultravox!* album the following year. Frontman John Foxx declared his intention to 'live without emotions', creating a certain tension with the assemblage. Falling into a black hole between glam-rock, punk and new wave, the group struggled, despite dropping the exclamation mark, and after three albums were dropped by Island. After changing their line-up and style, however, Ultravox became a great success.

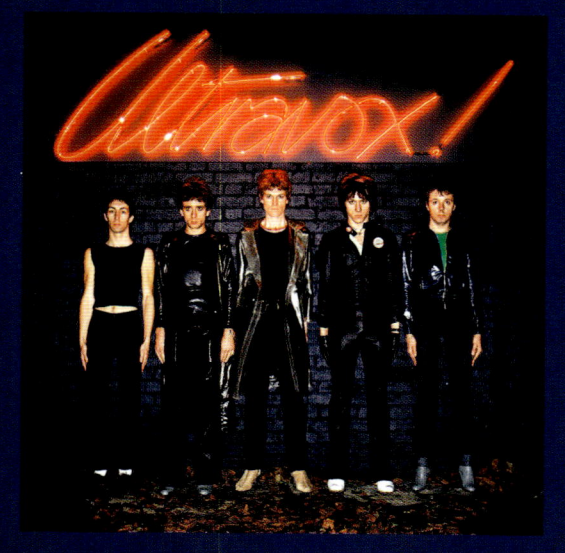

Not long before my departure, Blackwell was approached by the Warner-Elektra-Atlantic combine, whose board was thinking of buying Island and using it as the armature for their UK labels. That was how far little Island had come: its infrastructure and methodology were seen as superior to those of the industry's giants. There were discussions about how the extra labels would all fit into the Hammersmith office, and who was going to take charge of which (I fancied running Atlantic, envisioning a life of repackaging masterpieces by Ray Charles, Aretha Franklin, Ornette Coleman and John Coltrane). It came to nothing; perhaps just as well.

Soon after I went, Grace Jones – whose most inventive new wave dance confections were jointly produced by Blackwell and Alex Sadkin – and U2 came along: the conquest of the discotheque and the stadium, on a global scale in both cases. ZE Records followed, the result of Blackwell's friendship with the music-crazy Michael Zilkha, bringing the heady aromas of Paradise Garage and Studio 54 into St Peter's Square, along with the sounds of Kid Creole and The Coconuts, Cristina, Material and Was (Not Was). All of them were able to make use of the groundwork that had been laid at Island in the days when a musician in eyeliner and a feather boa seemed an affront to what a well intentioned but deeply misguided friend of mine used to call rock 'n' dignity.

Keep On Running | 77

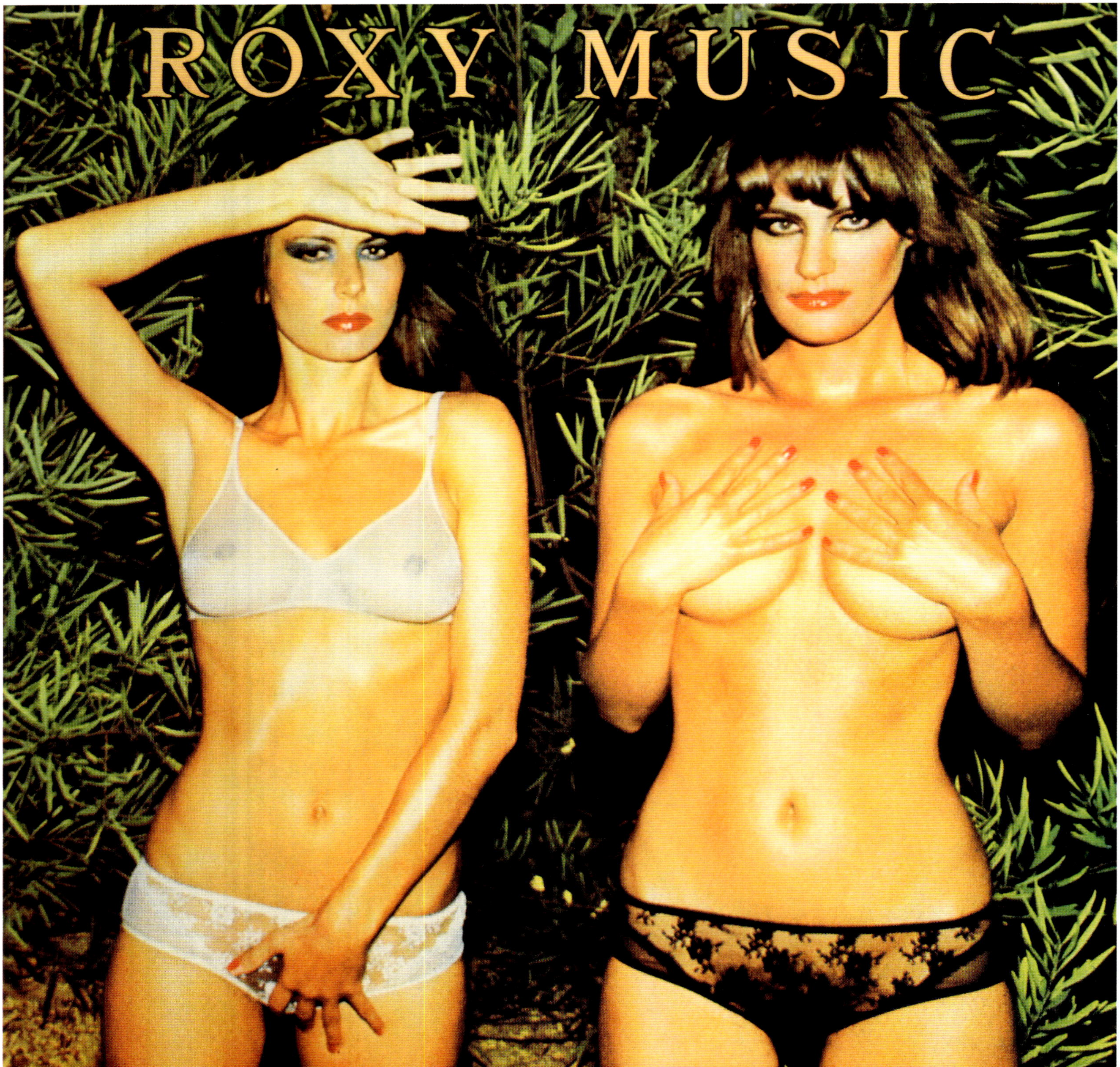
ROXY MUSIC

Keep On Running | 79

A move to New Orleans funk sophistication with The Meters (above); and a similar outlook with Steve Winwood's *Talking Back to the Night* (right).

80 | Keep On Running

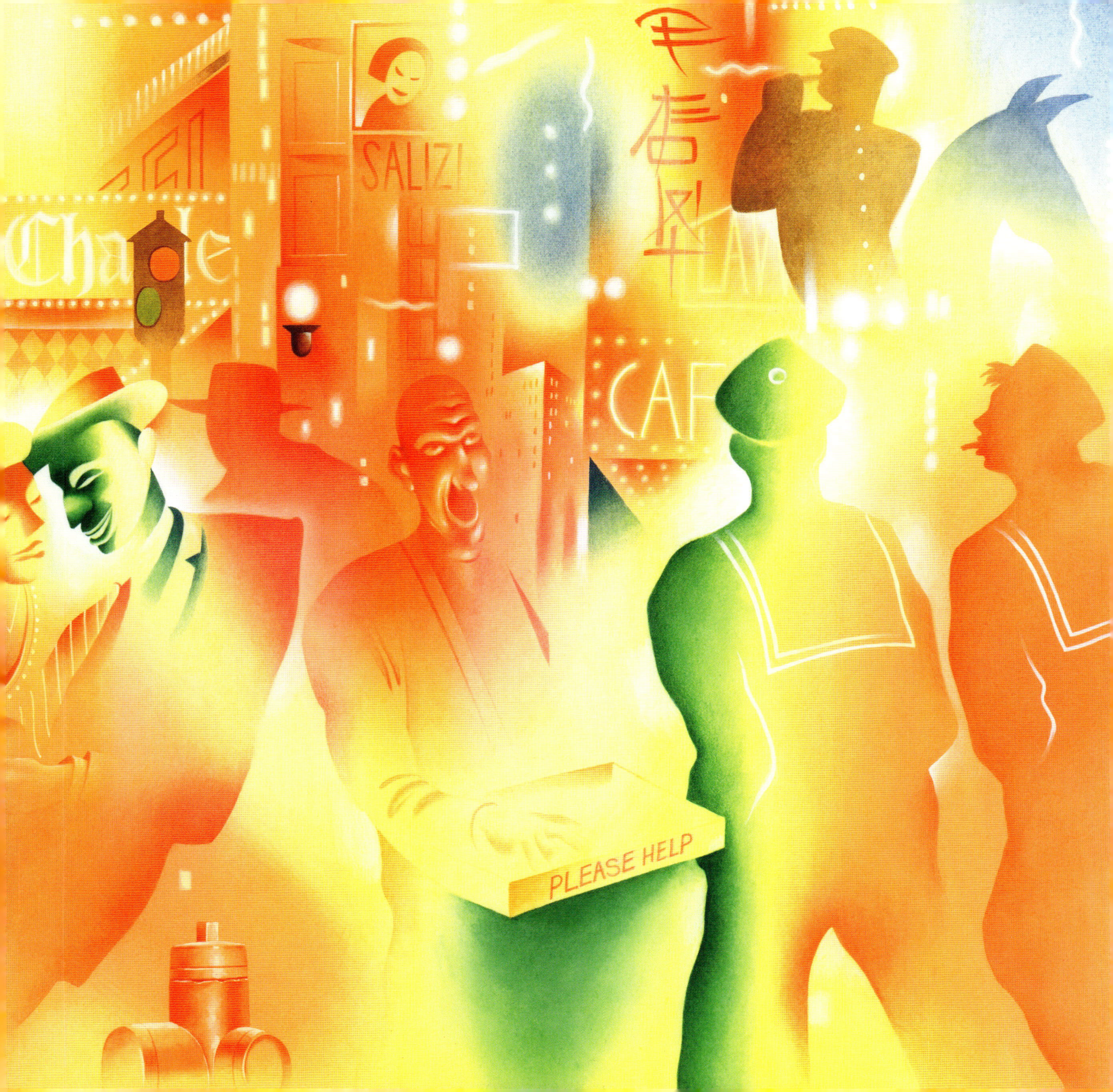
SALIZI
PLEASE HELP

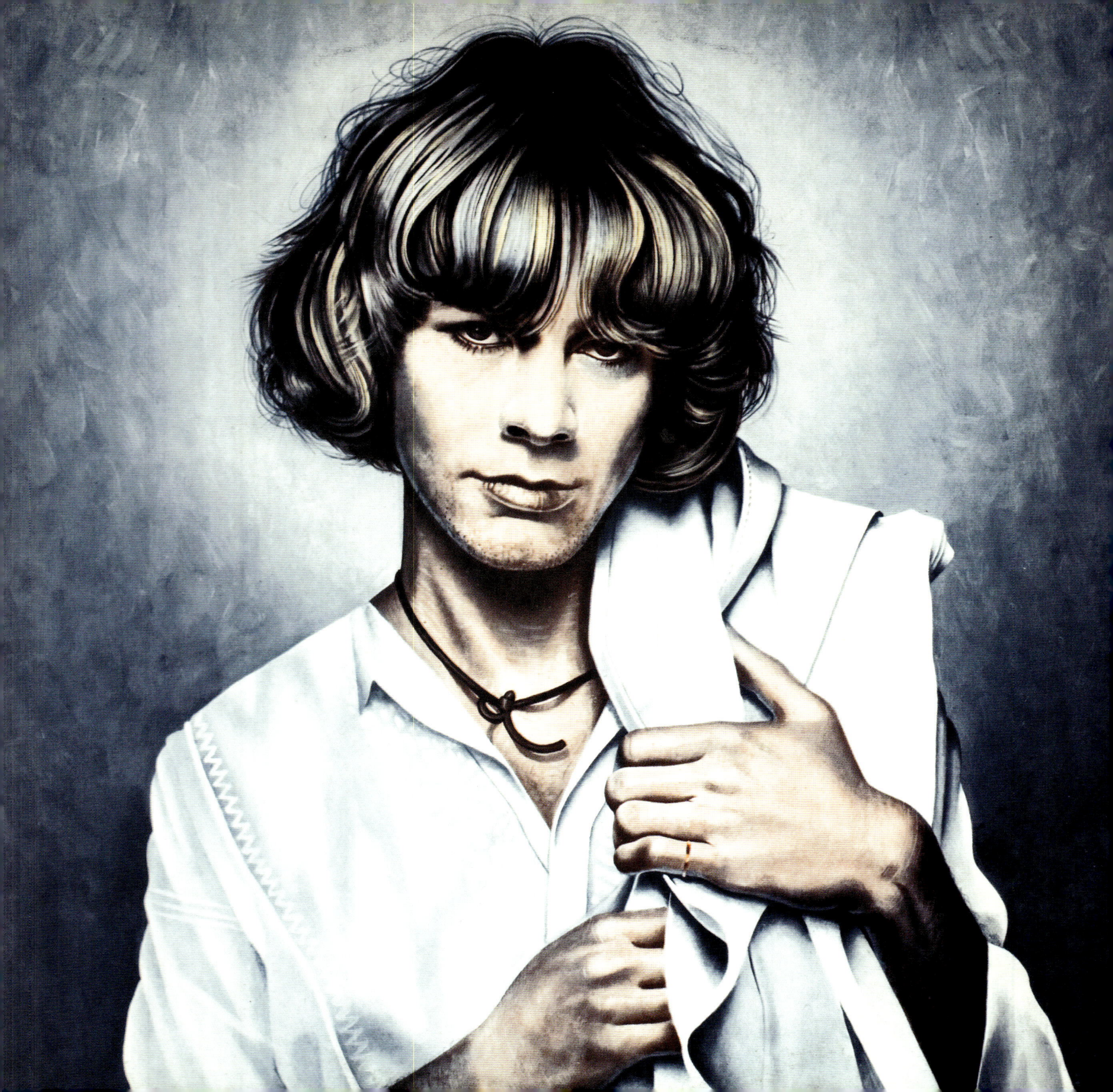

ANOTHER GREEN WORLD ENO

As Chris Blackwell had licensed Jamaican ska and American R&B, setting up specialist labels for these and other releases, so in the late 1960s he began to distribute labels through Island Records. An extremely profitable alliance was the licensing deal with E.G. Records, through whom first King Crimson, then Emerson, Lake and Palmer – who soon launched their own Manticore label – and later Roxy Music came to appear on Island. In a completely different style, Gerry Bron's Bronze label was distributed through Island, bringing the likes of 'Very 'Eavy' Uriah Heep to the roster. Mountain came to Island through a deal with the exhilirating *enfant terrible* Gary Kirfurst. Meanwhile, the likes of Jethro Tull and Blodwyn Pig appeared on Island through the auspices of Terry Ellis and Chris Wright's Chrysalis operation. A similar distribution deal with Richard Branson's Virgin Records brought enormous sales with Mike Oldfield's extraordinary *Tubular Bells*, the first Virgin release.

MOUNTAIN
LIVE
FEATURING
LESLIE WEST
FELIX PAPPALARDI
(the road goes ever on)

URIAH
HEEP
...very
'eavy

TUBULAR BELLS
Mike Oldfield

BLODWYN PIG
AHEAD RINGS OUT

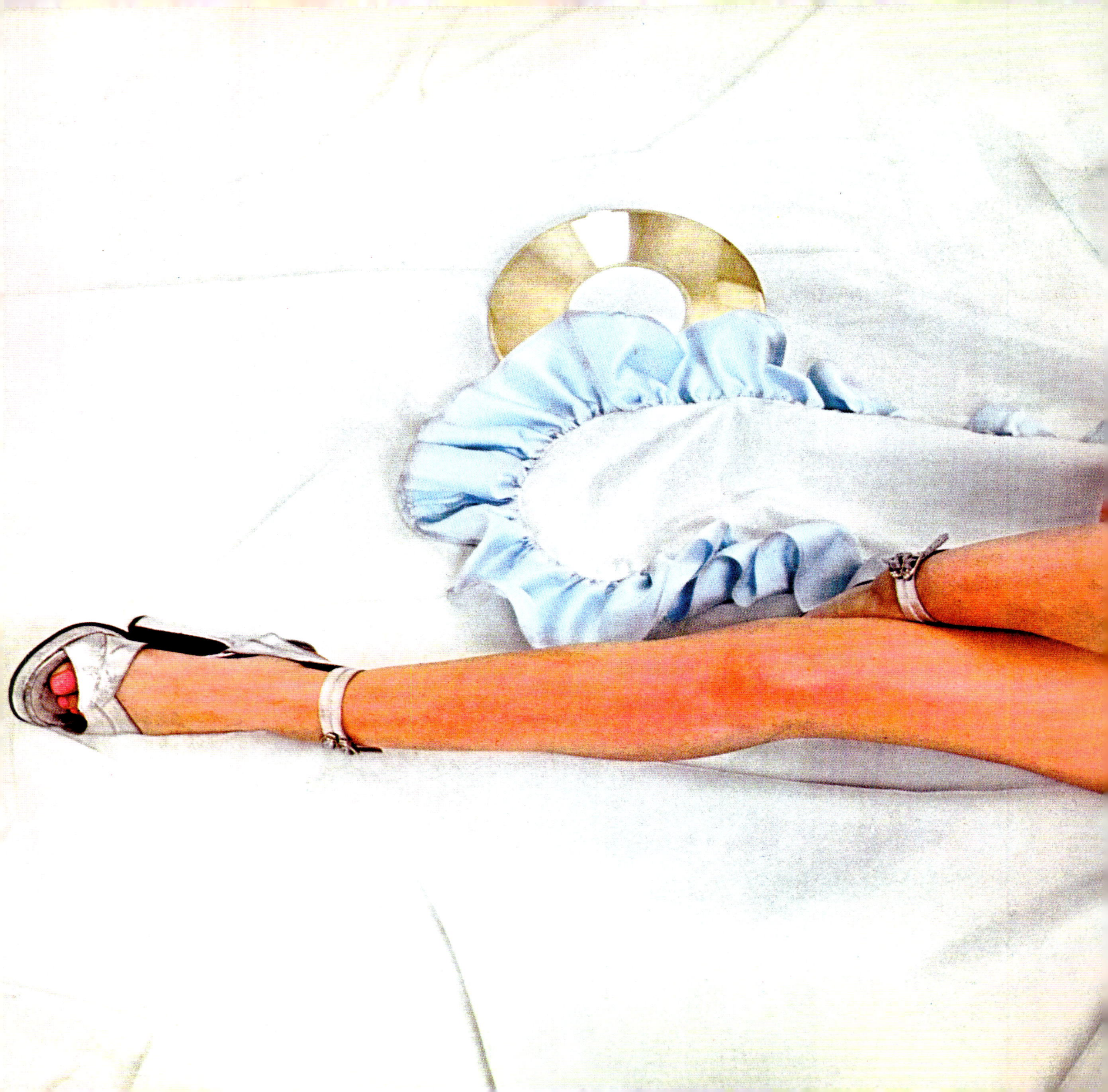

Roxy Music

88 | Keep On Running

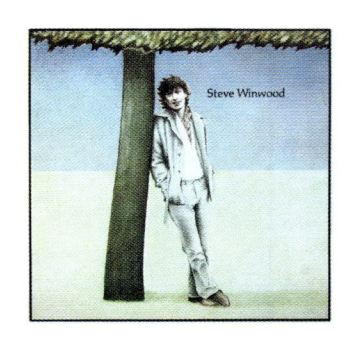

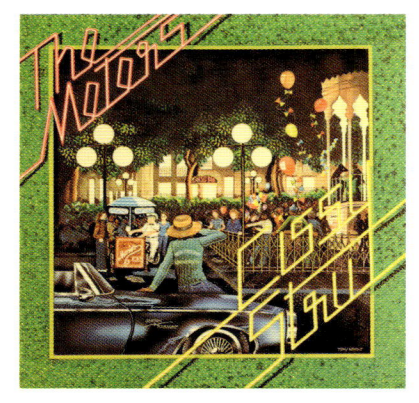

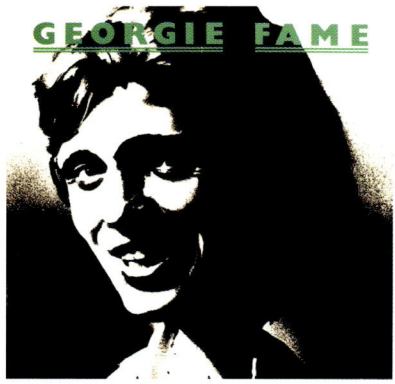

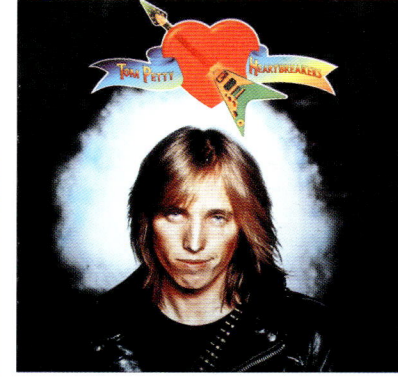

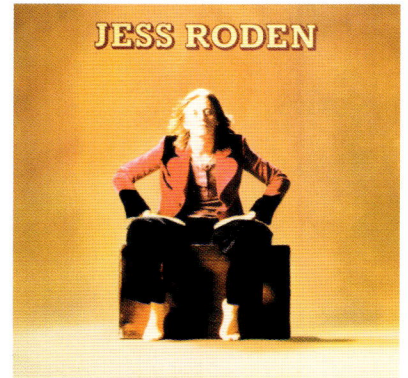

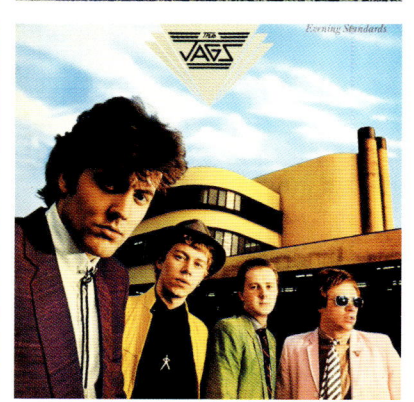

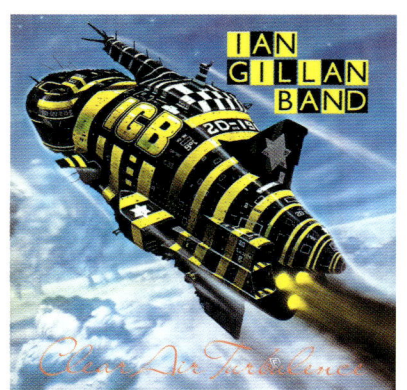

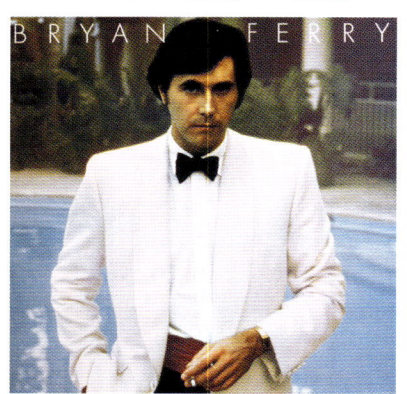

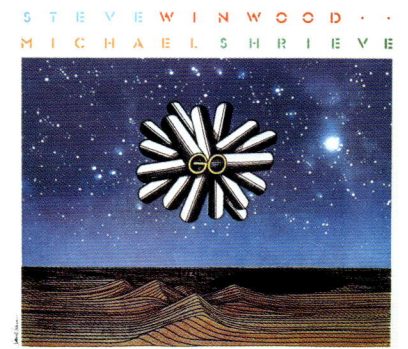

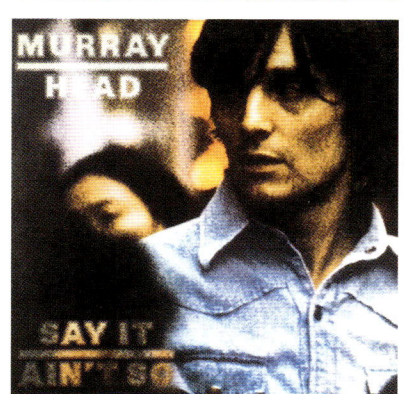

Keep On Running | 89

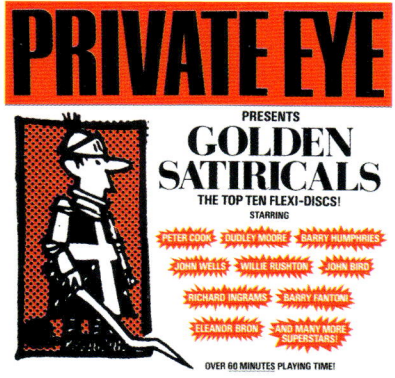

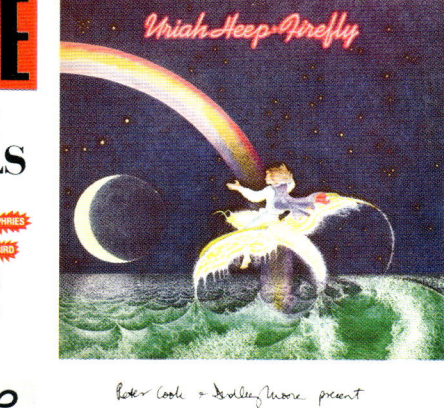

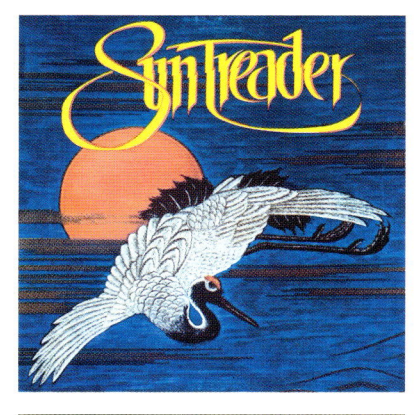

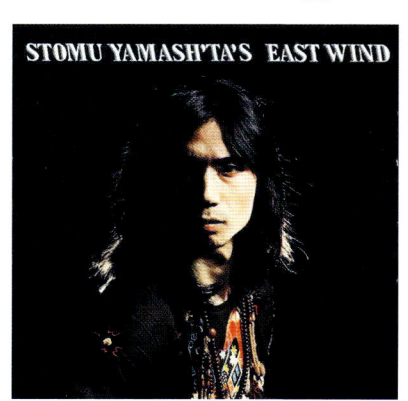

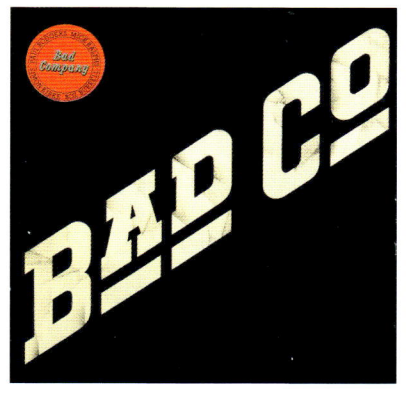

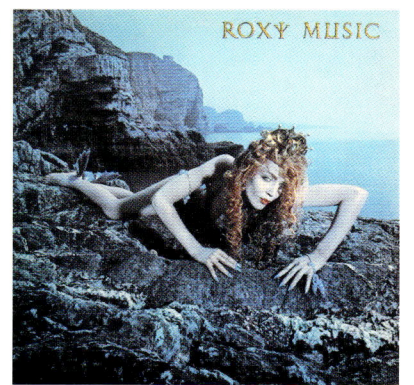

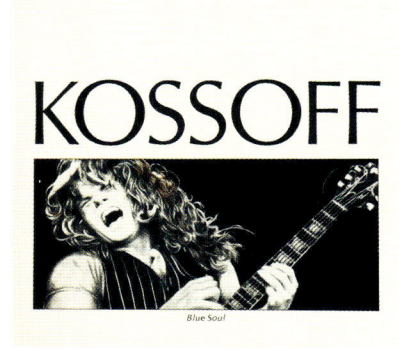

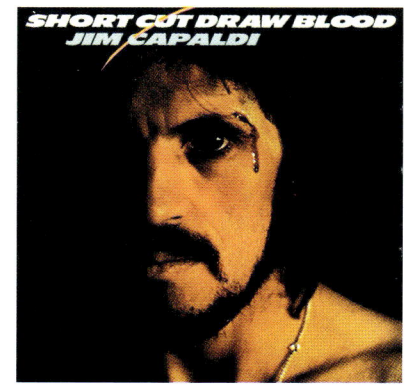

roots-rock reggae

by Lloyd Bradley

To the world at large, the concept of roots'n'culture "officially" began in 1972 with Perry Henzell's classic home-grown Jamaican movie *The Harder They Come*. At that point Jamaica was ten years into Independence, and the first generation to grow up with it felt deceived. Post-colonial economics did not add up, and the growing dissatisfaction was finding its way into song. Groups like The Wailers, The Ethiopians and The Maytals were supplementing reggae's time-honoured subject matter – affairs of the heart, dancing and cowboy films – with a biting commentary on life as it was being lived by the masses.

But although titles like 'Pressure Drop', 'Poor Me Israelite', 'Everything Crash' and '400 Years' were self-explanatory, to anybody born and brought up off-island the whole notion of sufferation was theoretical rather than tangible.

Until *The Harder They Come*. Equal parts violent thriller, gritty documentary and alternative travelogue, the film gave substance to everything you'd heard in those new-fangled 'conscious' records; and just as crucial in this educational process was the soundtrack album. As well as acting as the perfect introduction to Jamaican music for a non-indigenous market, it formed the perfect bridge from one era to the next, bringing us into a far more cerebral space without messing with the music too much – that would come later. The album put down Island's marker as reggae moved into this latest phase, and the biggest players on their budding roots roster – beyond Bob Marley, obviously – were Burning Spear, Lee Perry and Toots & The Maytals.

It speaks volumes for The Maytals' broadminded approach that while they were racking up chart-busting albums around the world, they remained the act with the most number one hits at home in Jamaica.

If ever an artist embodied roots'n'culture it was Burning Spear, and it had been that way throughout his career. Back in the 1960s, before dreadlocks in reggae were either fashionable or profitable, Winston Rodney had renamed himself after the Kenyan revolutionary leader Jomo 'Burning Spear' Kenyatta and was recording hymns of pan-African solidarity and righteous dread at Studio One, the only studio in Kingston to allow Rastas on the premises. By the time Spear signed to Island in 1974 he had matured as both an artist and as a thinker, and the four albums he cut for them – *Marcus Garvey*, *Man In The Hills*, *Dry & Heavy* and *Social Living* – remain the most consistently brilliant body of work in roots reggae's entire catalogue. Toots & The Maytals were never as openly committed to The Cause as Burning Spear, but it would be a brave man who questioned their roots credentials. The archetypal Jamaican trio drew on their wider musical method to move the message into hitherto uncharted areas, notably the USA, with such huge international-selling albums as *Funky Kingston*, *Reggae Got Soul* and *In the Dark*. But, as anybody who has seen *The Harder They Come* will be aware, it is in a live situation that the group's true soul shows through, and to celebrate this, Island set a remarkable record with them: their sell-out show at London's Hammersmith Odeon on September 29, 1980, was recorded, mastered, pressed and put into sleeves overnight – meaning that the first copies of *Toots & The Maytals Live* were in the shops less than 24 hours after the actual gig.

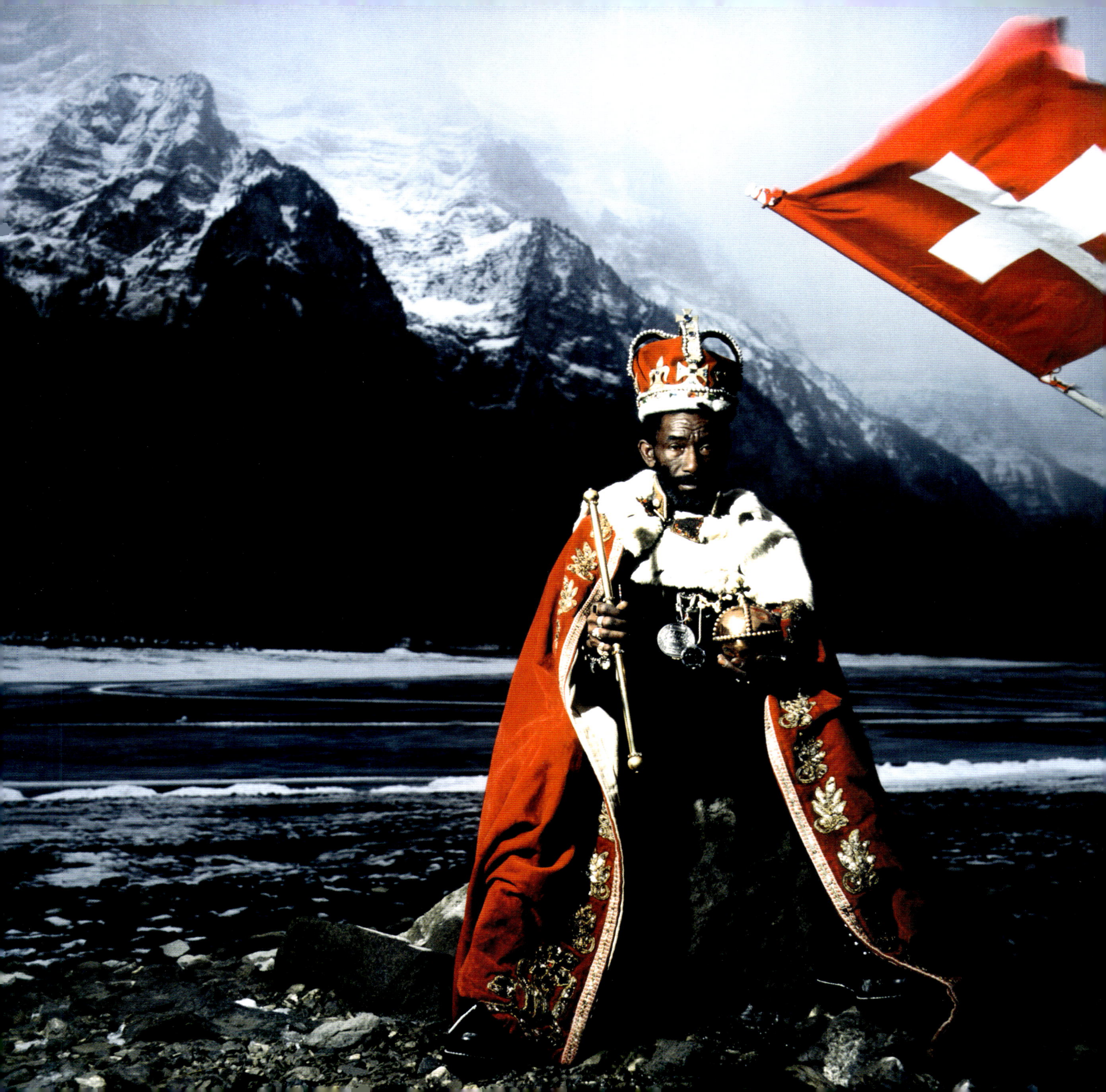

It speaks volumes for The Maytals' broadminded approach that while they were racking up chart-busting albums around the world, they remained the act with the most number one hits at home in Jamaica, a far-from-easy balancing act. As it is based on sound system competition, the reggae industry is driven by rapid turnover of singles, meaning tunes are usually parochial in outlook and exist purely in the present tense. The notion of an album would be little more than a vague promise of money for nothing, by gathering up a dozen or so of those singles and trying to sell them again. Exciting as this might be, this Jamaican practice is almost diametrically opposed to how any major record company likes to do business, and most of the producers there saw no need to change things. It is therefore no mean feat that Island Records managed to cultivate acts that were able to produce albums that remained true to their local roots yet entirely credible within the global marketplace.

The solo Bunny Wailer made a bona fide album for the company too, *Blackheart Man*, displaying a degree of thematic cohesion – dread in its various manifestations – that elevates it into an experience every bit as transcendental as anything Marley or Tosh achieved post-The Wailers. It leaves you wondering, had Bunny been more amenable to the demands of global marketing – his reluctance to travel was a factor in The Wailers' break up – how big a star he would have become? Likewise Jimmy Cliff, as we can only speculate what might have been had he stayed with Island building on his audience from *The Harder They Come*.

Perhaps unsurprisingly, Lee 'Scratch' Perry refuses to be covered by any such cosy singles-vs-albums theory. A producer of prodigious, if uneven, output, in 1976 Perry demonstrated all the requisite albums-making skills with *Superape*, but made sure it ruled itself out of mainstream contention as ten beautifully-fitted-together examples of hyper-smoked melodic dubs – you could almost hear the chalice bubbling. Reggae aficionados loved the LP, but it left everyone else somewhere on the outside. And it wasn't as if 'Scratch' didn't know how to balance the often exclusive demands of the sound system crowds and the mainstream rock audience: during the mid-1970s, at his Black Ark studio, he produced a succession of soft, organically multi-layered tunes that deftly straddled the divide – Junior Byles's 'Curly Locks', Junior Murvin's 'Police & Thieves', Max Romeo's 'War Ina Babylon', Scratch's own 'Dreadlocks In Moonlight', The Heptones' *Party Time* LP and so on.

The year after *Superape*, Perry produced another expertly paced, super-woozy roots work of genius, but this time conventional vocals gave The Congos' *Heart of The Congos* a keener commercial edge. It was widely acknowledged as The Best Reggae Album Ever, but it was also the best reggae album ever not released by Island. Through no fault of their own either. Never the easiest man to deal with, Perry blamed the company for *Superape*'s relative lack of success and, regardless of his contract with Island, released the Congos' masterpiece on his own Black Ark label. As a result this brilliant album all but disappeared for twenty years.

Such behaviour vividly illustrates the inherent tension between the needs of the music industry in Jamaica and what it took to manage an international roster. As the roots era established itself, Jamaica's music scene was an explosion of free-market enterprise; by the mid-1970s there were so many small studios and record labels in Kingston it was impossible to keep track of who was recording what, for whom, and where.

Such behaviour vividly illustrates the inherent tension between the music industry in Jamaica and what it took to manage an international roster.

92 | Keep On Running

BURNING SPEAR

MARCUS GARVEY

MAX ROMEO & THE UPSETTERS
WAR INA BABYLON

Local reggae boys Aswad signed to Island as a working, gigging band – similar to how Chris Blackwell had envisaged The Wailers. They brought a distinctly London tang to reggae music.

Singers and musicians worked for cash-in-hand, with few concerns as to who put it there. Any talk of a 'contract' rarely involved anything written, let alone a signature, and it was not unusual for artists to record for several different labels in the same afternoon. Maybe even singing the same song. This was because the copyright act had yet to be applied to music in Jamaica, ownership of a song resting with whoever held the mastertape of that particular recording of it.

Because Island enjoyed an inside track on how things worked in Jamaica, they seemed to use it to their advantage, cherry-picking tracks from artist catalogues that were being added to on an almost hourly basis. This meant that such superb roots singles as Leroy Smart's 'Ballistic Affair', George Faith's 'To Be A Lover', The Wailing Souls' 'Bredda Gravalicious' and 'Very Well', and Jacob Miller's 'Tenement Yard' received widespread international release. As did some of the best of Gregory Isaacs: the *Night Nurse* album made available the title track as well as 'Cool Down the Pace' and 'Objection Overruled', but spared us too much of the throwaway end of Gregory's Herculean output. Island also had the good sense to record him in concert, and *Reggae Greats: Gregory Isaacs (Live)* is one of the best live reggae albums ever made, showcasing exactly what it is that made the Cool Ruler so special.

Of course this method did not always come off. But when it did, the consequences could be transcendent, the classic dub outing 'King Tubby Meets Rockers Uptown' a case in point. For years Island had been releasing roots singles with dub mixes on the flip, but this time they had the good sense to realise that Augustus Pablo's King Tubby-mixed 'B'-side dub was more interesting than Jacob Miller singing 'Baby I Love You So', and made that the 'A' side. The single flew off the shelves, introducing the world at large to the delights of dub, but Island missed out on the album of the same name, which remains the standard by which other dubwise longplayers are judged.

This is not to say that Island dragged their feet when it came to dub. As the 1970s progressed, so did affordable studio technology, meaning that far more Jamaican producers had the facilities to do far more with vocals and instrumentation than simply accurately reproduce them. Dub was developing into an accepted musical art form, therefore having its place in the LP format.

In a move that appealed to Island's album-buying audience and kept them firmly in touch with the music's sound system roots, the record company offered dubwise takes on some of the favourites in the catalogue: Burning Spear's *Marcus Garvey* album was transformed into the otherworldly *Garvey's Ghost*; tracks from Linton Kwesi Johnson's *Forces of Victory* and *Bass Culture* were reworked into the muscular *LKJ in Dub*; Rico reapproached *Man From Wareika* and came away with the ethereal *Wareika Dub*; Aswad's *New Chapter* became *Chapter of Dub*; and at the end of the decade Sly & Robbie remixed a selection of their productions into the *Raiders of the Lost Dub* album.

> Because Island enjoyed an inside track on how things worked in Jamaica, they seemed to use it to their advantage, cherry-picking tracks from artist catalogues that were being added to almost on an hourly basis.

What might have come as a surprise to reggae fans is that Island more or less opted out of the deejay phenomenon that gripped the music through the roots era. But on reflection perhaps that was not so remarkable. By the time reggae was well into the 1970s, the difference between a good sound system and a killer sound system was increasingly down to its deejay's microphone skills. But toasting was largely a matter for the sound systems and, as regards the recording industry, still an optional extra – a parochial appendage to a pre-proven piece of music rather than a stand-alone statement. Unless, of course, you were U-Roy, I-Roy, Big Youth or Dennis Alcapone, or, slightly later, the Princes Far-I and Jazzbo. On record these stars approached deejaying with the same structural care over music and lyrics as any top singer, and so did not need to rely on the popularity of the original tune to court an audience. Thus they all sold huge amounts of albums. But none of them were recording for Island.

However, this should not be interpreted as the company couldn't do deejay, more like they couldn't do mundane deejay. Without access to the abovementioned, Island simply waited until another genuinely special deejay came along – or, as it turned out, two genuinely special deejays. In 1976 Island signed former Dennis Alcapone protégé Dillinger and to instant international acclaim released his *CB200* album; then in the same year came Jah Lion's *Colombia Colly*, another roots classic that masterfully combined the deejay's gravel-voiced militancy with Lee Perry's airy, intricate production.

During this period, the biggest market for reggae in the world was the United Kingdom – it had been this way for a while, but during the 1970s, roots reggae's messages gave the music meaning among large numbers of rock album buyers. It was only natural that the music would be made here too.

Jamaican music had been produced in Britain virtually for as long as there were large numbers of Jamaicans in the country – since the 1950s – but twenty years later it was being made by boys and girls who had been born or brought up in the UK. This introduced some radical changes, as it began to soak up other influences, from its environment and from the background of those who were making it – not every British reggae musician was of Jamaican descent. The best seemed to gravitate to Island, where their broader sensibilities found support, creating a sub-genre of roots music rarely seen in Jamaica: reggae as made by self-contained groups, instead of singers working with backing musicians.

Steel Pulse and Aswad led the way. The former's *Handsworth Revolution* album was groundbreaking in its use of rock sensibilities into a crisp reggae framework. Aswad operated in a more straightforward roots situation, but were perfectly capable of subverting the format by ushering in elements of pop, soul and jazz-funk – the singles 'Three Babylon', 'Warrior Charge' and 'Back to Africa' are vivid illustrations. Another major contributor to Island's UK roots roster was ska trombonist Rico Rodriguez, who moved to London in the early 1960s. His 1977 album *Man From Wareika* was as much about jazz as it was roots reggae, and while it may have been recorded in Jamaica, its fusion sensibilities were a consequence of fifteen years on the UK music scene.

Great Britain's biggest stylistic contribution to international reggae was the dub poetry of Linton Kwesi Johnson with Dennis Bovell's Dub Band. LKJ's *Forces of Victory*, *Making History* and *Bass Culture* albums, all Island releases, are fantastic examples of this spoken word form that had all the immediacy and militancy of toasting, the considered, cerebral qualities of conventional poetry, and some kicking riddim tracks.

Denise Mills (top), the spine of Island Records. Ini Kamoze (centre). Suzette Newman (bottom), with Sly And Robbie, in her role as Island ambassador-at-large.

Keep On Running | 97

Winston Rodney (left), the man called Burning Spear, relaxing at his home in St Ann, Jamaica.

Black Uhuru (opposite), who took up the mantle of Sly and Robbie's digital feel to international critical and commercial acclaim.

98 | Keep On Running

On record these guys approached deejaying with the same structural care over music and lyrics that any singer would, and so didn't need to rely on the popularity of the original tune to court an audience.

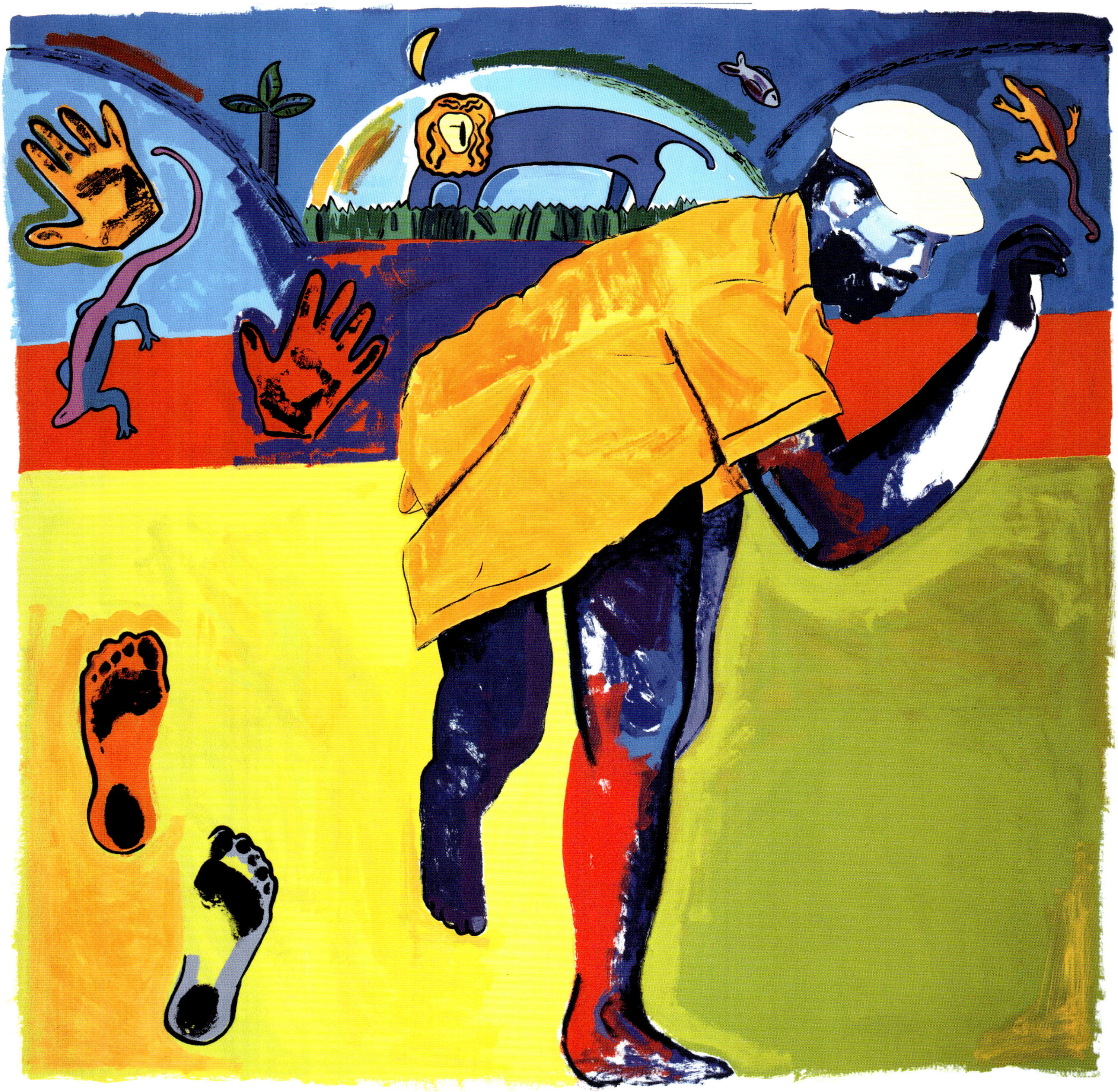

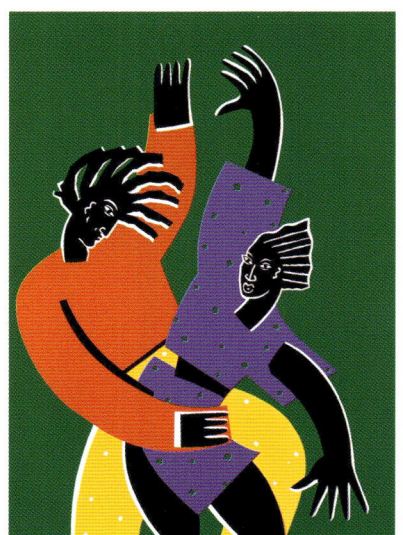

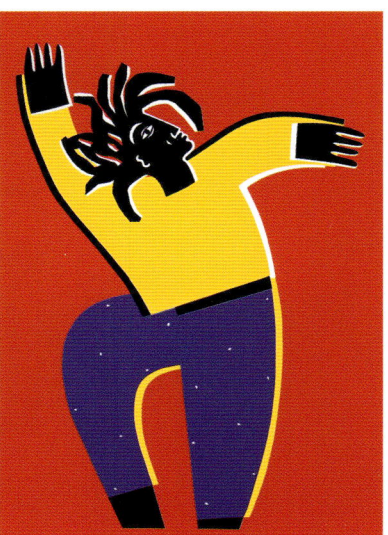

Part of the Reggae Greats series, the artwork for the Lee 'Scratch' Perry record (left) in the series perfectly captured the surreal flavour of the legendarily eccentric producer's yard. Meanwhile, Paul Wearing's imagery on the right provided all the hallucinatory spirit of a Friday night Kingston sound system dance.

Tony Wright (artwork following pages) at first had a hip shop on London's Kings Road called Lucky's Design. Among other products that the store sold were the bumpers sneakers featured on the Bumpers album sleeve. Tony and Chris Blackwell hit it off. Increasingly Tony Wright came to be highly influential, the prime motivating force, in the creation of Island Records' landmark artwork, becoming the label's art director, and acting as a constant in the stream of iconic images that played a large part in the public's understanding of the label; Tony was, it seemed, instinctively suited to being Chris Blackwell's visual interpreter, as testified by the many awards he would win over their years working together. It is a relationship that has continued to the present day.

Keep On Running | 101

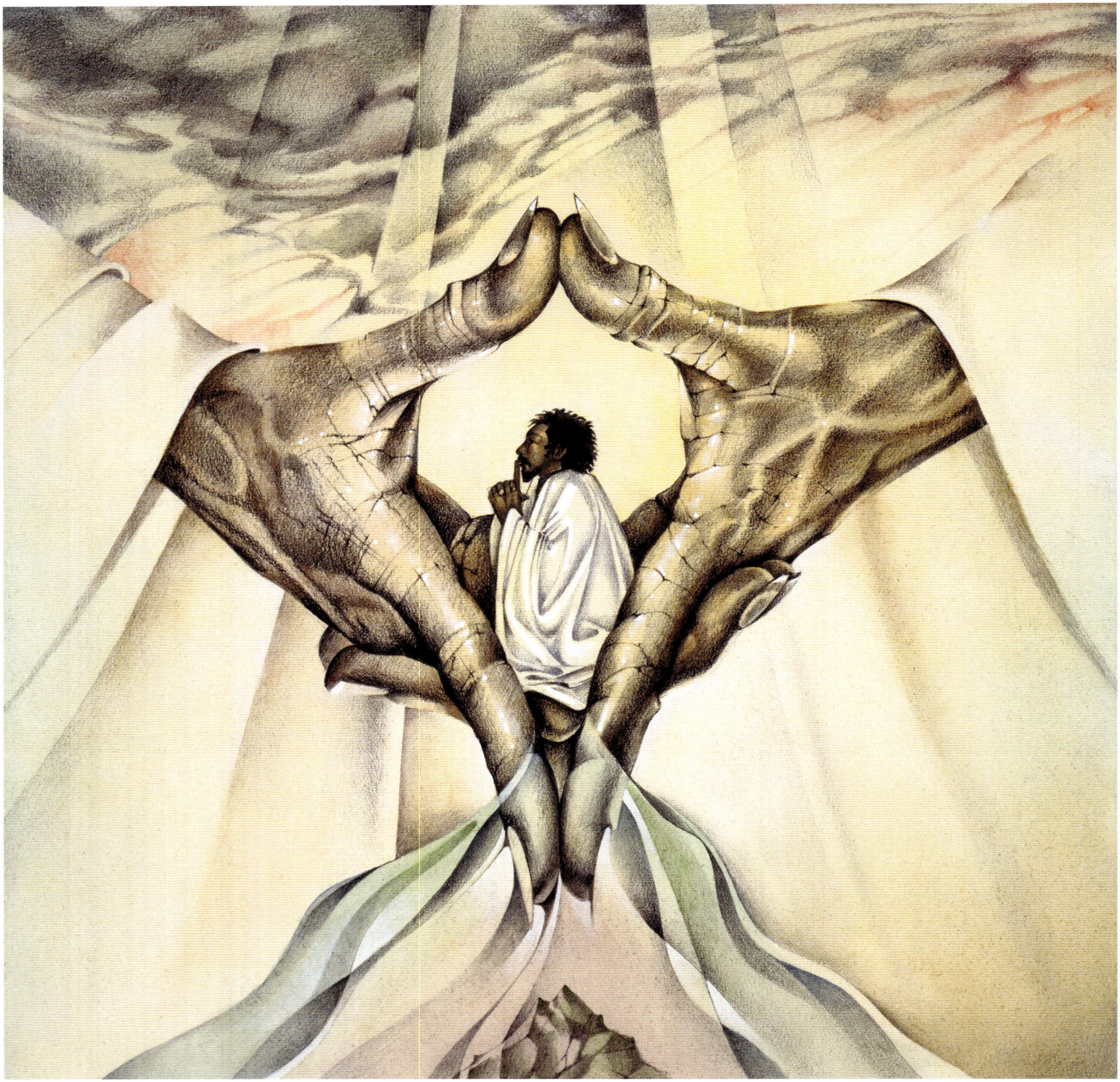

Keep On Running | 103

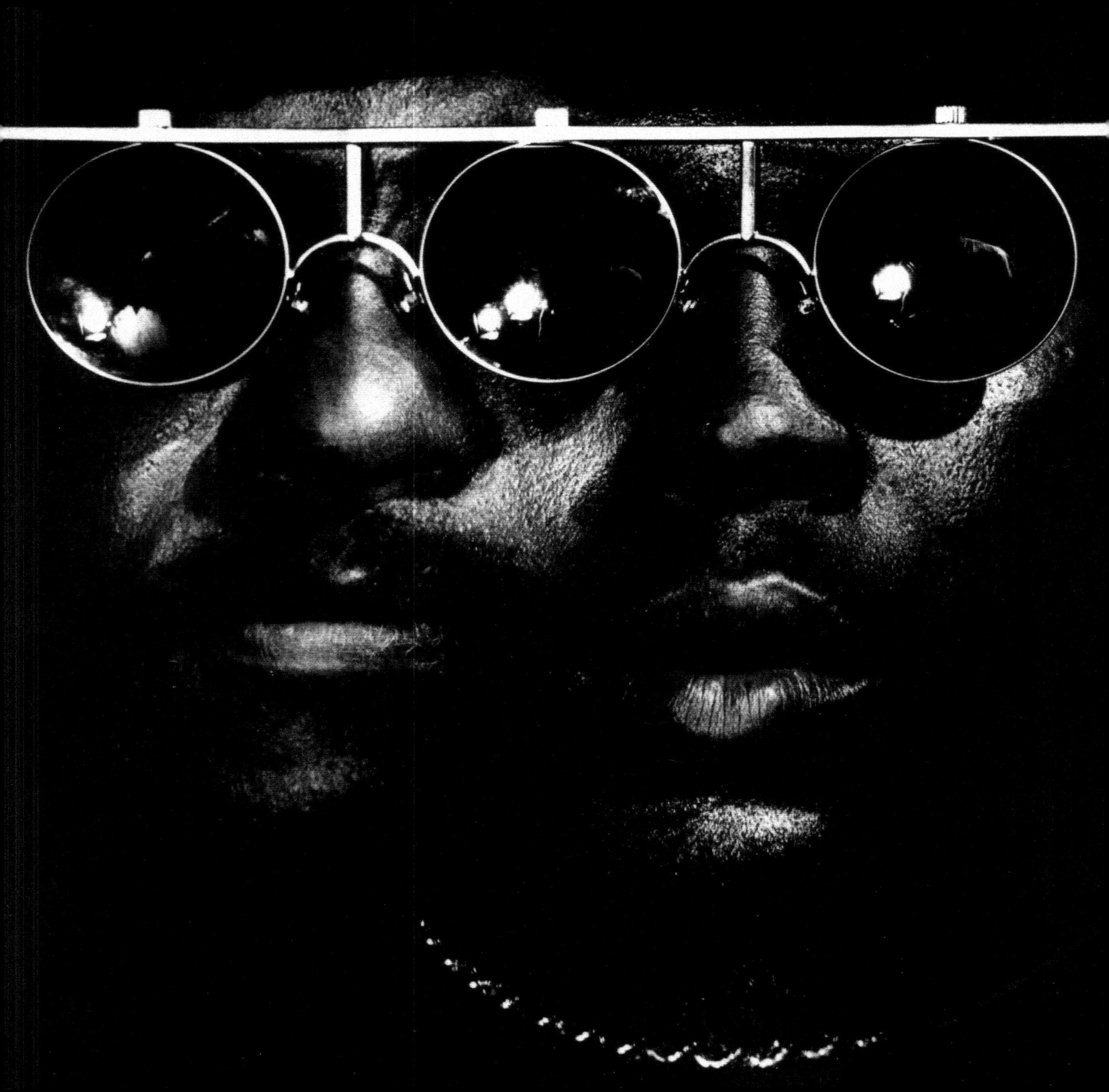

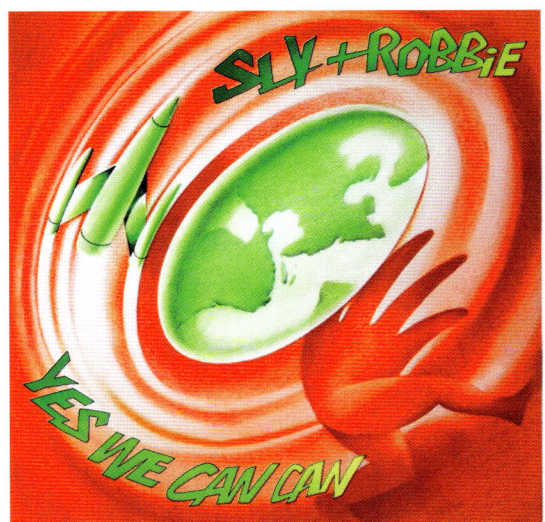

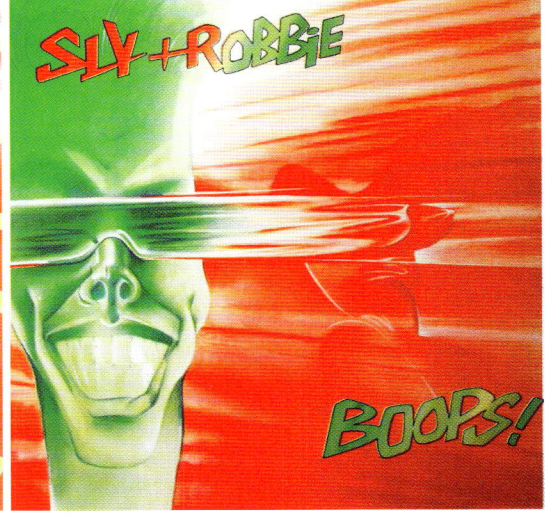

By now, Island was becoming something of a magnet for those who wanted to move roots music on. Third World played as a fully-fledged group, with their dreadlock'd sensibilities clearly influenced by soul and disco; by the time they hit their stride with their second album for Island, *96 Degrees in the Shade*, this clever, laidback fusion had earned them an international audience and a massive club hit with 'Now That We've Found Love'. Their follow-up album *Journey to Addis* consolidated matters, and seemed to pave the way for Inner Circle and their 1979 LP *Everything Is Great*. Disco-tinged? Sure, but very definitely with reggae roots, and a resulting two international hit singles – 'Stop Breaking My Heart' and the title track.

By the end of the decade, roots reggae's landscape was virtually unrecognisable from what it had been when *The Harder They Come* blew up. The most significant change was that reggae now had a life beyond the island and its diaspora. In Bob Marley's global slipstream, what was once a cottage industry had transformed itself into a bona fide world music, and to continue its trajectory artists were needed with a world view. Enter Sly & Robbie.

Established in the Kingston reggae business as master musicians, this self-contained rhythm section (Sly Dunbar, drums; Robbie Shakespeare, bass) had an international outlook, a shared love of US soul and a fascination with studio technology. They had also struck a deal with Island for their Taxi label and productions. With a string of impressive singles from acts like Dennis Brown, Jimmy Riley, Jacob Miller and Junior Delgado, their taut, computerised sound borrowed from American studio innovation and pushed roots reggae from the woozy 1970s into the harder-edged 1980s. This supplanting of the traditional one drop beat with something deliberately synthetic-sounding peaked with vocal trio Black Uhuru. Their albums *Sinsemilla*, *Red*, *Chill Out* and *Anthem* were big sellers all over the world, with the last winning the inaugural Reggae Grammy in 1985, and *Red* being voted in at number 23 in a Rolling Stone magazine poll of the 100 Best Albums of the 1980s.

But Black Uhuru also were the last big stars of that roots reggae era. True, Jamaican roots music has never gone away and Island continued to enjoy conscious success with acts like Ini Kamoze, Luciano, Buju Banton and Damian Marley. But as the 1980s got underway reggae's emphasis was on pleasures of the flesh set to digital rhythms. Island opted to concentrate on building a legacy, hence nearly all of their carefully-selected roots reggae remains available, the most vibrant documentation of that most fertile of musical eras.

> By now, Island was becoming something of a magnet for those who wanted to move roots music on.

106 | Keep On Running

Keep On Running | 107

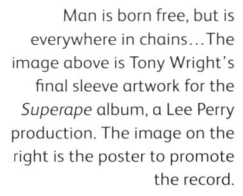

Man is born free, but is everywhere in chains…The image above is Tony Wright's final sleeve artwork for the *Superape* album, a Lee Perry production. The image on the right is the poster to promote the record.

Keep On Running | 109

Reggae and – more specifically – Rastafari evolved a set of archetypal images that were implicit in first the artwork and then the culture of the age. Ubiquitous were the red, gold and green colours of the Ethiopian flag; the star of David; and the image of the Conquering Lion of Judah, one of the several titles of His Imperial Majesty Haile Selassie I, Emperor of Ethiopia. Portraits of Haile Selassie, and also of Marcus Garvey, the Jamaican prophet of black conciousness, were omnipresent. And then there was always the herb plant, and the living art of the spliff…

Painting by Paul 'Groucho' Smykle.

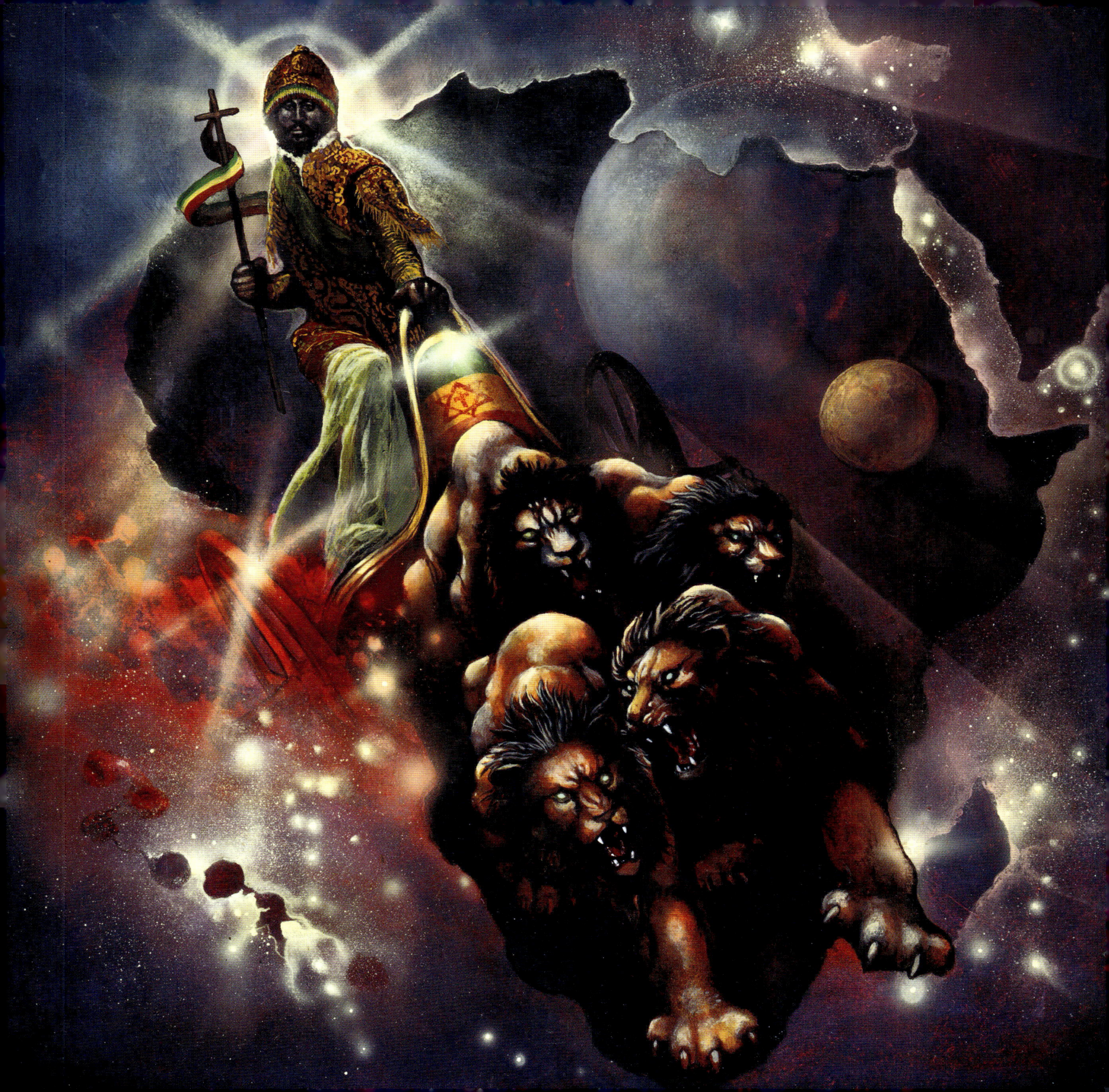

112 | Keep On Running

Rico Rodriguez, a trombonist of unparalleled ability, was a sometime player with assorted Jamaican combos. Moving to London in 1961 he played with – among others – Georgie Fame's Blue Flames. A true Rastafarian musician, in 1977 he released his inspirational *Man From Wareika*. The album became regarded as a classic, as was the dub version which enjoyed a more informal release.

Keep On Running | 113

Linton Kwesi Johnson's dub poetry was both edgily Jamaican and simultaneously distinctly English: LKJ's cool, understated delivery drew the listener into his stories of everyday oppression and aggro.

LINTON KWESI JOHNSON

BASS CULTURE

The Harder They Come is a rough-hewn masterpiece, the first and best home-grown Jamaican feature film. When the movie was first shown in Kingston in 1972, it provoked riots by people unable to gain admission to the sold-out Carib cinema.

Based on the life of Ivan Martin, a self-styled ghetto Robin Hood who had died in a shoot-out with police in 1948, the film's director Perry Henzell added an extra element by turning the gunman into an innocent country youth desperate to succeed in the cut-throat Kingston reggae world. With Ivan played by the local singer Jimmy Cliff, an Island signing, Henzell created a Jamaican rebel archetype; inspired by such an image, Island Records' creator Chris Blackwell - who had part-financed the movie - seized upon it in promoting his new signing, Bob Marley. In some ways the groundwork for Marley's eventual success had been laid by *The Harder They Come* having one of the best soundtrack albums ever released, an indispensible accompaniment to chic dinner parties of the early 1970s, introducing Jamaican music to the white album market; Perry Henzell had personally chosen the record's reggae gems.

Another Jamaican hit, *Countryman*, released in 1982, was an early release by Island Alive – this company would soon mutate into Island Pictures, the imprint formed to further the cinematic ambitions of Chris Blackwell and the Island team. Directed and written by Dickie Jobson, *Countryman* was a romantic comedy, starring a genuine Rastafarian fisherman, a personal friend of Jobson, who saves a woman whose plane crash-lands from political and drug-related intrigue. On the 'recommended' list of many video-stores, *Countryman*'s surreal plot was driven by magic realism, something that was a norm in the life of Dickie Jobson.

After this pair of Jamaican classics, the emphasis of Island Pictures shifted from the island where the record business had begun to the world of high-end art movies.

A TALE OF MODERN ADVENTURE AND ANCIENT MAGIC

COUNTRYMAN

A FILM BY DICKIE JOBSON

FEATURES CLASSIC REGGAE TRACKS FROM
BOB MARLEY, STEEL PULSE & TOOTS AND THE MAYTALS

118 | Keep On Running

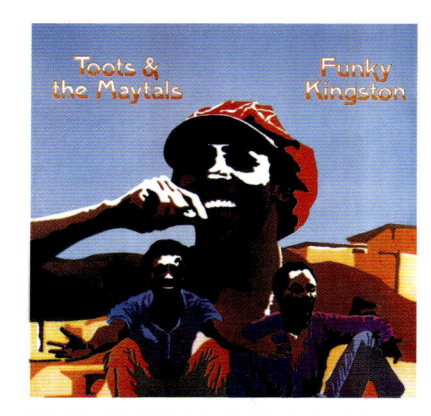

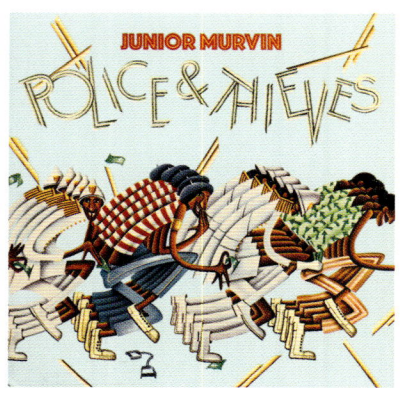

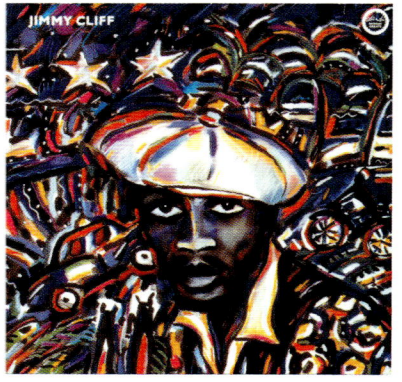

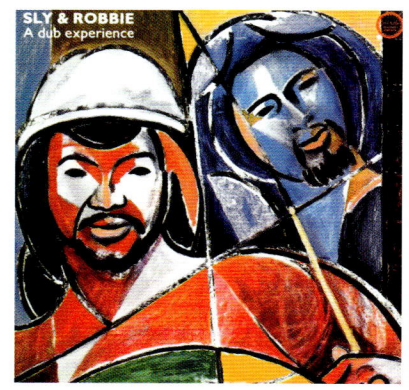

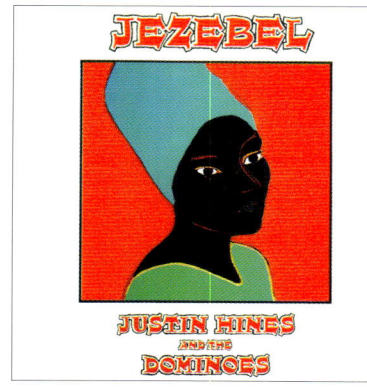

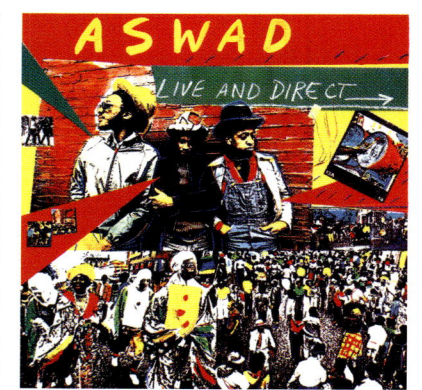

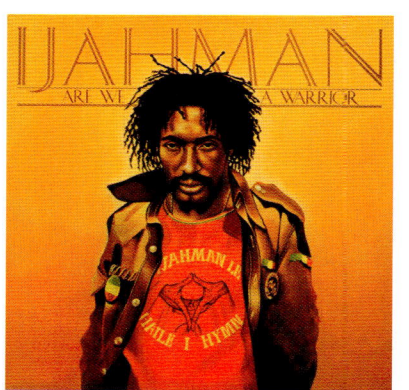

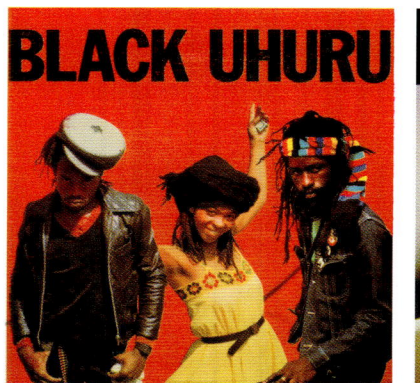

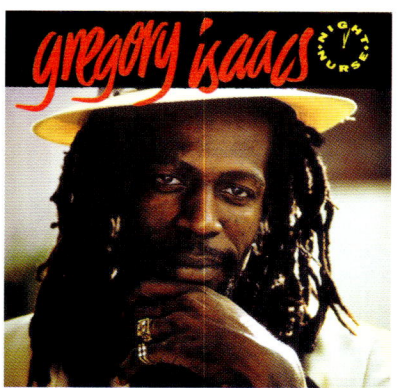

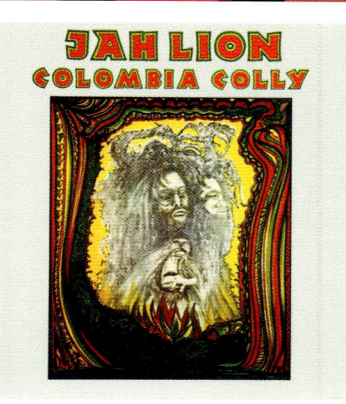

Keep On Running | 119

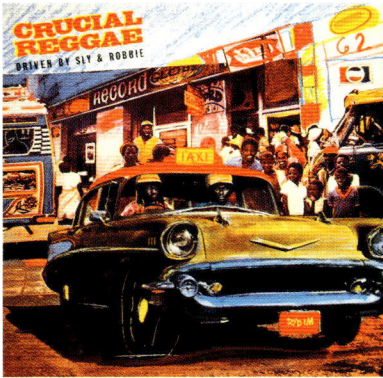

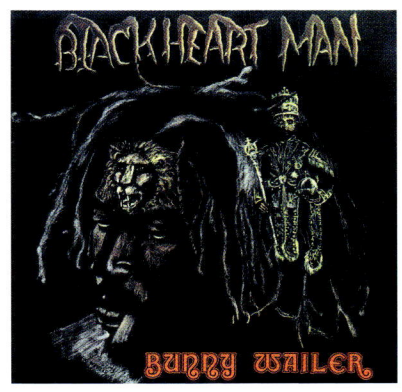

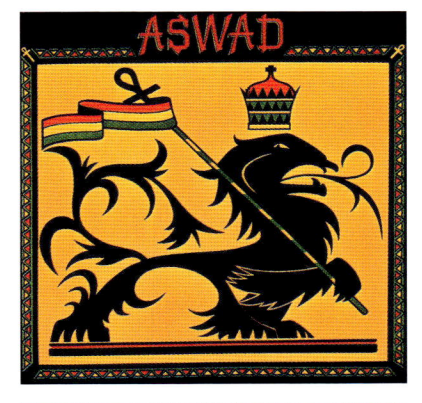

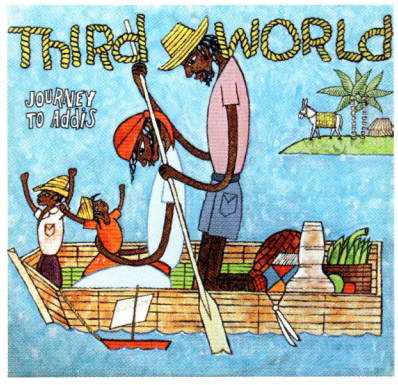

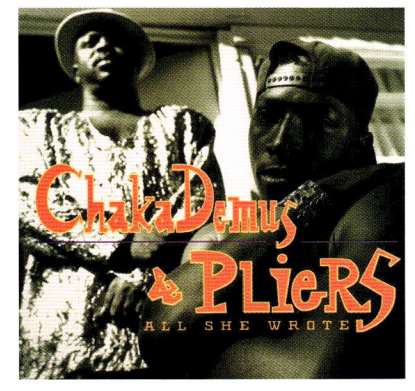

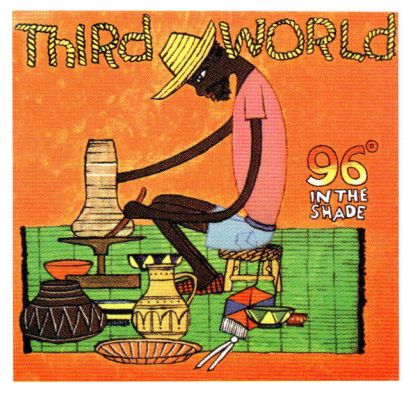

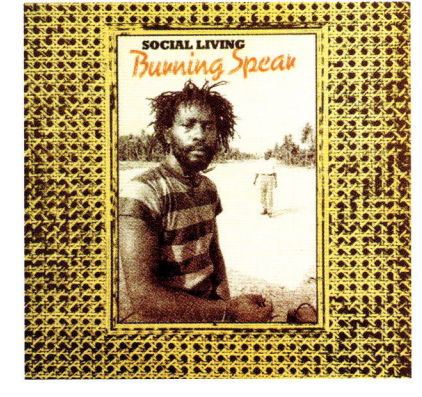

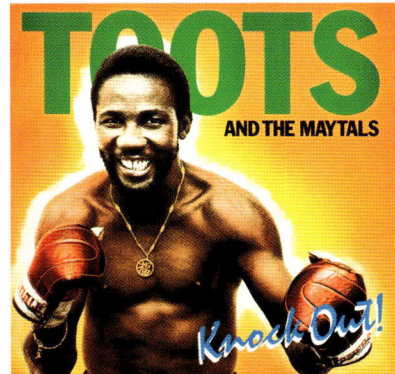

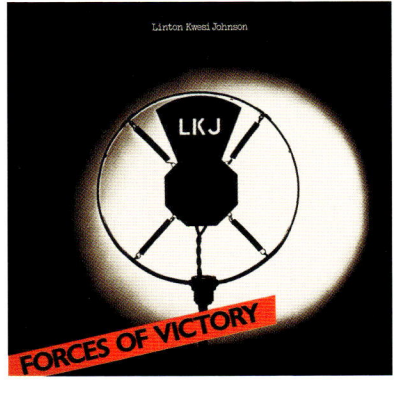

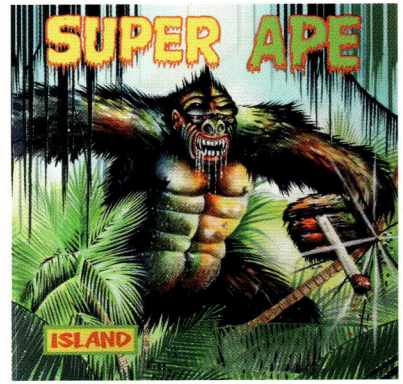

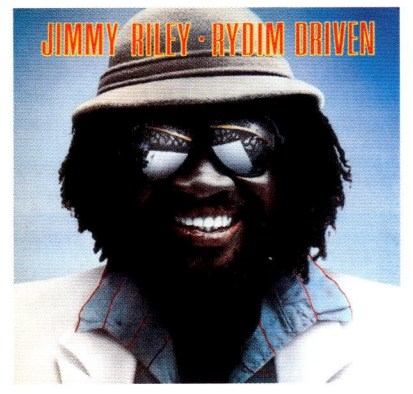

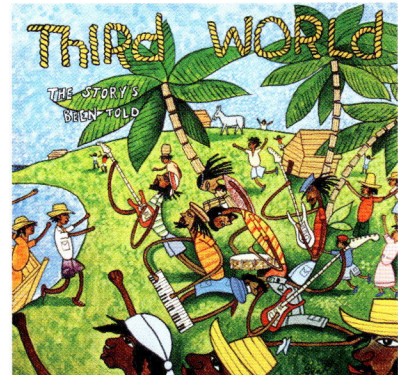

singular voices

Grace Jones, with Jean-Paul Goude.

by Sean O'Hagan

In the late 1970s and early 1980s, Island Records stayed true to its initial independent ethos by signing a handful of maverick artists that probably would not have found a home on any other mainstream label. The first, and most extravagantly eccentric, was Grace Jones, a Jamaican born ex-model whose three early singles had earned her a certain cult status on the European and New York gay disco scenes and made her a muse for Andy Warhol.

'I really had nothing to do with the signing with Island,' she told journalist Chris Salewicz in 1980, 'I didn't even know which record companies were around - I just came from a totally different world.'

It took Chris Blackwell a while to realise that Grace's otherworldliness might be exaggerated to dramatic effect if grounded by a music that sounded unearthly funky to the point of futuristic. After the commercial failure of her first three disco-oriented albums, *Portfolio* (1977), *Fame* (1978) and *Muse* (1979), Blackwell installed Jones in his state-of-the-art Compass Point studios in Nassau and together with Alex Sadkin, who had worked with artists as diverse as KC and The Sunshine Band and Bob Marley, set to work transforming Grace Jones the disco diva into Grace Jones the androgynous ice maiden of eighties' dub-funk.

All three of Jones's statement albums – *Warm Leatherette* (1980), *Night Clubbing* (1981), *Living My Life* (1982) – were recorded at Compass Point with the ace reggae rhythm section of Sly Dunbar and Robbie Shakespeare, several Jamaican session men and French synth player Wally Badarou. Like the modernist reggae group Black Uhuru, Grace Jones used Sly & Robbie's propulsive rhythms to create something both new and urgent sounding, a merging of funk, dub and dark-edged, hypnotic, post-disco beats. Her singular vocal style – a mixture of the deadpan and the defiant, with a trace of aristocratic *hauteur* thrown in for good measure – lent this already heady sound a darker, almost Germanic, edge. It remains one of the more original and forward-sounding musical signatures of the eighties.

Then there were the songs, most notably the covers that she made her own: Daniel Miller's 'Warm Leatherette', Bryan Ferry's 'Love Is the Drug', Iggy Pop's 'Nightclubbing', Chrissie Hynde's 'Private Life', Joy Division's 'She's Lost Control'. All of them became Grace Jones songs: imperious, exotic, chillingly sexy. She could do light, too, but it was always Grace Jones' light, even the buoyant pulse of 'My Jamaican Guy' is undercut with a sense of dark possibility – just what would it take to be Grace Jones's Jamaican guy?

The extended 12-inch single format was a medium made for Grace Jones and Sly & Robbie, a form on which those propulsive rhythms – repetitive, heady, insistent – perfectly suited the emerging club culture of the time. On the provocatively titled

> **It took Chris Blackwell a while to realise that Grace's otherworldliness might be exaggerated to dramatic effect if grounded by a music that sounded unearthly funky to the point of futuristic.**

Keep On Running | 121

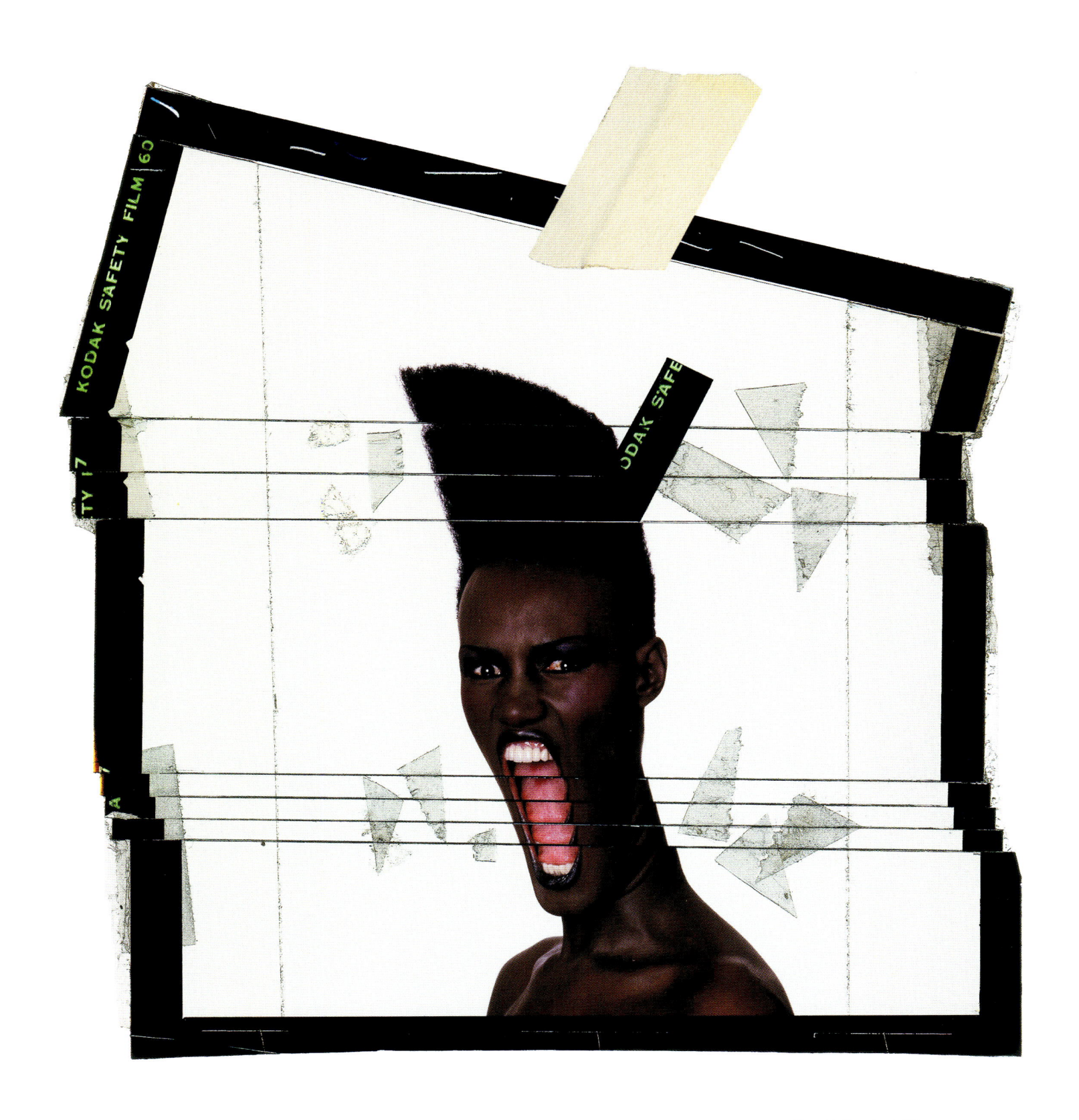

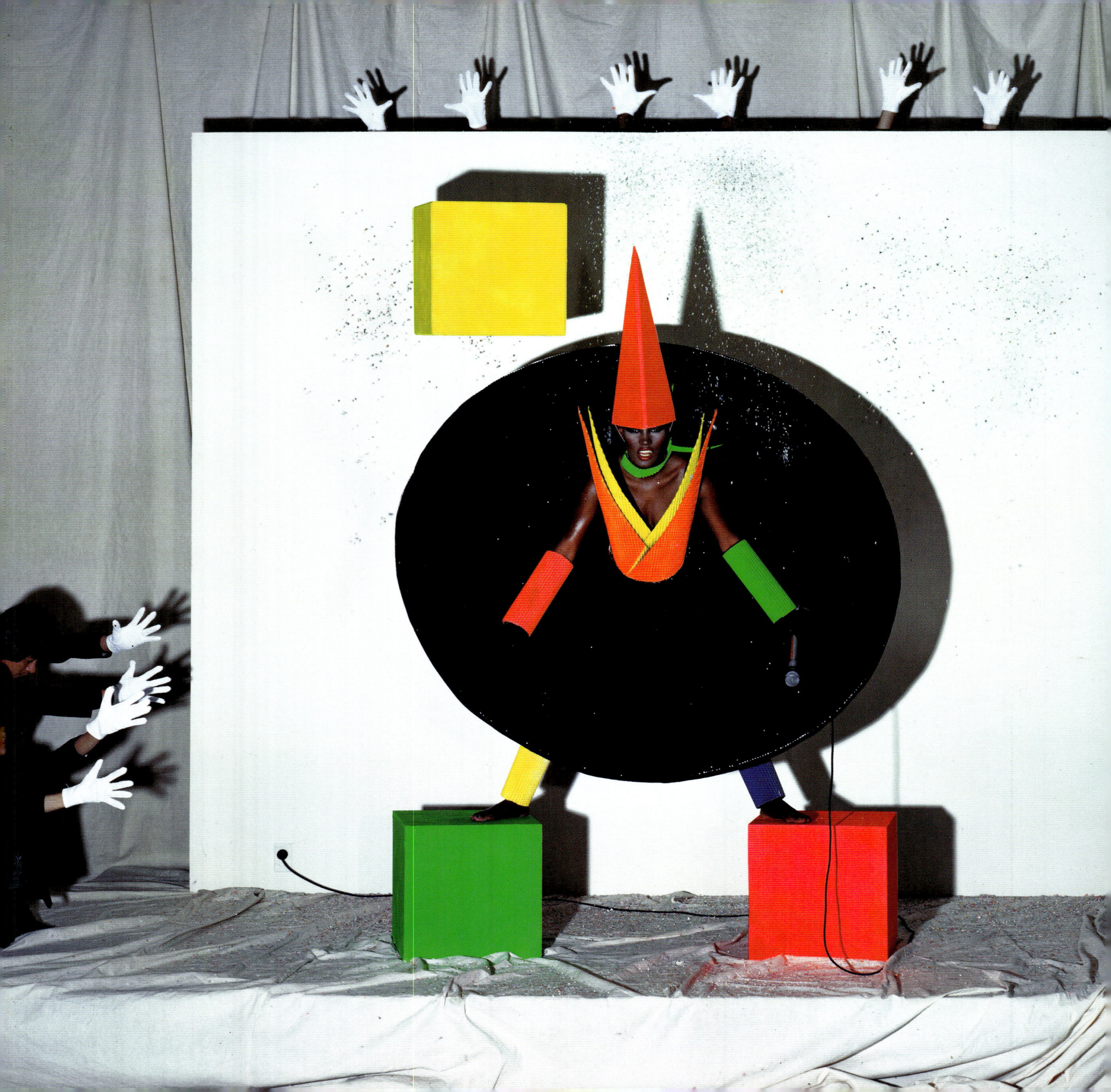

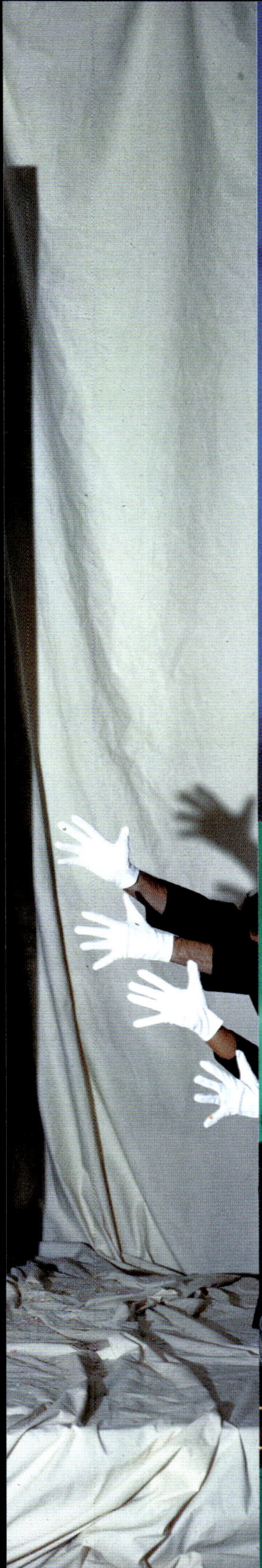
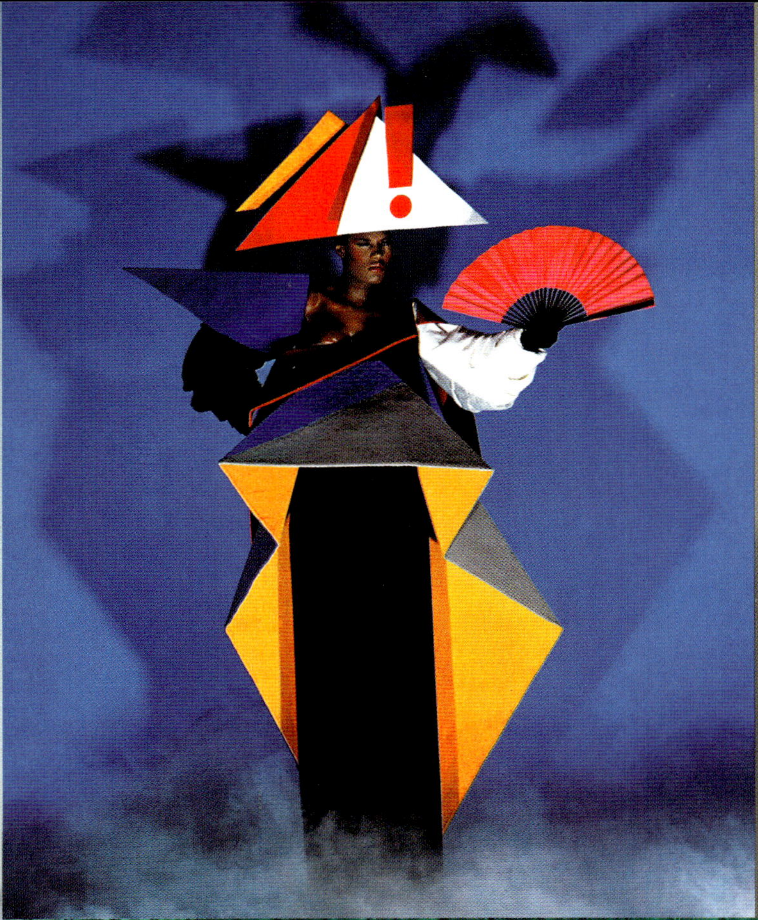
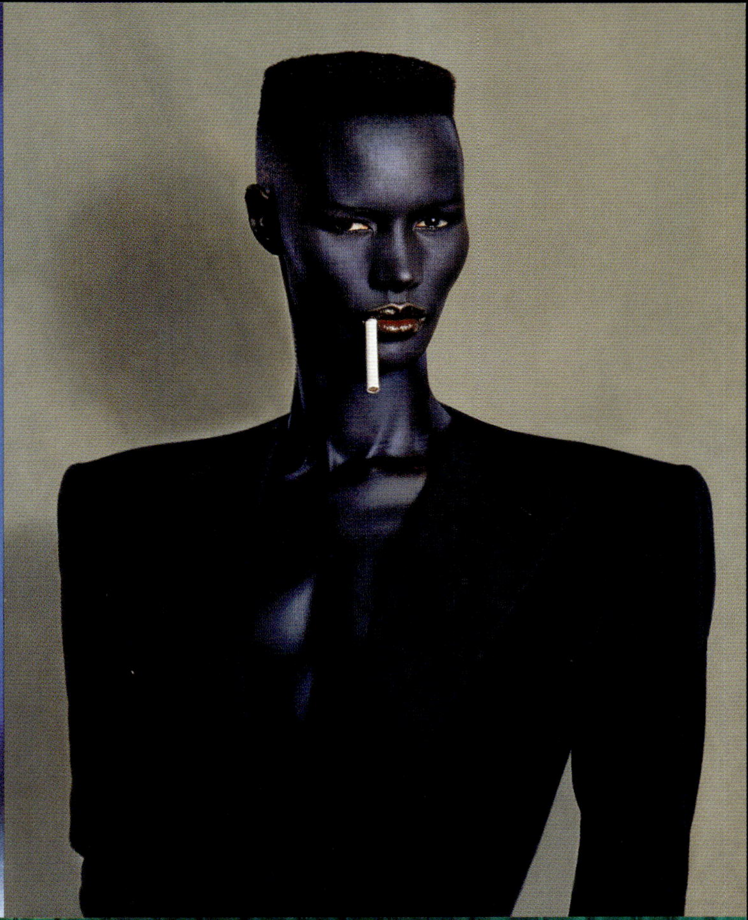
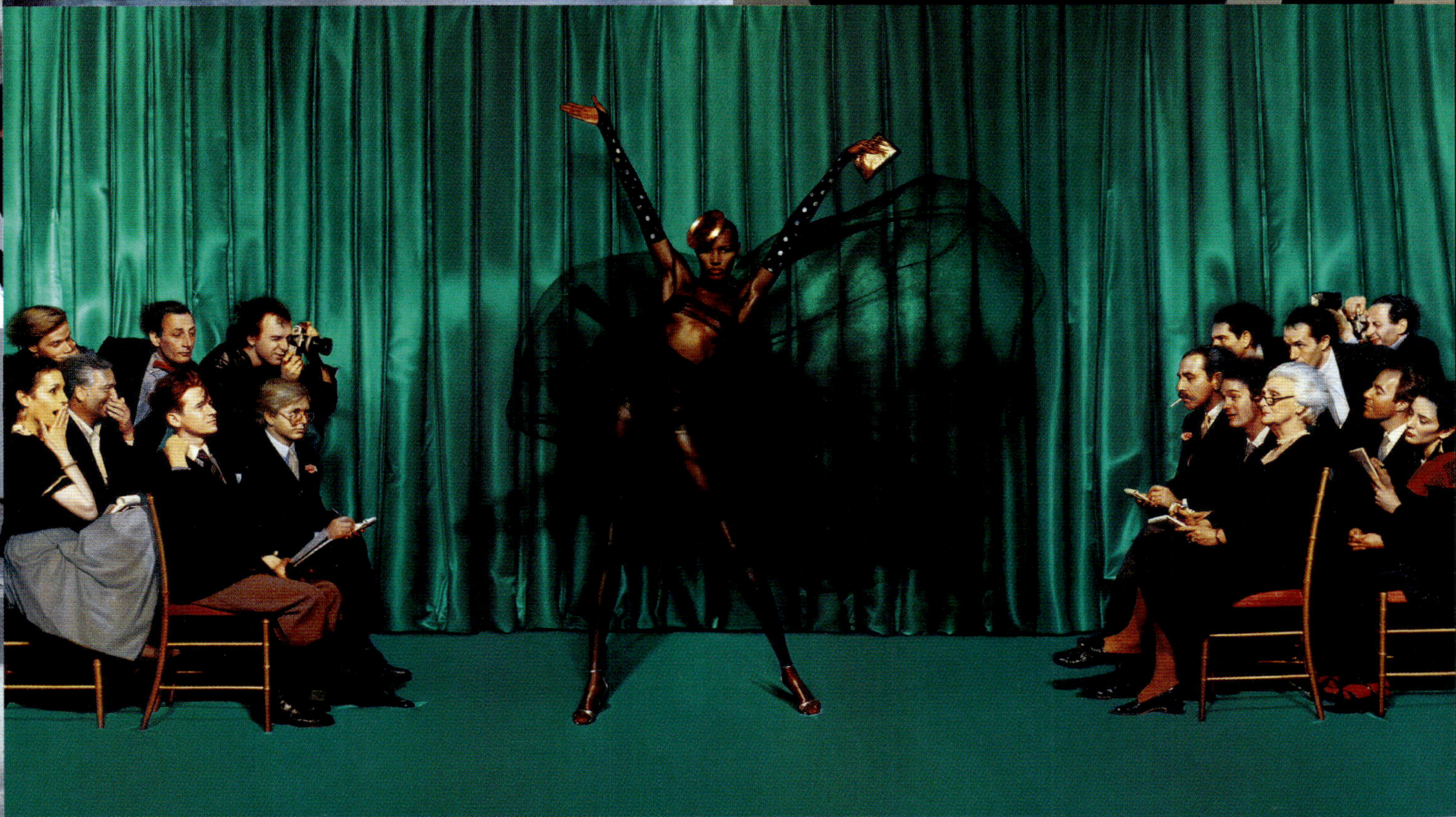

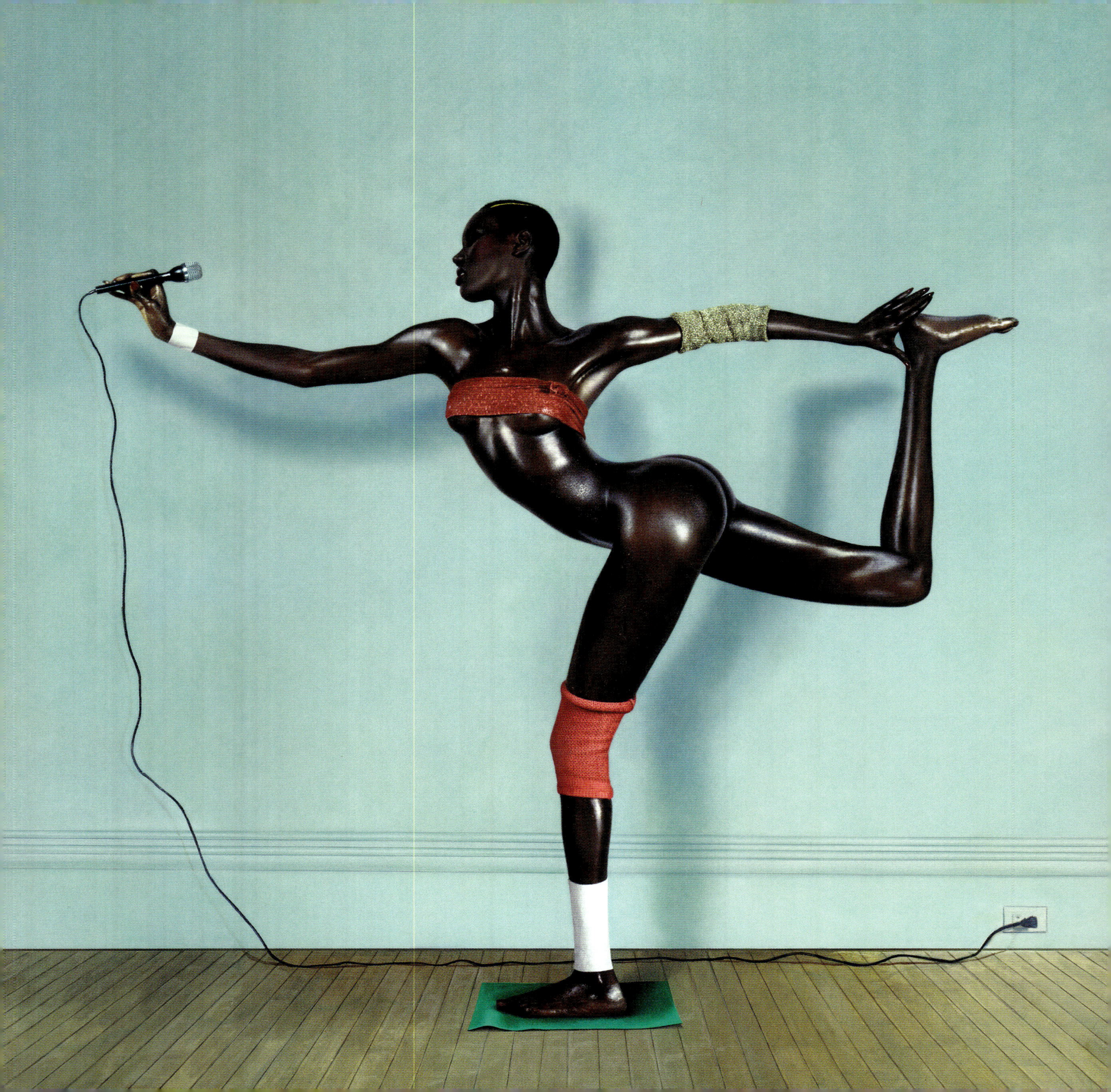

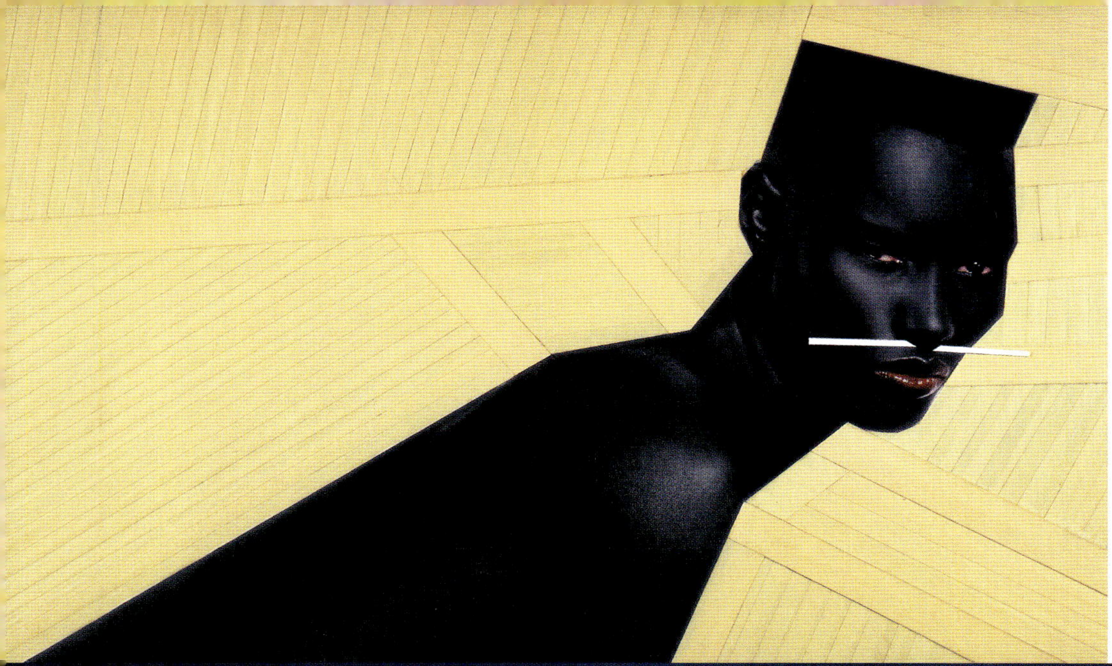
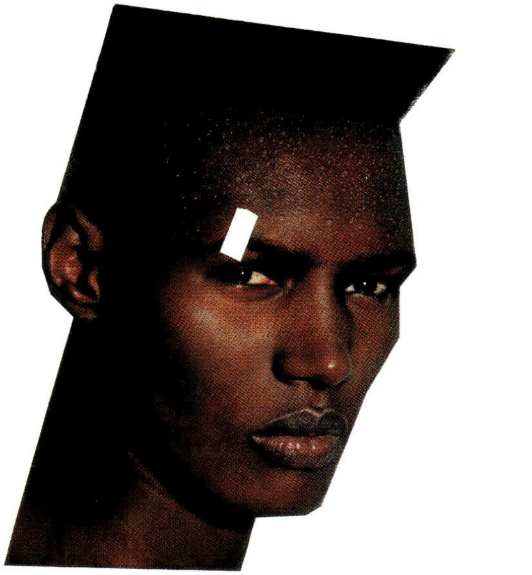
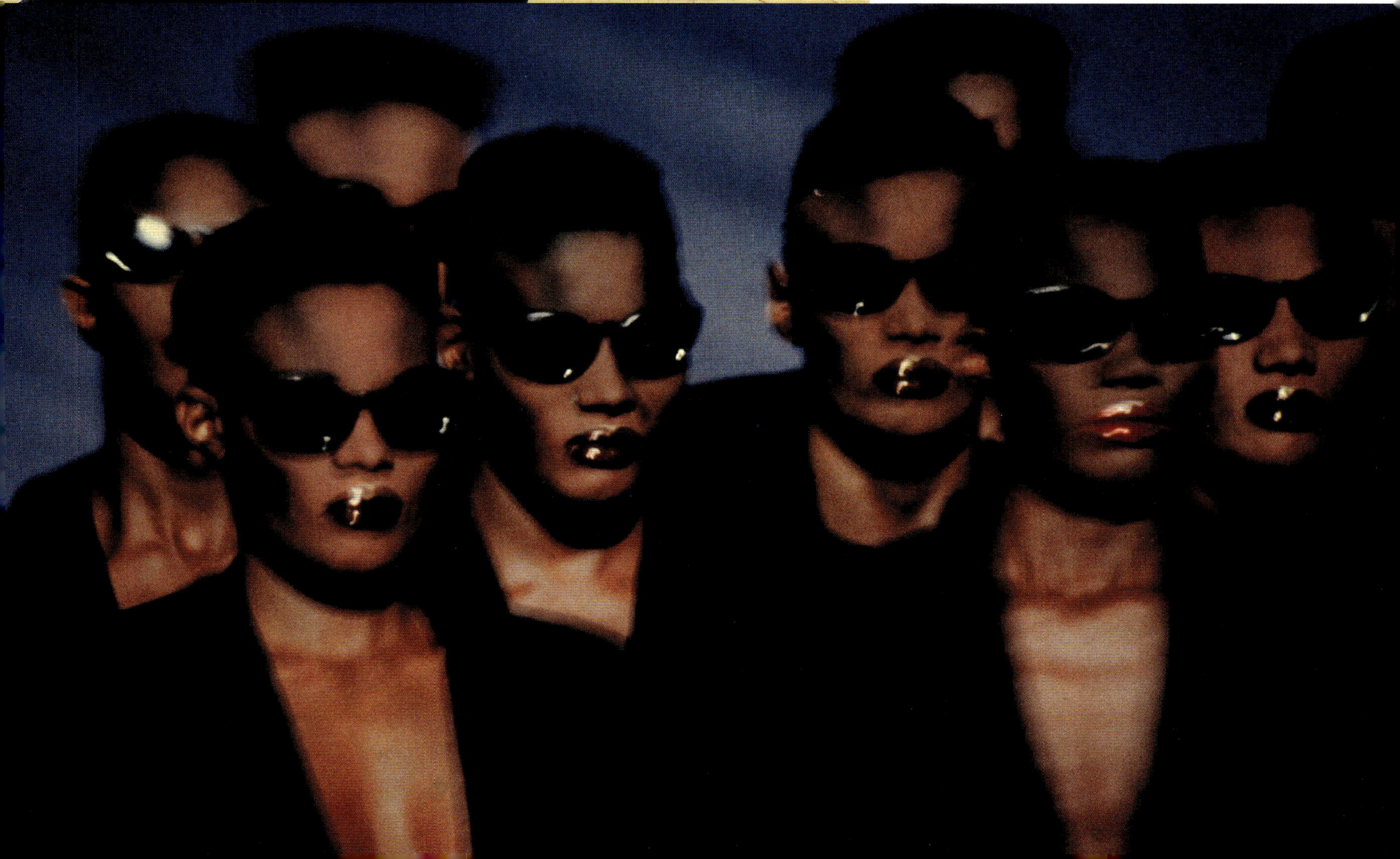

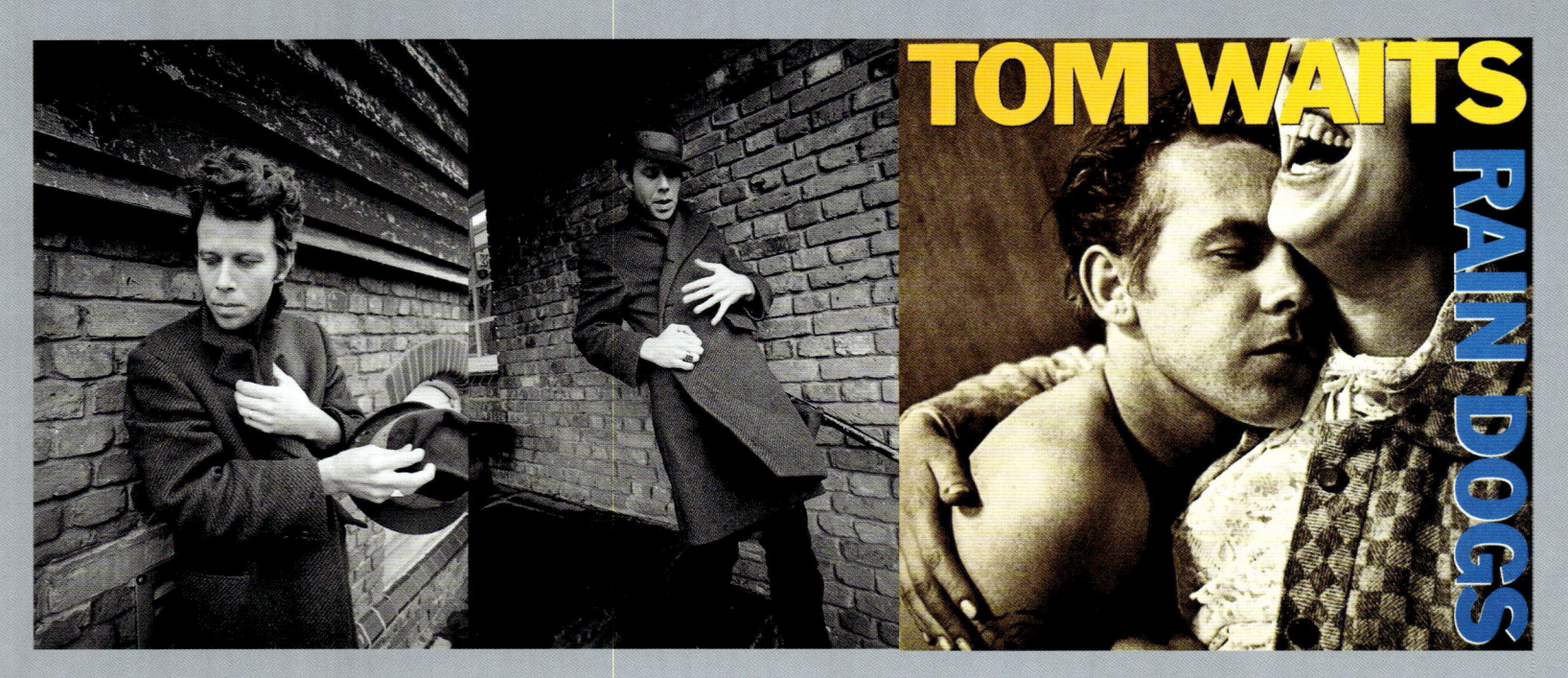

Tom Waits, too, was a man who came to Island Records trailing a persona. He was the bar-room bard, the beatnik with a piano, a broken heart and a broken down voice, gravelly and gin-soaked.

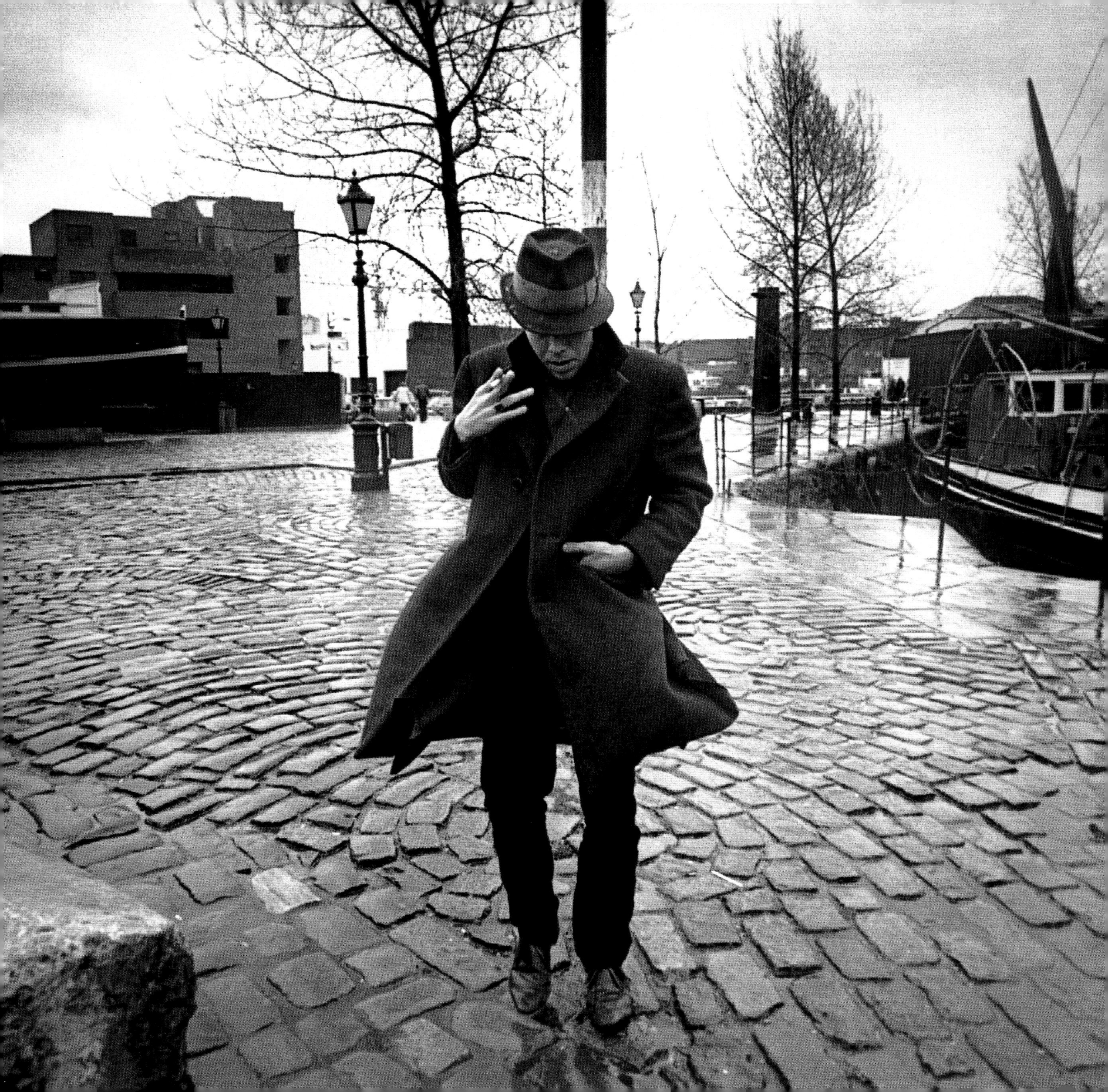

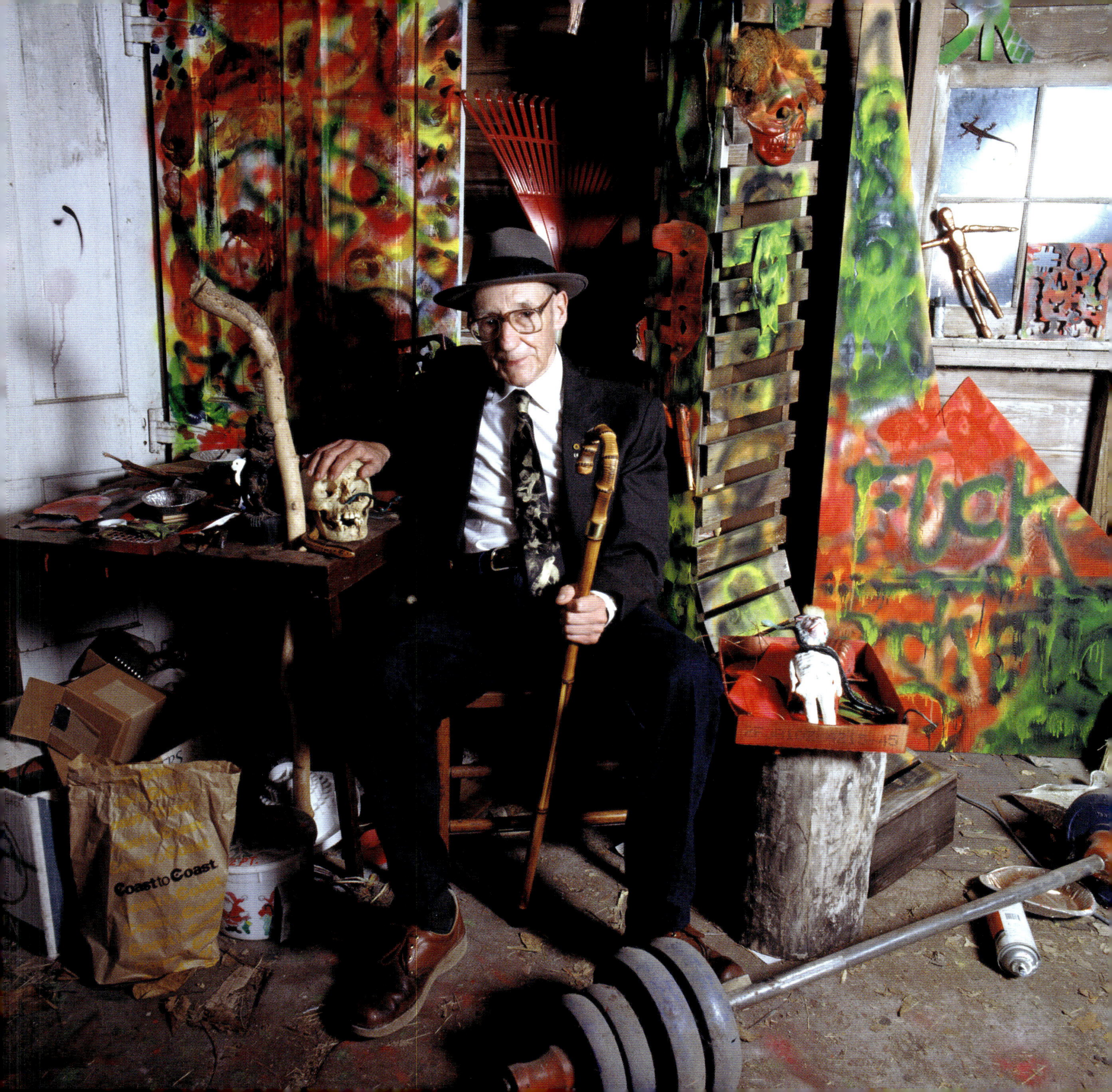

Working with innovative conceptual producer Hal Willner at the suggestion of poet Allen Ginsberg, the (in)famous American writer William Burroughs recorded and released *Dead City Radio* on Island in 1990. With musical contributions from – among others – John Cale, Steely Dan's Donald Fagen, Sonic Youth, and Blondie's Chris Stein, Willner's personal brief was that *Dead City Radio* would be 'the image of a true and great American writer with "The Star-Spangled Banner" behind him ... a timeless album that would sound as if it could have been recorded tomorrow.' One of the record's high points is Burroughs' reading of 'A Thanksgiving Prayer': he gives thanks for matters he considers to have shamed American life, including the destruction of the environment, and the slaughter of the Indians and buffalo. Three years later William Burroughs sang on 'T'Ain't No Sin' on Tom Waits' *The Black Rider*.

'Nipple To the Bottle', she delineated, in her own abstract way, the contours of her wilfully wayward life over another thudding bassline. It still sounds both licentious and controlled, out there in its celebration of unbound sexuality.

In concert, Grace Jones was a thing to behold. Her entire persona had been created by her mentor and then companion Jean-Paul Goude, a French photographer, graphic designer and conceptual artist who had created a persona for Grace Jones that exaggerated everything about her – her height, her haircut, her cheekbones, her androgyny, her imperious manner, as well as her sexuality. In performance, the result was spectacular and not a little unnerving.

In interview, she seemed unbridled going-on-unhinged. She famously thumped the late chat show host, Russell Harty, for turning his back on her to interview another guest: 'She's Lost Control' suddenly sounded autobiographical. That incendiary thrust is there in her best music, too, a constant, edgy and unsettling. Listening again to the great Island years' compilation, *Private Life: The Compass Point Sessions*, her voice still startles with its difference, its sense of not belonging to any tradition, be it soul, blues or even disco. On those Island albums, she sounds both detached and urgent, the ultimate club singer, signalling the digital future in all its libidinous intensity.

Tom Waits, too, was a man who came to Island Records trailing a persona. He was the bar-room bard, the beatnik with a piano, a broken heart and a broken-down voice, gravelly and gin-soaked. Over seven albums on the Asylum label, Waits had articulated a sleazy, after-hours world of drinkers and hookers, drifters and losers, sounding, at times, like he was perhaps too deeply involved in that world for his own good. He had achieved cult status, his songs occasionally covered by other more mainstream artists – Bruce Springsteen ('Jersey Girl') and The Eagles ('Ol '55') – but, in the process, his persona seemed to have taken him over.

In 1980, Waits recorded the acclaimed soundtrack for Francis Ford Coppola's film, *One From the Heart*, and wed Kathleen Brennan, whom he had met on the set. He stopped drinking soon after and, together, they started writing songs. The first indication of what Waits called the post-Brennan 'paradigm shift' in his music was 1983's *Swordfishtrombones*, his first album on Island Records. It remains an astonishing artefact, the songs augmented not just by piano, bass, guitar and drums but by bassoons, pump organs, marimbas and all manner of found percussion. Here, brass band melodies, Irish balladry, medicine show spiels and industrial noise all merged into a mutant end-of-the-world blues that paid homage to the likes of Howling Wolf, Captain Beefheart, Kurt Weil, the

> Waits had articulated a sleazy, after-hours world of drinkers and hookers, drifters and losers, sounding, at times, like he was perhaps too deeply involved in that world for his own good.

After spending much of the 1970s in the wilderness, Marianne Faithfull revived not only her career but her life with 1979's *Broken English*. Although the almost religious image above would suggest otherwise, Marianne still knew how to have a good time.

avant garde composer Harry Partch and the Irish tenor, John McCormack. As reinventions go, it was truly radical.

Swordfishtrombones was followed two years later by *Raindogs* (1985), the album that spawned 'Downtown Train', which has since become Wait's most well-known song courtesy of Rod Stewart's workmanlike cover version. Again the instrumentation was exotic, the songs moving from the jaggedly surreal to the downright romantic. With the likes of Bob Quine and Marc Ribot at his side, Waits was creating songs that seemed both utterly out-of-time and timeless.

In 1987, following an acclaimed acting role in Jim Jarmusch's equally acclaimed *Down By Law*, Waits released the soundtrack to his ambitious stage-play, *Frank's Wild Years*. It was followed by 1992's *Bone Machine*, a starker, harsher-sounding album that made for uneasy, if rewarding, listening. It somehow won a Grammy for Best Alternative Album. Tom Waits was still a cult artist but his stock was rising.

In 1993, Waits released *The Black Rider*, songs from another stage-show on which he had collaborated with the experimental theatre director, Robert Wilson, and the beat writer, William Burroughs. Waits' farewell to Island Records was the 1998 compilation, *Beautiful Maladies*, a collection that was a reminder, if one was needed, of his years of reinvention and experimentation.

During the Island years, Waits had formed a bond with the late Rob Partridge, the label's one time head of press who subsequently became his manager and confidante. Both Waits and Brennan attended Partridge's funeral in December 2008, where his favourite song of theirs, the poignant 'Gonna Take It With Me When I Go', was played as a farewell. One was reminded once again that Island, even in the increasingly corporate eighties, was a place where music makers were looked after by music lovers.

Rob Partridge also managed Marianne Faithfull, another wayward talent that gravitated to Island. She had tasted stardom early as a late sixties pop idol and subsequently fell into years of drug-addiction and obscurity. Such was the extent of her fall from grace – in the depths of her addiction, she had lived on the street – that Faithfull's comeback on Island Records was nothing short of a resurrection.

Reviewing her first album for the label, 1979's *Broken English*, the American music critic Greil Marcus, noted that '15 years after making her first single, Marianne Faithfull has made her first real album'. One would have been hard pressed, without prior knowledge, to identify the parched voice that articulated the songs of anger and despair on *Broken English* so far

130 | Keep On Running

MARIANNE FAITHFULL BROKEN ENGLISH

removed was it from the angelic tones of her best known sixties teen ballad, 'As Tears Go By'. A world of abjection and struggle separated the two.

Broken English still makes for uneasy listening. It is an album of extremes: despair, desire, rage, jealousy and loathing; a catalogue of survival, and its cost. Faithfull's voice, by turns guttural and raspy, turns John Lennon's already scathing 'Working Class Hero' into something almost vindictive in its thrust. Shel Silverstein's 'The Ballad of Lucy Jordan' is perhaps the closest Faithfull has come to the creation of a personal anthem. Neither, though, prepare you for the coruscating disgust of 'Why D'Ya Do It?', in which the poet Heathcote William's words take on the hue of a feverish rant delivered by a woman consumed with sexual jealousy and self-hate. There is nothing like it in contemporary music.

Broken English re-established Faithfull's musical reputation but it was too extreme even for the post-punk audience. Its follow-up, 1981's *Dangerous Acquaintances* was a more muted affair, almost buoyant in comparison. She was mapping out more intimate territory: love and loss, and an undertow of deep regret that may have had its roots in her continuing struggle with heroin addiction. Like Nico, she was a woman whose life seemed to enthrall many of her fans as much as her songs.

In 1983, she released *A Child's Adventure*, an album that seemed too much in thrall to her own mythology, the songs unfocussed and adrift. Five years later, having undergone a long stint of drug rehabilitation, Faithfull made *Strange Weather*, an album of cover versions – Dylan, Billie Holiday, Jerome Kern – with eccentric producer Hal Willner at the helm. The record also included her reworking of 'As Tears Go By', the song now a kind of elegy for her lost years. 'Forty is the age to sing it', she told an interviewer, 'not seventeen.'

Faithfull began the new decade with 1990's *Blazing Away*, a live recording of a show in St. Anne's Cathedral, Brooklyn, featuring guest appearances by Dr. John and The Band's Garth Hudson. In many ways, it is the consummate Marianne Faithfull album, intimate and powerful, honest and yet still imbued with that self-mythologising artfulness that has been a constant of her solo work. When she released *A Secret Life* on Polygram in 1995, Vanity Fair dubbed her 'one of the great interpretive singers of our time'.

Each of the three artists above found a home, and a place to become themselves, on Island Records. That, as much as the extraordinary global success of U2 or the enduring influence of Bob Marley, is a testament to the label's uniqueness, its maverick genius.

Out of Athens, Georgia, The B-52's were definitively American New Wave. Looking like the cast of a John Waters' movie, wearing thrift-store outfits, they perpetually had a sheen of camp neurosis behind their distinctive vocals, the consequence of the duelling female harmonies of Cindy Wilson and Kate Pierson, counterpointed by the almost spoken-word style of male vocalist Fred Schneider. But they also gave the sense of life-as-a-party with highly danceable rhythms behind such trademark tunes as 'Rock Lobster', 'Planet Claire' and the later 'Love Shack'. Although on one hand very much of their time, they continue to perform to large audiences.

HIGH FIDELITY

the B-52's

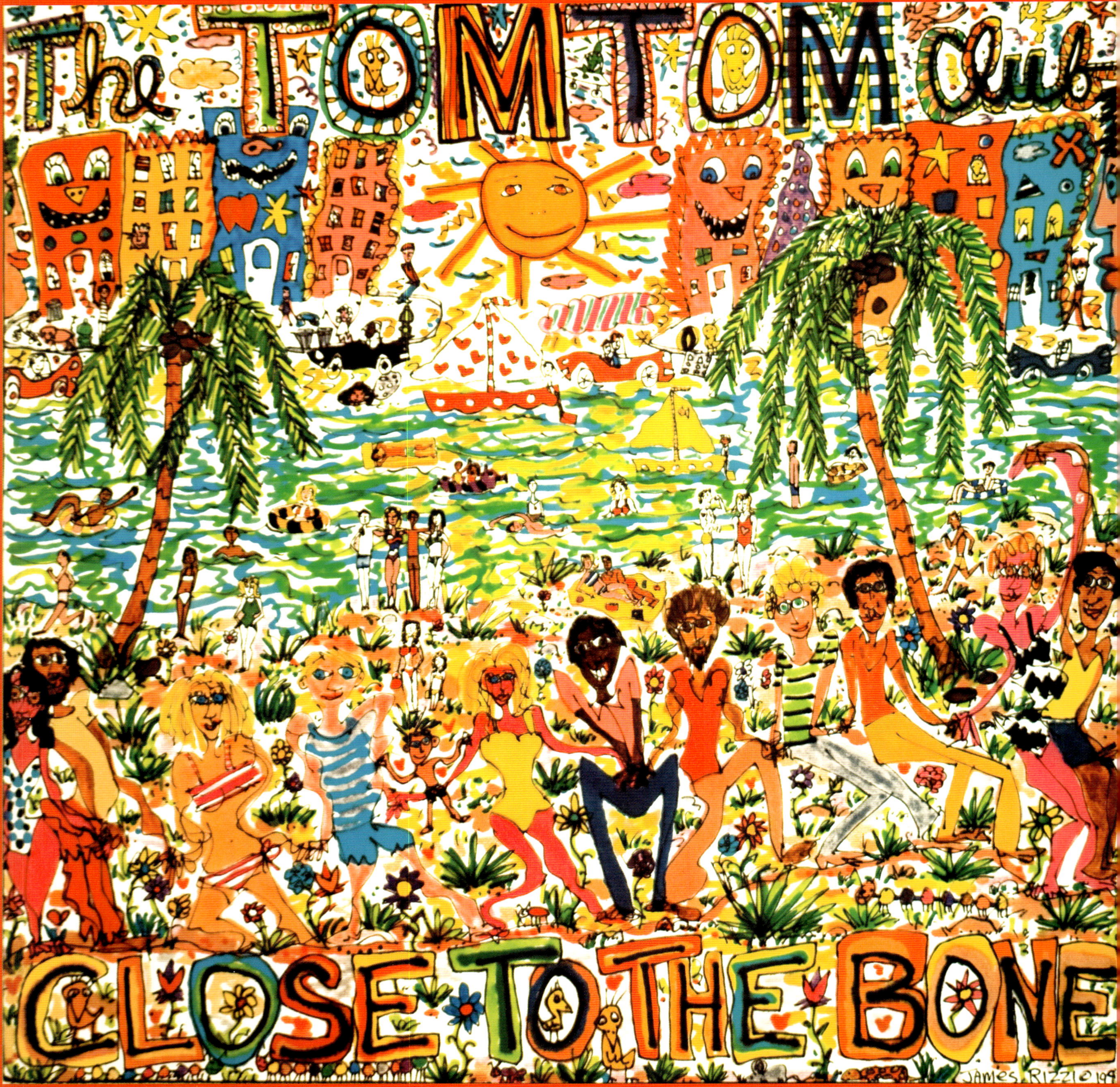
The TOM TOM club
CLOSE TO THE BONE
JAMES RIZZI ©

compass point

by David Katz

Compass Point is one of a handful of recording studios whose exceptional qualities and particular circumstances have earned them legendary status. Inspired by the studios of Stax and Motown, the definitive markers of soul during the 60s and 70s, Chris Blackwell constructed Compass Point in 1977 chiefly to allow Island acts greater artistic freedom, unfettered by problematic time constraints. Located some ten miles outside Nassau, capital of the Bahamas, its serene situation was also important, as with little nearby other than fantastically picturesque views of the Atlantic Ocean, it allowed for an ultimately relaxed recording experience, unencumbered by the kinds of distractions artists perpetually face in metropolises like Los Angeles, Kingston or New York.

Although Talking Heads, Dire Straits, The Rolling Stones and other non-Island acts worked at Compass Point in its early days, after the mixing of Steel Pulse's *Tribute To the Martyrs* and the recording of Third World's *Journey To Addis*, the first notable Island project focussed on Grace Jones, the Jamaican preacher's daughter who had already made her mark on the New York disco scene. To give her new work an outstanding difference, Blackwell put together the house band known as the Compass Point All Stars, joining ace rhythm duo Sly and Robbie, guitarist Mikey Chung and percussionist Sticky with Barry Reynolds, the guitarist on Marianne Faithful's *Broken English*, and Benin-born, Paris-based keyboard wizard, Wally Badarou. Aided and abetted by engineer Alex Sadkin, a perceptive perfectionist, and later by the young wildcard, Steven Stanley, the result was an unprecedented blend of reggae and funk, tinged with the jagged edges of new wave and avant-garde rock, a forward-facing tropical dance fusion that would come to typify the Compass Point sound.

'I wanted a new, progressive-sounding band,' said Blackwell, 'a Jamaican rhythm section with an edgy mid-range and a brilliant synth player. And I got what I wanted, fortunately.'

As *Warm Leatherette*, *Night Clubbing* and *Living My Life* were all cut at the studio, yielding gems such as 'Private Life,' 'Pull Up To The Bumper' and 'My Jamaican Guy,' Compass Point will forever be associated with Ms Jones, yet Grace's work is just the tip of the iceberg. Much adventurous material of the late 70s and early 80s was recorded or mixed there, including Talking Heads' *Remain In Light* and the genre-bending 'Genius Of Love' by Heads spin-off group, the Tom Tom Club, as well as U2's *Fire*, AC/DC's *Back In Black*, Ian Dury's *Lord Upminster*, Serge Gainsbourg's *Mauvais nouvelles des étoiles*, Joe Cocker's *Sheffield Steel*, the B-52s' *Whammy*, Gwen Guthrie's *Padlock*, Lee 'Scratch' Perry's *History, Mystery, Prophecy*, and portions of Black Uhuru's *Red*, *Chill Out* and *Anthem* – winner of the first reggae Grammy. There was also an infamous James Brown session that remains unreleased.

Following Sly and Robbie's 1985 solo masterwork, *Language Barrier*, chaos reigned at Compass Point. Alex Sadkin's tragic death in 1987 placed the facility in limbo until 1993, when engineer Terry Manning and his wife Sherrie reopened it on Blackwell's behalf, continuing its legacy to the present.

'I don't believe anything could ever sum it up,' said Wally Badarou of Compass Point's heyday, 'like nothing could ever sum up the Motown or Stax sound. So much goes into the fabric of those sounds: the studio itself, the engineers, the producers, the artists, the vibes of the time, and only the specific combination of elements does the job.'

Steven Stanley at Compass Point Studios.

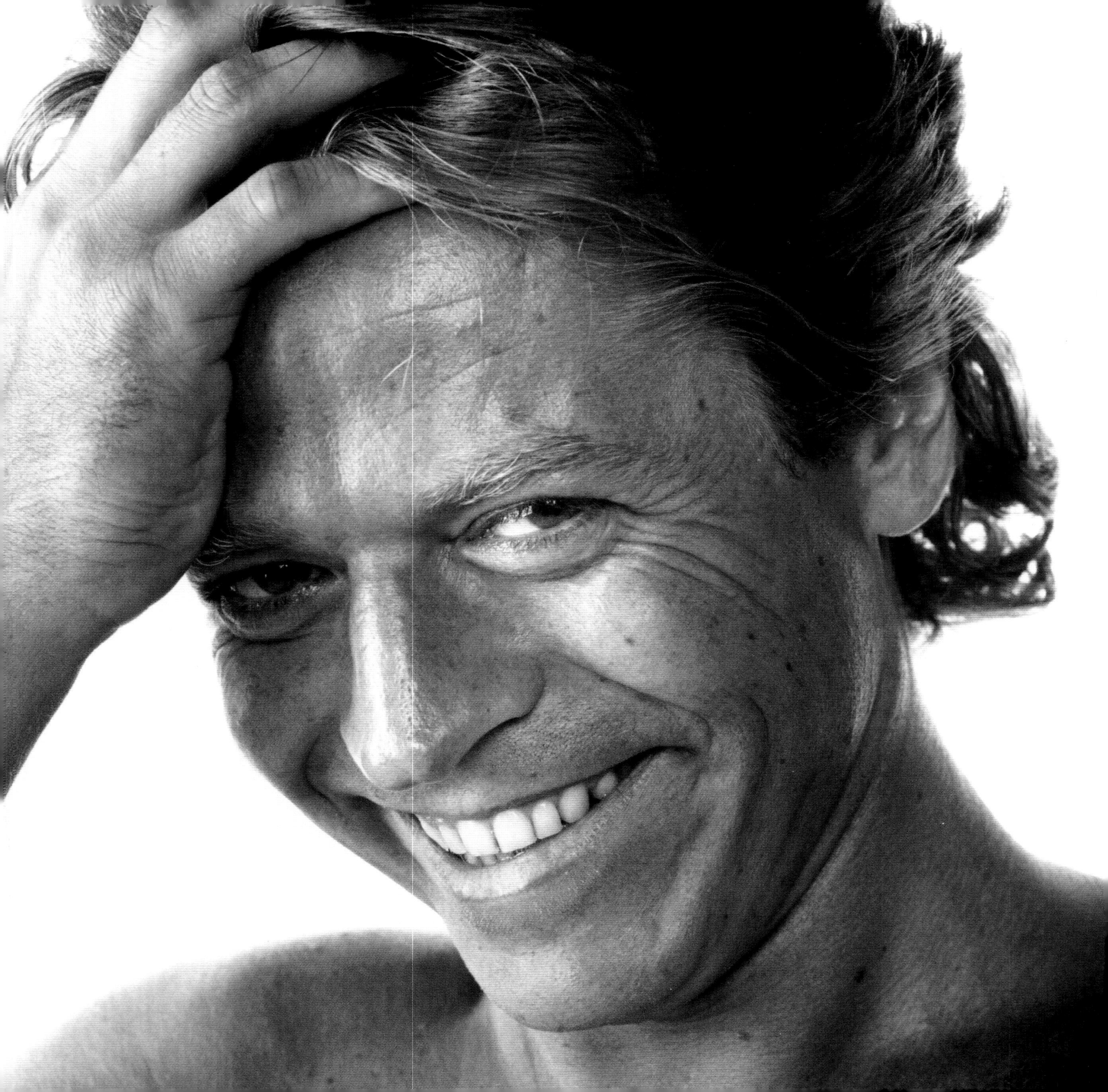

From the embers of the unsuccessful college-circuit band Vinegar Joe he plucked Robert Palmer, a Yorkshire-born singer with good looks, a smooth manner and a blue-eyed soul voice to die for.

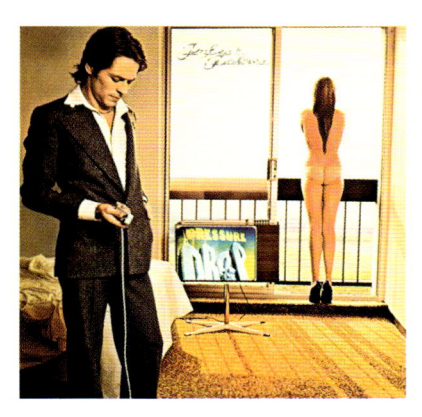

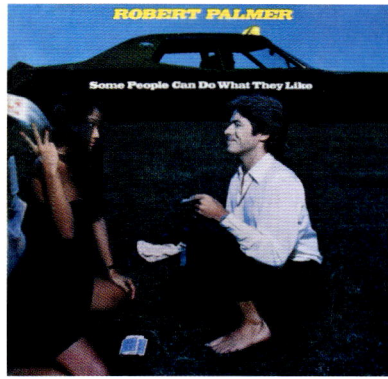

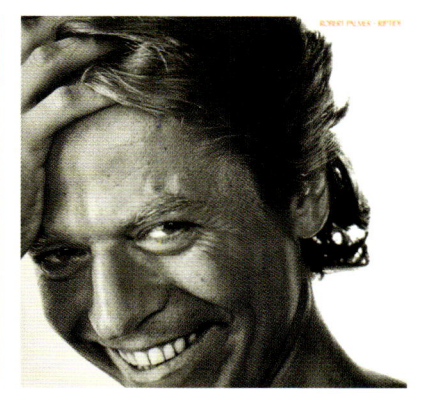

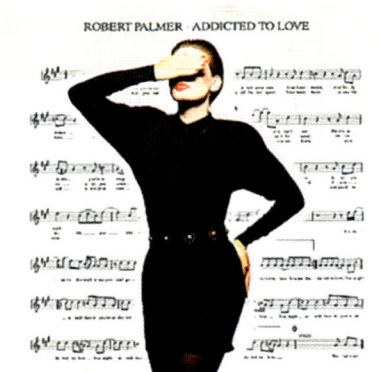

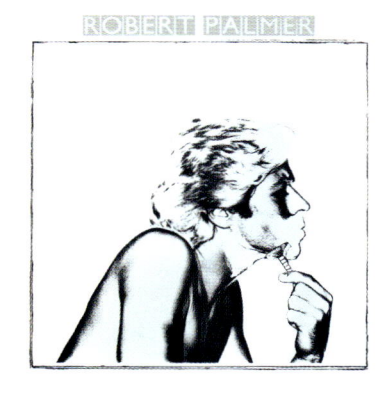

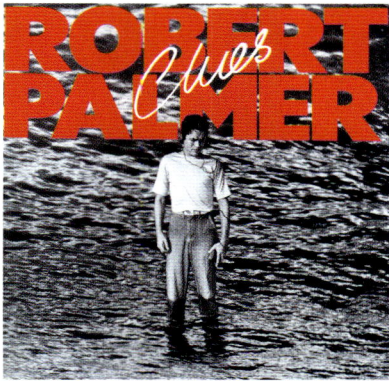

From Batley in Yorkshire, Robert Palmer proceeded on a unique course for an English artist. His funky soul boy tunes and sexy image, nurtured by album artwork that was sometimes outrageous, was only enhanced by the credibility he earned from working with the acclaimed Little Feat and The Meters on his 1974 debut LP, *Sneaking Sally through the Alley*. A cool individual, his enigmatic persona enhanced his appeal.

Keep On Running | 137

Always his own man, Julian Cope (left) enjoyed a typically difficult relationship with Island Records. During his time with the label, Cope's lateral urges led him from the relative commerciality of his third solo album, *Saint Julian*, with its hit single 'World Shut Your Mouth', to the more controversial *Peggy Suicide*, with its outright condemnations of the excesses of the Thatcher era. Later, he fell out with the label, at a time when he had sold out three nights at a prime London venue.

From Bristol, Tricky (right) had been part of the Massive Attack collective. After recording a tune called 'Aftermath' with vocalist Martina Topley-Bird, which he released as a white label, Island Records signed him to a deal. For Island he recorded his *Maxinquaye* album; this exercise in trip-hop was hugely successful, the NME's Album of the Year in 1995, breaking through to the United States where it was a Top 10 record. His second solo CD, *Nearly God*, had a much more aggressive punk-tinged feel that was reflected in his later Brown Punk project.

Polly Jean Harvey (far right) is a former art student – she remains an accomplished sculptor – whose unique musical take has drawn her to the hearts of the world's music fans. Signing to Island Records in 1993, she quickly released her *Rid of Me* album. 1995's *To Bring You My Love* was a global hit, selling over one million copies; especially popular in the United States, it was voted Album of the Year by a multitude of publications, including Rolling Stone and The New York Times.

By the turn of the millennium PJ Harvey was an established facet of the music scene. 2007's *White Chalk*, her eighth album, was comprised largely of piano ballads, a sign of her utter lack of compromise, a characteristic she has also employed to great effect in her visual appearance.

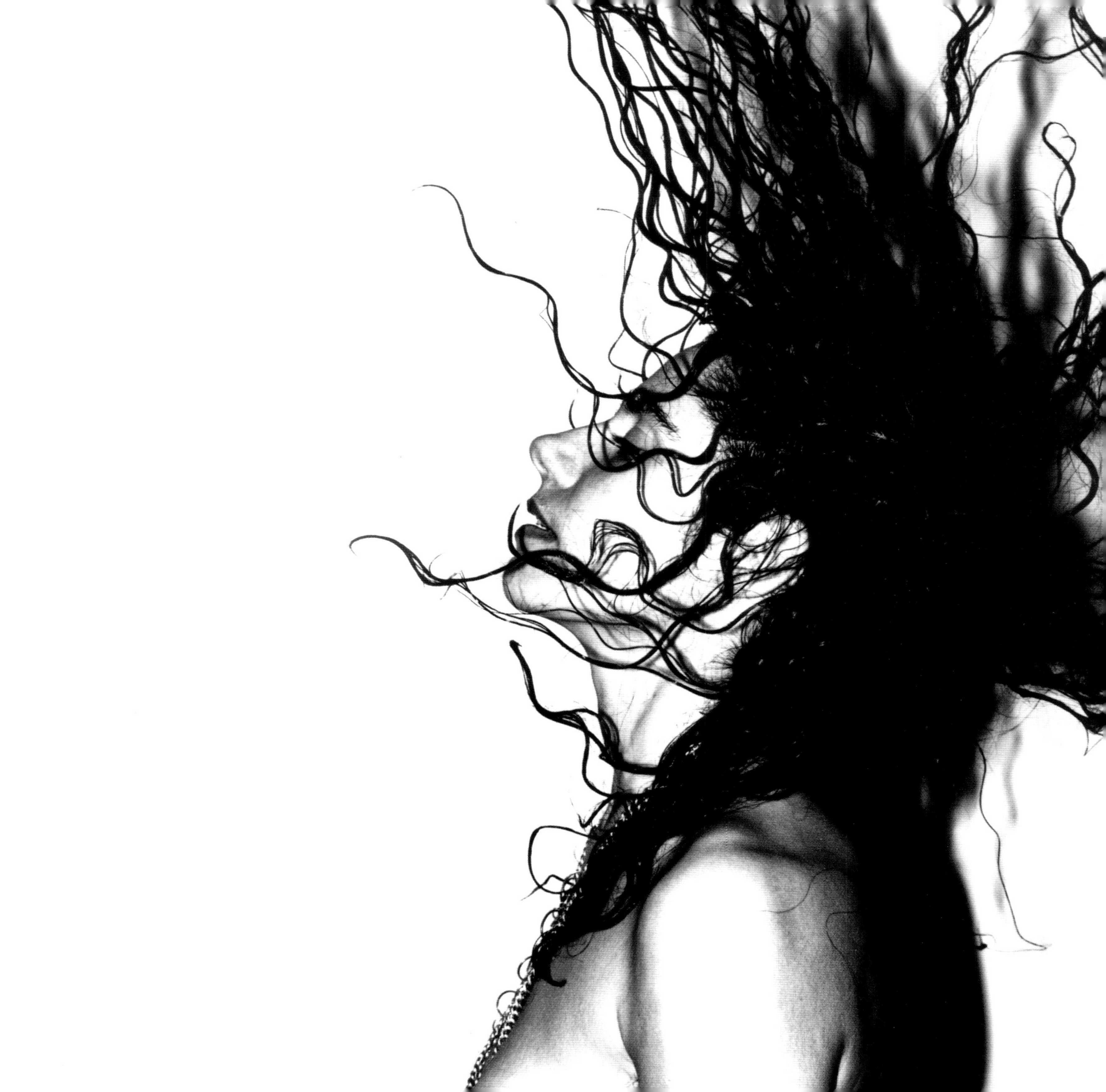

the tuff gong

Island Records, The Old Laundry, St. Peter's Square, Chiswick, 1975.

by Vivien Goldman

Word that Bob Marley and The Wailers were practicing in Island Records' rehearsal room at the back blew through the Edwardian building like a breeze. There were lots of exciting artists on Island but in many ways, The Wailers' militant message, easy-skanking riddims and charismatic singer/songwriter, Bob Marley, represented the soul of the label. Everyone was proud to be working for them, and the band knew it.

The bare-bones rehearsal room was so heavily soundproofed that you had to slip inside to really hear Carlton Barrett's stuttering drums and Aston 'Family Man' Barrett's fulsome bass. Many employees did skive off out of the office to do so. But it didn't lower productivity, rather the reverse.

At that time Island was bubbling with creativity. Several lively departments worked together in the former laundry – Art, PR, International, the radio pluggers, the rehearsal room, Blackwell's own bright, plant-filled office and the Press Office where I was briefly employed before *Live At the Lyceum*. Then there was the basement studio, a bunker called The Fallout Shelter, with a concrete hallway Bob liked to sing in because of the echo. The pool table in the canteen just upstairs was well-used by artists and employees. And, especially when The Wailers were in, that breeze would blow fragrant ganja out from the rehearsal room and through the canteen.

After those rehearsals, The Wailers played the London gig which was later released – immortalised – as *Live at the Lyceum* (1975), with its 'No Woman, No Cry' track which turned everything around commercially for the band. The hit enabled Island to start seeing a return on their investment. For their tour supporting *Exodus* (1977), a further sales breakthrough, Jah People moved with a greater degree of comfort: a proper tour bus, better hotels and their own sound system.

Bob didn't believe in being greedy, but as he told me, 'I want some improvement. It doesn't have to be materially but in freedom of thinking.'

These improvements came about through a virtually unique partnership between label founder Chris Blackwell and Bob Marley that began in 1972. When Marley sauntered like a lion into the Island office at Basing Street Studios in West London, Chris Blackwell felt a familiar tingle. It indicated the possible imminence of great music, a challenge, money in the bank – and fun. He'd already proved his instinct for Jamaican music a decade before with the worldwide success of Millie Small's bouncy ska hit 'My Boy Lollipop'. But Blackwell's focus had wandered from Jamaica, seduced by discovering best-selling UK rock superstars like Stevie Winwood and Traffic, Paul Kossoff and his band Free, as well as Cat Stevens the prototypical bedsit troubadour. Yet meeting the rebel soul Bob Marley, Blackwell felt the urge to push Jamaican music again.

He handed over £4,000 to the band from the downtown Kingston ghetto, and the result amazed his more cynical peers. 'Every penny went into the record,' emphasises Marley's lawyer and confidante, Diane Jobson of *Catch a Fire*, which was proudly delivered a couple of months later.

Bob Marley and The Wailers knew when they were being correctly treated. Prior to signing with Island, The Wailers and their associates were already music biz veterans who'd done it all – been the artist, the producer, the label, the distributor, the promoter.

In their Rude Boy period of the early 1960s, The Wailers had boldly sung of being the 'Small Axe', ready to cut down the existing monopoly of the 'Big T'ree' – really a reference to the Big Three producer/labels, Coxsone Dodd, Duke Reid and Prince Buster who controlled the Jamaican music scene.

In reaction to enough rip-offs to drive a musician mad, the band were among the first local artists to set up their own indie label, Wail'n'Soul'M. At that time, The Wailers often recorded and distributed their music through Vincent Chin's Randy's Records, the island's most popular studio/ store. His producer son Clive recalls, 'Rita Marley would come in with one hand holding one kid and another holding her box of Wailers records - and pregnant on top of it. Their label made enough to pay the bills and feed the kids, but Rita would ask to be paid upfront, to clear certain expenses. She always got it. There was no doubt that every Wailers' single would always sell out.'

That local success was soon mirrored abroad. Though he didn't realise it at their first meeting, Blackwell himself had already done well selling Wailers' music in the early 1960s when he first worked in England. Ten years on, when Bob met Blackwell, he was songwriting for American soul star CBS artist Johnny Nash and manager Danny Sims. In fact, problems with that camp had left The Wailers stranded with no work visa, staying in a street called The Circle in Neasden in north-west London. They spent their days playing football on Neasden Common and jamming with local artists like the Cimarons band and a young actor/guitarist, Brinsley Forde, who would soon co-found another Island group, Aswad.

Originally entitled Knotty Dread, the sleeve of Natty Dread, Bob Marley's first album without Peter Tosh and Bunny Livingston, enjoyed further controversy. Followers of Rastafari are adamant about the need to refrain from shaving facial hair. However, Tony Wright had inadvertently neglected to provide Bob with his habitual straggly beard. In certain circles, this provoked a considerable hullabaloo.

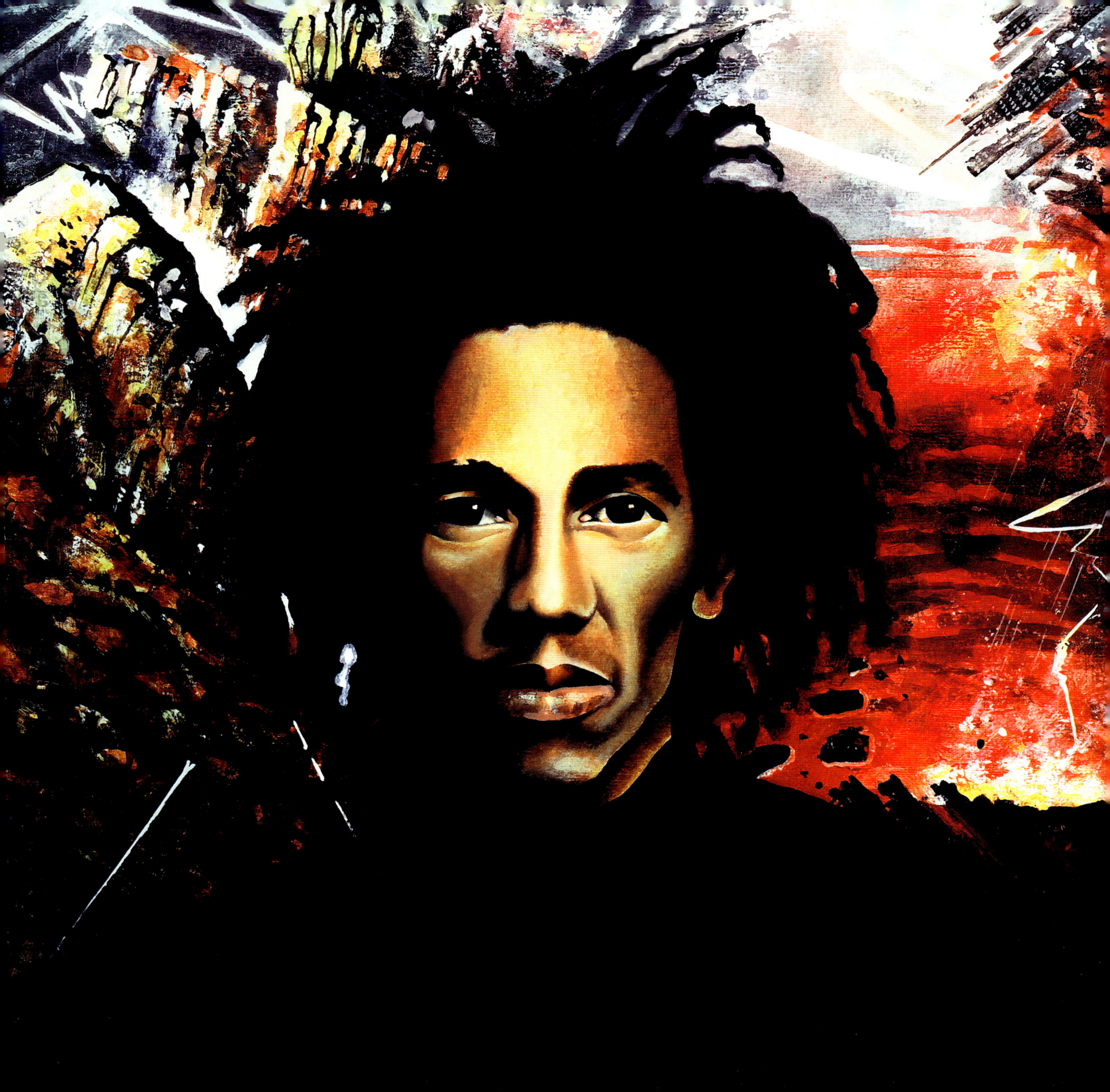

Bob Marley was far from desperate when he encountered Blackwell. But he was definitely receptive to a new route to the international market.

With Island, the original Wailers brought the fire this time to a wider public, defining Rasta and a post-colonial Caribbean identity with their first two Island albums *Catch a Fire* and *Burnin'*, in 1973. Sales didn't match the records' brilliance, but the label stuck with them, a commitment to career development that's unusual now.

Then The Wailers group went through their mythic 'death and rebirth' cycle as the original trinity of Bob, Peter & Bunny imploded.

With Bob at the helm, the band was re-invented as Bob Marley and The Wailers for *Natty Dread* (1974). The original Barrett Brothers rhythm section were joined by young guitar bloods Boston's Al Anderson, then later, Junior Marvin from London; plus the I Three's Marcia Griffiths, Judy Mowatt and Rita Marley.

In this new form, The Wailers re-committed to Island. Through every album, the bonds intensified. Recalls guitarist Junior Marvin, 'Island people like Suzette Newman and Denise Mills helped us with everything - from shipping things to Jamaica to helping us organise our tours with Alec Leslie. We all worked together as a team and it was a lot of fun.'

Ultimately, with Island being a private company owned by one individual, Chris Blackwell, the connection between Island and Bob Marley and The Wailers was personal and the partnership between artist and producer and label grew into an unusual creative symbiosis. 'I wouldn't say that we were friends, exactly: we didn't socialize,' Blackwell explains. 'But we always worked well together. I never knew what music Bob was going to bring me, but it always turned out to be astonishingly good and quite inspiring.'

Thinking back on his path from the start of his career to the new level of global success he was enjoying around the time of the *Exodus* album, Bob once told me fiercely, 'I had to work hard – HARD – me a tell ya,' as if to emphasise that Blackwell hadn't simply waved some magic wand to ensure the band's success.

Equally, as Diane Jobson observes, 'Blackwell's opinion and input always mattered a lot to Bob. The creative force was definitely Bob: but Blackwell's good ear added to the music.'

Crucially, Bob entrusted Blackwell with key ideas and choices, like overdubbing rock guitar on *Catch a Fire*; the slow build-up of sound that introduces the song 'Natural Mystic', at the opening of the *Exodus* album; or the introduction of neo-disco drum flourishes on that album's title track.

Over the years, the business dealings between Island and Bob Marley were comparatively flexible and human. At *Rastaman Vibration* time in 1976, sales had soared and the deal was changed, including an eccentric clause giving Marley the house at 56 Hope Road (now The Bob Marley Museum) where he'd been living – for as long as he remained signed to Island.

Respect between the creative and business partners was shown in Marley's steadily increasing control of his own work. He retained all the Caribbean rights to his music. Gradually he enlarged his Tuff Gong label, as well as the pressing plant on Kingston's Marcus Garvey Drive that used to belong to one of those 'Big T'ree' recording companies he'd sung about in 'Small Axe' so long ago.

By the time of 1979's *Survival* and *Uprising* the next year, Bob was happily recording in his own home studio at Hope Road.

Towards the end of his livity, Marley was planning his own independent Jamaican answer to Motown. It was a logical next step to his increasing independence throughout his years with Island.

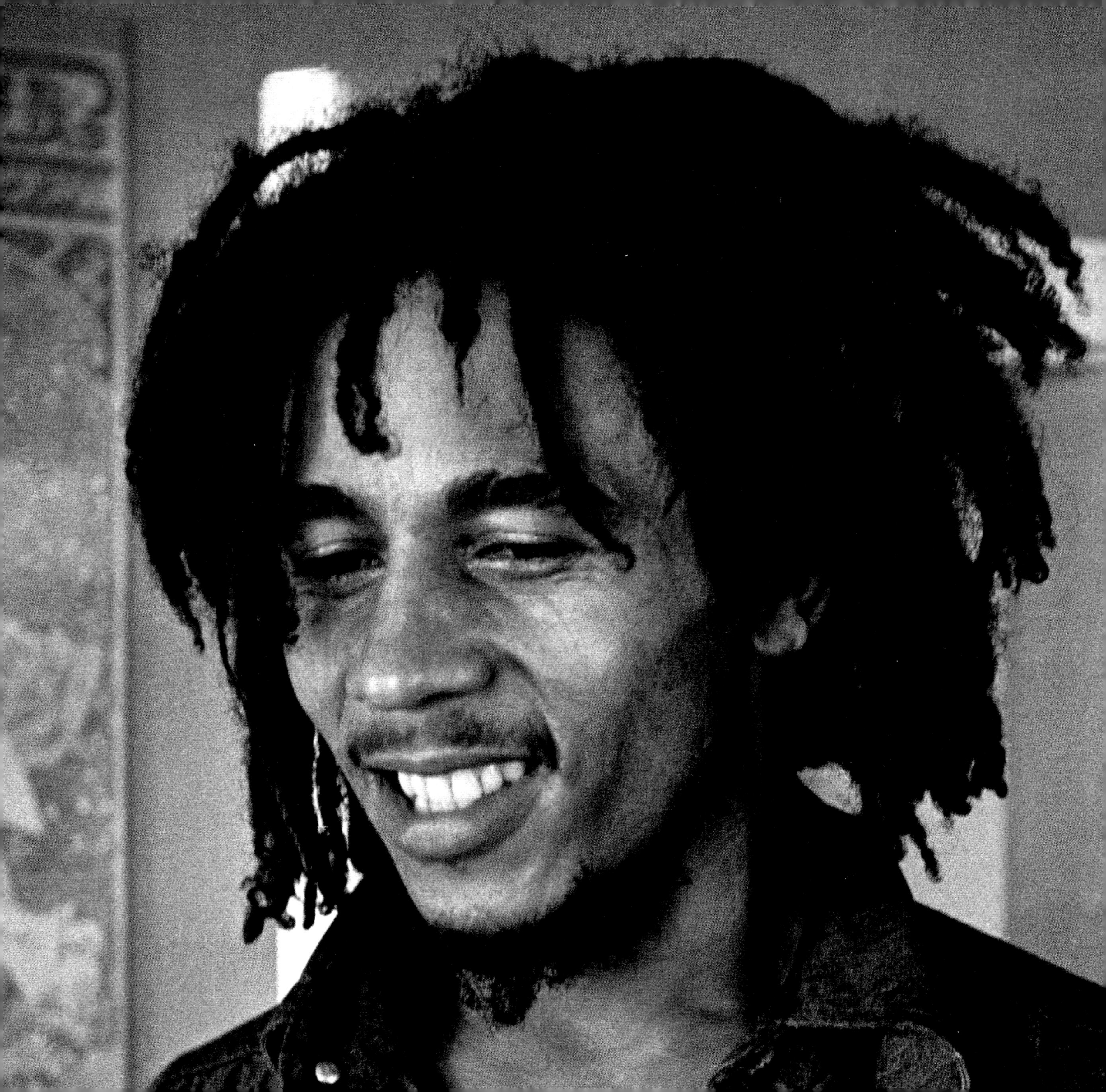

144 | Keep On Running

The unusually intimate connection Marley enjoyed with the label was evidenced by the fact that during the singer's last days, Blackwell's right hand woman, the late Denise Mills, was with him constantly.

Three years after Bob's passing in 1981, the idea of promoting a compilation with then-novel TV advertisements was implemented by Island veteran Trevor Wyatt and then label head Dave Robinson, who'd never actually known or worked with Bob. Prophetically, they called it *Legend*. It became a ten times platinum seller and as Island Records geared up to celebrate its 50th Anniversary, *Legend* was still top of Billboard's pop compilation charts.

from new york city…

> There was a distinct ZE ethos. The lyrics were invariably at odds with the music. We were merging punk and funk, creating mutant disco by adding heavy metal guitar to the mix.

by Michael Zilkha

In the summer of 1975 I moved to New York City where I had landed a job as a theater critic for the *Village Voice*. It took me three days to discover CBGBs, where 'punk rock' was being invented, and before long I was a fixture there, meeting the musicians who were making new music.

Some months later I met Chris Blackwell through a mutual friend and sat next to him at dinner after a Bob Marley concert. I looked up to Chris and Island Records as cultural beacons, probably the same way that he looked up to Ahmet Ertegun and Atlantic Records, but that didn't stop me from questioning him about why he hadn't done a better job promoting John Cale, the Velvet Underground polymath who was then an Island artist. He could tell I loved music as much as he did, and we became friends.

A year later John Cale was playing CBGBs and I interviewed him for Andy Warhol's *Interview*. Soon after that John suggested that we start a label together and get in on the punk explosion in England. I, of course, thought that was a wonderful idea.

Our label was called Spy and our first single was by Harry Toledo and The Rockets. We made a few more, including one by the great rock critic Lester Bangs, but neither of us was equipped to run the label as a real business and it fell apart.

At the time John and I were making a single called 'Disco Clone' with my then girlfriend Cristina singing lead. It was an ironic duet about the interchangeability of girls on the dance floor, with actor Kevin Kline as the male. Chris Blackwell mixed it and agreed to release it in the UK. This was the first ZE record, and it followed a trajectory that kept repeating itself until 1982: excellent reviews, limited sales.

I told Chris about a band I was really excited about, The Contortions. Coincidentally Brian Eno was producing a compilation of underground bands called No New York for Island's Antilles label. That and my enthusiasm impressed Chris enough to offer to pay for a Contortions record and distribute it. But my enthusiasm didn't impress The Contortions. They didn't want to sign as the first band on my new label.

People aren't as aware of it today but punk and disco happened at exactly the same time, in the same cities, sort of polarizing nightlife in an era when everyone went out. Why not combine them, I thought, and so I talked The Contortions manager Anya Phillips into signing The Contortions non-exclusively to ZE, spinning off another identity as James White and the Blacks to make a commercial disco record. It was an idea perverse enough to appeal to Anya. Our first album was called *Off White*. James and Anya were then comfortable enough to let me have The Contortions as well, and the buzz was good enough that I was able to put together a roster for the fledgling label, all artists that no one else wanted but that in my innocence I believed should be stars.

Island licensed our releases for Europe, providing enough money for ZE to function like a real label. I set about building a repertory company, with all the musicians playing on each other's records. Although it crossed genres, from singer songwriters to punk to disco, there was a distinct ZE ethos. The lyrics were invariably at odds with the music. We were merging punk and funk, creating mutant disco by adding heavy metal guitar to the mix, and blending it all with Kid Creole's cosmopolitan synthesis of world cultures and Tin Pan Alley writing skills. Hipsters around the world loved our records and we had great critical support from Glenn O'Brien at *Interview Magazine*, Robert Christgau at *The Village Voice*, and from *The Face* in England which wrote: 'If it's on ZE, buy it!' ZE wasn't rich, it was poor, but it had enough buzz and sales that advances from Island and a variety of American labels and, especially in times of crisis from Lionel Conway at Island Music, kept us in business.

We lived for the studio, seeking to subvert and entertain in the same groove. Lydia Lunch's band Teenage Jesus and The Jerks was jarringly abrasive. On *Queen of Siam* she transformed into a torch singing diva with the help of Bob Blank, whose studio was our base of operations. He enlisted Billy VerPlank who had written the *Flintstones* theme tune as the album's arranger. Cristina's anthem of disaffection 'Is That All There Is' was arranged by August Darnell, the original song's wistfulness utterly negated by her one bitter vocal take, and James Chance's saxophone wailing in the background. ZE's essence was best captured on two compilations. *Mutant Disco* was the brainchild of Rob Partridge, Island's head of publicity and our greatest supporter there. Consisting of six very long dance tracks, these were our greatest hits so far, showcasing the multiplicity of tonal and lyrical variants that could be layered over disco's traditional bass and drums. *A Christmas Record*, the following year, united eight ZE artists, and included our one indisputable standard, The Waitresses' 'Christmas Wrapping'. Here was an Xmas soundtrack for a recessionary world: realistic and ultimately triumphant – I may not be in control, life may be tough, but we're all in this together and I will dance my way out of this mess.

Between 1980 and 1984 we released three albums by Kid Creole and The Coconuts (who proved huge everywhere but America – thus justifying Island's investment in a matter of a few weeks in the summer of 1982), The Waitresses ('I Know What Boys Like'), two albums by Was (Not) Was, one by Suicide, two by Suicide's Alan Vega, two by Davitt Sigerson (who one day would be chairman of Island Records), two albums by my then wife Cristina, and three by John Cale. Over it's brief lifetime ZE also released music from Junie Morrison, Material, Teenage Jesus and The Jerks, Coati Mundi, The Aural Exciters, Ron Rogers, Lydia Lunch, Lizzy Mercier Descloux, and Rosa Yemen.

ZE had fabulous producers and songwriters on its roster, but the vocals were rarely as strong as the songs, which with hindsight proved a limiting factor. Davitt Sigerson, August Darnell (Kid Creole), and Don Was all achieved enormous success as outside producers. Almost as an answer to my first question to Chris Blackwell, the question that got me into the business, I got my hero John Cale to finally let loose on *Music for a New Society*, his most personal record.

It was a very exciting time and also very stressful, as we were always operating on the edge of bankruptcy, but if success were only artistic we were on top of the world. In retrospect my problem as a record executive was my emotional attachment to the product. I honestly believed that all my records should be hits. I finally got out when I produced a record with a band I believed in, Breakfast Club, and Dave Robinson, then head of Island, would not put it out, saying I should put together a multi-cultural extravaganza instead (another Kid Creole and The Coconuts, I suppose). Breakfast Club had a top five hit in the States but I was out of the music business by then.

It seems like a lifetime was packed into those few short years, and I believe the results have stood the test of time. I loved it while I was doing it, but I'm thoroughly gratified today to buy album downloads for $9.99 and be a fan, just like I was when I started.

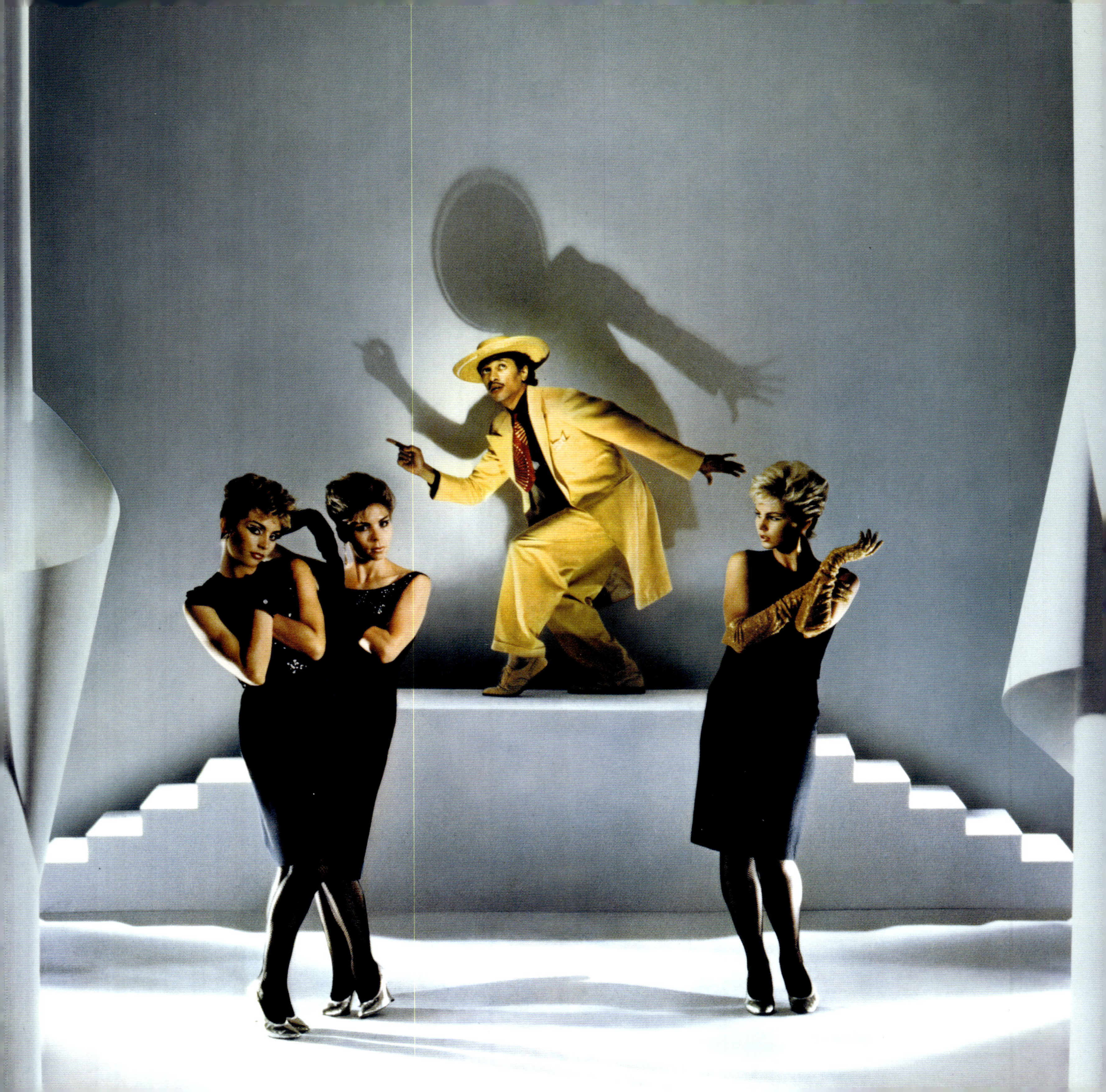

WAS (NOT WAS)

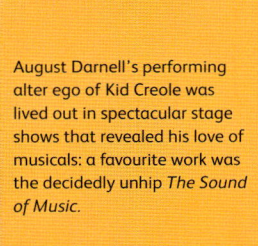

August Darnell's performing alter ego of Kid Creole was lived out in spectacular stage shows that revealed his love of musicals: a favourite work was the decidedly unhip *The Sound of Music*.

Keep On Running | 149

FRANCOIS KEVORKIAN PRESENTS
JAH WOBBLE THE EDGE HOLGER CZUKAY / snake charmer

MINI LP 33·3

MELISSA ETHERIDGE

RATTLE AND HUM

The legend goes that it was the late great Irish music journalist, Bill Graham, who told the late, great Island press officer, Rob Partridge, that U2 were going to be bigger than Thin Lizzy. So it was that Partridge dragged Chris Blackwell away from the Crystal Palace Bowl on a Saturday night in July 1980, where Bob Marley and the Wailers had just mesmerised fifty thousand people, to a south London pub, the Half Moon in Herne Hill, where U2 were struggling to keep the attention of about fifty punters.

The legend may be true but it was A&R maverick, Nick 'the Captain' Stewart, who pitched up in Dublin when U2 headlined at the National Stadium in 1980 and, there and then, offered them a deal. The contract with Island Records was signed by the band a few weeks later in the ladies' toilet of the Lyceum Ballroom in London, where apparently the light was better than in the gents. Thus, rock history was made.

One of the first things U2's manager, Paul McGuinness, told Chris Blackwell was, 'We're not in the record business, we're in the U2 business, which is different.' How different the world would soon find out. Blackwell, as McGuinness admitted later, 'saw the bigger picture… he was very smart, very worldly, and a great ally for U2. He picked up on the intelligence of the band, and the commitment they showed.'

That commitment has since made U2 the biggest rock band in the world. The band were nurtured on Island, growing steadily in confidence and popularity over their first four studio albums, *Boy* (1980), *October* (1981), *War* (1983) and *The Unforgettable Fire* (1984), the latter the beginning of their long-term collaboration with the production duo, Brian Eno and Daniel Lanois. On songs like 'Pride' and 'New Year's Day', they broke with the conventions of post-punk rock, foregoing angst and adolescent rebellion for a joyous, uplifting sound.

In 1987, U2 released *The Joshua Tree*, which refined and deepened their early signature – Bono's soaring, heart-felt vocals, the Edge's chiming guitar and Adam Clayton and Larry Mullen's driving, insistent rhythm pulse – and became one of the biggest selling albums of all time.

In the 1990s, their sonic invention continued apace with albums like *Achtung Baby!* and *Zooropa*, and the group redefined the term stadium rock with the groundbreaking technological ambition of the *Zoo TV* and *Pop Mart* world tours. Simultaneously, Bono began his relentless campaigning for Africa aid and debt relief, and has since become not just the world's biggest rock star, but the world's most well-known celebrity activist. With their twelfth studio album, 2009's *No Line On the Horizon*, U2 show no signs of the fatigue or formularisation that dogs most rock groups who manage to stay together for three decades. The commitment that Chris Blackwell recognised back in the early eighties continues to underpin the group's extraordinary success and their unassailable position as the world's most popular – and most credible – rock group.

Sean O'Hagan

globalisation

by Paul Morley

At the end of 1982, the record producer Trevor Horn, then of The Buggles, surprisingly asked me, a journalist for the NME with no particular thoughts about entering the music industry, 'Do you fancy inventing a record company?' I remember how in more or less the very first sentence of this invitation, he mentioned the name Chris Blackwell, and therefore the name, the company, the entity, the history, the atmosphere, the reputation, the imagination, the separate, experimental essence of Island Records. Along with the idea of 'inventing' a record label, the thought of working with Island was enough for me to instantly accept his offer. The idea would not have had the same appeal if his new label was going to be set up in collaboration with CBS or Warners, where I was sure there wouldn't be much room for the kind of invention I had in mind.

I imagined a kind of label that would be directly influenced by the defiantly European, definitely ideological post-punk labels of the time – Factory, Mute, Fetish, Fast – but which was also influenced by the Island label itself, and the way that it didn't necessarily have a sound, or a particularly militant sensibility, but was somehow consistently, elegantly in favour of the iconoclastic. The independent punk and post-punk labels that had emerged since 1975/6 had made many labels seem rigid, old-fashioned and institutional. Island was not put out by the arrival of these radically inspired, enthusiastically anti-corporate labels. They'd actually set many of the precedents as a founding independent for the imaginatively self-conscious, creatively intimate ways these labels worked, in how they found their acts and made their records, and then packaged, marketed and distributed them. (Subsequently, we can see that the labels that have inventively extended the traditions of the record label through the confused first decade of the 21st century – Domino, XL, Bella Union, Warp, Matador, Heavenly, etc. – are all descendents of Island as much as they are descendents of Elektra, Rough Trade or Factory.)

It was the Factory influence that led me to naming Trevor's label Zang Tuum Tumb after a militant, noise-infatuated gang of early 20th century Italian futurists. It was Island where a label with a name like that was encouraged to come to life, and given the kind of practical support where it could issue its grand, passionately boastful pre-launch manifestoes as expensive full page music paper ads. I could immediately see how there would be room for the invention I had in mind because when those three words Zang, Tuum and Tumb were passed over to Blackwell for his thoughts on whether a label with that name interested him, or perhaps seemed a little daft, or unnecessarily obscure, something best left in the pages of the NME, the response was swift and unfussy. Something along the calm, almost disinterested lines of 'fine.' The implication being, get on with it, and make it work. If you have hits, then the label will mean whatever you want it to mean, it will become for everyone what you think it is, and the label name will be the label name. If you don't have hits, make it glorious anyway.

It was initially odd to me that Buggles were an Island act. They seemed a little on the novelty side, perhaps the absolute synthetic opposite of the Island artists you immediately thought of, Cat Stevens, Nick Drake, Bob Marley, Free, the earthy, ethereal, spiritual or lusty. Buggles were in fact the very first Island act to have a UK number 1 single, and perhaps it was inevitable that Island, when they issued their warning that, in their own way - now that the 1980s were upon us, surely where the future was to really begin - they were ready to take on the world, it wouldn't come in any expected way. It wouldn't be as such a record you could faithfully, logically, trace back to soul, blues, jazz, or to Chicago, Jamaica or New York, but a record rooted in machines that accidentally anticipated a glib, grabbing, sensationalist MTV video pop world (and then became an historic part of it) far removed from the kind of virtuous, thinking rhythm music favoured by Blackwell and Island. The music that Trevor started to produce after leaving The Buggles, the flamboyant, literate northern soul pop for ABC and the fractured absurdist, internationally biased post-funk for Malcolm McLaren, seemed closer to an Island ideal. This music demonstrated that what Blackwell had seen in the Buggles, the machine age avant-techno visually explicit ingredient, was just where 80s pop was destined to go.

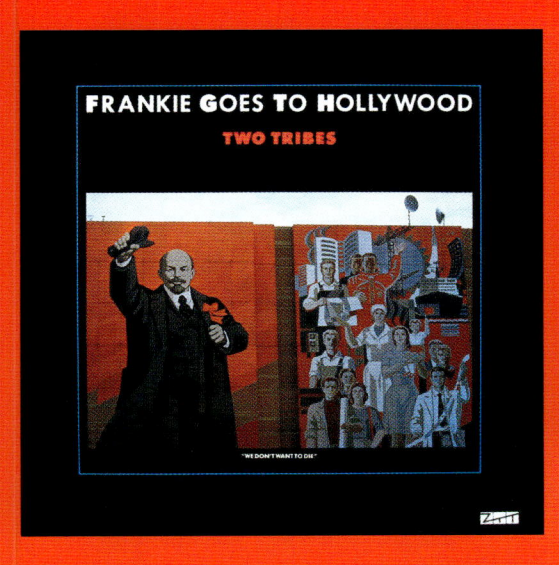

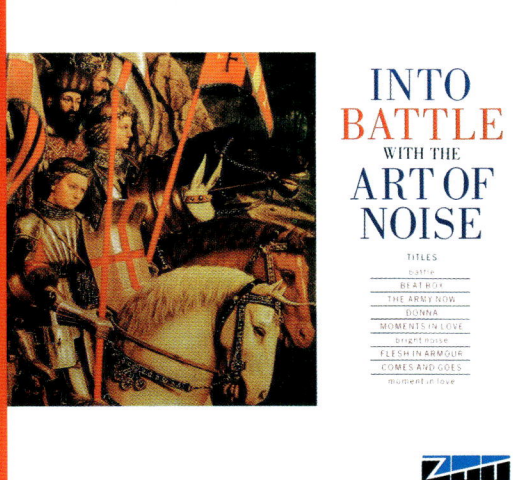

The group Trevor and I invented to be the ZTT house band – a label needed a house band, I decided, like Motown, and then like Sly and Robbie for Island – were called Art of Noise, and they used the protean, extremely English musicians and technicians that played on the Malcolm McLaren and ABC records. Art of Noise turned out, accidentally and a little intentionally, to be the haywired ZTT version of a classic unclassifiable Island act, not least because the image of the group was masked so successfully no one guessed when we released the debut EP 'Into Battle' that they were the group, a little neo-novelty themselves, in the way ultimately all pioneering pop is, that Trevor Horn had formed after the Buggles.

Some reviewers faced with the deliberately cryptic puzzle of their origins decided the Art of Noise were cloaked black Detroit, or maybe surreptitiously avant-Berlin. Being an Island act definitely helped the illusion. We had created a disguise for Art of Noise in much the same way we had created a kind of entertaining disguise for our main pop act Frankie Goes To Hollywood, following enshrined Island rules that you never made the obvious, plainer decisions when it came to advertising the merits of your acts, and that the whole point of a great pop or rock record was that it was a fabulous performance collision of original image, innovative sound and a certain portion of mystery. A record wasn't just music. It was music and furtive, or completely conspicuous, atmospheric presence. Music, and the promise that something important was about to happen.

Perhaps Buggles were an Island act in the way that, say, White Noise, Roxy Music, Sparks, Eno, B-52's and Grace Jones were, reflecting that side of the label, and therefore that side of Chris Blackwell, that watched with keen interest where the world was heading, and reflecting how Island took certain clues about its direction and identity from the past, but was always moving, one way and another, into the future. Buggles, this cartoon electro-pop group compressing inevitable commercial and sonic change into a flash, gimmicky pop song, were part of the research and development area of the label, one you could never pin down, but which was always operating, behind the scenes, under the radar, as a fundamental, motivating part of the Island aesthetic.

Even as the label was having their success with Traffic, or Cat Stevens, or Bob Marley, or E.L.P., or Free, roots and yearning, conscience and heritage, truth and salvation, insolence and drama, fixing themselves in our hearts and minds as the label that does this and that, and only this and that, the sensually abrasive, reality twisting Jamaican reggae and the evocative, outsider British underground, and the way that Blackwell shrewdly bound them together, there was a research and development department working in mysterious ways on ideas, suggestions, new paradigms and possible futures that didn't seem to be the Island we thought we knew. This covert research and development exhibited how the restless, questing Chris Blackwell moved around the world, glimpsed various secretive new things, quickly diagnosed cultural switches happening in the shadows, and integrated them into his philosophy, a philosophy inspired by the liberating force of change.

The unofficial, abstract research and development department was always on the look out for what Island Records would become, extending and refreshing its traditional

Keep On Running | 155

A dogged four-man gang, U2 assiduously pursued success for their addictively commercial, mesmerising material, finally transmogrifying into The Biggest Band in the World. Their influence growing far beyond music alone, they wore their responsibilities with dignity.

values, and only Blackwell fully knew what that was going to be. Everything was in flux, always, in the world, in music, and the label never settled down to be what now and then it seemed to be, because there was always something else starting to happen, and Chris would always be standing by, seeing what interested him, what made sense to him based on his love for music and the sudden merger of talent and organisation, instinct and incident, art and trading.

Island, born in 1959, along with Berry Gordy's bold, pioneering Motown, took the baton from Chess, Sun, Atlantic, Imperial, King, these great unprecedented American independent labels run by alert, audacious Record Men, who invented and defined this scintillating new form of anti-corporate creative and entrepreneurial intelligence. These new Record Men, catching fire, making a business out of art, out of the three-minute 45 rpm single and soon the carefully sequenced two-sided 33 and a third rpm album, these tantalising, world-shaking new inventions, spotted, relished and exploited whatever new energy was happening. Blackwell picked up from where these groundbreaking record-loving talent-spotting mavericks had taken the hot-off-the-press idea of a record label, and through the 60s and 70s handed over this music and commercial history produced by these hustlers, futurists, visionaries, traders, operators, idealists, poets, pioneers and merchandisers to a succession of modern versions of those hustlers and poets.

He handed over this energy and craving, this addiction to hits, and the influence hits gave you, hits not just because of their sales but because of their subversive emotional and cultural impact, to those that formed Witchseason, Chrysalis, EG, Virgin, ZE, to those dedicated to discovering new talent, new genres, and new directions, and, eventually to those in the Eighties who found themselves on the edge of their own futures because of Island Records.

As the 80s began to take over from the Seventies, there were the fresh-faced post-punk neo-traditionalist Irish zealots U2, and the label formed by Trevor Horn of The Buggles: Horn's label that was to be based at the Basing Street recording studios where Chris Blackwell and company had set up and developed the Island Records that went from Stevie Winwood to Bob Marley via Cat Stevens and John Martyn. Here was Chris explicitly passing the baton over to the next generation – those facing up to life in the Eighties – never afraid to contradict the assumed identity of Island with a brand new programme of beliefs, sometimes ones he didn't initially identify with.

In a way, even as Blackwell was suggesting the route forward to U2 and Horn's Zang Tuum Tumb, making available various tools and environments, patiently watching developments, he also kept handing that 1950s' baton back to himself. While he was encouraging new guards to embellish and enhance the Island story, he was maintaining his own momentum, and the enterprising, at-an-angle Island spirit of the 60s and 70s kept pace with the charging, chopped up, uncontrollable 80s, through Tom Waits, Robert Palmer, Grace Jones, and the immortal Bob Marley. He thrived on change, and anticipated that music-inspired change would accelerate throughout the 1980s, as a culmination of the pop story he'd help started at the beginning of the 1960s. He wanted to be a part of this latest climax, as direct practitioner and undercover catalyst, responding in his own particularly resilient way as new inventions and new generations created new sensations.

Working with Island from inside the preposterously unstable ZTT, I eventually grew to appreciate how Chris Blackwell, and therefore Island Records, was not about one thing, or one style, or one system, or one way of doing things, but about reflecting how the world functions and reinvents itself precisely because it is a fluid, sometimes dangerous, always exhilarating union of systems and beliefs, and the best way of allowing the world to progress is to mix up, and place in glorious conflict, these various systems and beliefs. This is how he liked music to be made, it's how he made his music, or encouraged others to make it – by blending sounds, and theories, and words, and rhythms, and moods, and people, and histories that had previously not necessarily belonged together, noting what the connections and alliances were between them, or the disparities, and then exploiting all the sonic and conceptual possibilities that ensued because of the putting together of one strange thing with another strange, or even ordinary thing.

Island created a series of solid and liquid coalitions, one leading to another, so that in fact you could plot the sequence of events that led from 'My Boy Lollipop' to The Slits, from Dr. Strangely Strange to Ultravox, from John Cale to Frankie Goes to Hollywood, from Fairport Convention to U2, from White Noise to Eric B and Rakim, from Jethro Tull to Grace Jones, from Jimmy Cliff to Julian Cope, from Sue to ZE, and observe that as improbable as these journeys seem, they do in fact follow a kind of internal logic – and every journey of course follows a route proposed by Chris Blackwell, fitting into a map of discovery he drew up. And every journey passes through Chris Blackwell himself, who invested early into the tradition of the Record Man, and then fused that – his own unorthodox hybrid – with the role of desert pure, Caribbean loaded, pleasure seeking, creatively speculative, high-stake gambling, charismatic, technomadic Buddhist.

And then, to an extent, for the game, the experiment, and the quiet, unsettling glory, after having set up the union of one thing and another, and enabled the circumstances for these hybrids to be manufactured and distributed, he would stand back, he would almost disappear into the shadows, and watch what happens. He set up various unorthodox federations, junctions and alliances, based on his faith and appetite, his love of the untypical, unprocessed and up to date, and then allowed them to achieve their own momentum. Some achieved more momentum than others, but they all had their value, and were all of interest. This was how he kept up his search for his next fix, his next hit, his next moment, never satisfied with whatever commercial or artistic achievement he attained. This was how he entered the clamouring, new-fangled 1980s, still in positive transition, resetting in motion the Island Records that now contained U2, Zang Tuum Tumb and the enduring posthumous legacy of Bob Marley, an Island Records that in its own open-minded, mercurial way was set up to take over the world.

Because the invention of ZTT happened to be happening alongside the inexorable expansion of U2, the chimerical fabrication of Grace Jones, and the commercial establishment of Bob Marley as iconic revolutionary, and the development of Fourth and Broadway and Mango – experimental dance and internationally sourced music as self-generating brands years before their time – Island found a way to abstractly dominate the decade without sacrificing any of its rational avant-garde flair, without succumbing to the common and the vulgar. It flourished in the notoriously competitive and made-over 1980s without dirtying its hands, or its soul. Then again, for Island to blossom in the self-centred, brand-centric 80s, someone had to get their hands dirty.

By 1984 Blackwell had handed the managing directing role at Island over to a particularly aggressive version of the Record Man, Dave Robinson, who had set up Stiff Records. If there was previously a certain form of institutional delicacy, almost modesty, at Island that might have interfered with its indeterminate yet somehow incisive plans to achieve a deluxe form of entertainment world domination, and even meant the label's existence might be threatened by the cutthroat commercial fury of the 1980s, Robinson tore that apart. He arrived just after U2 had replaced Michael Jackson's *Thriller* at number 1 in the album charts, in place for the transformative performance by U2 at Live Aid and the release of October 1984's *Unforgettable Fire*. He arrived just as Frankie Goes to Hollywood's disco-mutant debut single 'Relax' was climbing the top 75 at the rate of about one place a week. 'Relax' ended up being insistently naughty at number one for five weeks in early 1984, and was established in this position when the second

For long supported by the camera-work of photographer Anton Corbijn, U2's myth was assisted by the sense of the epic employed in their image-making.

immodest Frankie single, 'Two Tribes', was released. Robinson was running things his way when Bob Marley's *Legend* compilation was released in May, three years after Marley's death.

If U2 were determined as loud-mouthed idealists, music fans and bloody minded self-mythologisers to be the biggest rock group in history, and the ZTT team, caught up in their own loud-mouthed fantasy of self-aggrandising hit-making glory, were determined to dominate the charts, and Chris Blackwell was determined to nourish the celestial legend of Bob Marley, for a few months the sheer marketing attack of Robinson helped turn these ambitions into reality. Robinson didn't last long as Island president, his tenacious commitment to the creation of hits was ultimately inconsistent with Island's intrinsic unhurried and uncynical psychology, but his stay helped ensure that 1984 was their greatest year for sales. It was the culmination of Blackwell's unshakable commitment to the idea of hit records not for their own sake but hit records that were the result of emotional intelligence.

When U2 were signed as a raw, almost babyish version of the incensed, stirring post-punk bands such as Joy Division, Public Image and Siouxsie and The Banshees, they also didn't seem a very typical Island act. They were maybe a sign of Island coming to punk a shade late, missing the moment, the movement, although their signing of The Slits actually meant that Island signed the most difficult, tantalising and enigmatically political of the original punk bands. (They didn't as such miss punk, just as Roxy Music showed they hadn't missed glam. They just found their own way into it, even though that sometimes seemed as though they'd gone AWOL at a key moment in history. Sometimes their absence, say around the time of 2-Tone, had its own kind of impervious poetic obstinacy. Then again, 2-Tone, a very Island combination of ska and pop, was an offshoot of Chrysalis, which had been formed though a licensing deal with Island, so there was a sort of (invisible) link between Island and 2-Tone.)

U2, though, were not just weaned on the expressive energy of post-punk. They were just as activated by Dylan, Van and Bruce, they could tell a tall story or two about how the blues, as anger, strain and melancholy, had made it into The Pistols and The Associates. It was this intense idiosyncratic relationship with the past that intrigued and turned on Island as much as U2's obvious crush on The Clash, Gang of Four and The Ramones. U2's early albums did not sell well, but Island stuck with them, indulgently allowing their emotional adolescent passions and obsessions to settle into grandiose, world conquering shape.

U2 stayed an Island band, and in a way even as the pure always progressive idea of Island disappeared behind its own success and history, replaced by a succession of compromised corporate versions, some more sincere than others, U2 keep the idea of Island alive. They are Island as much as Winwood, or Drake, or Marley, or Cat, or Grace, in the way they articulate so relentlessly the intangible, aspirational philosophy of Blackwell, this combination of sensitivity and intent, of faith and hedonism, of love and purpose. As long as U2 are intact, and calculating, instinctively and with rare cunning, how to channel tradition and invention into the future, whatever the circumstances, so is the original spirit and nerve of Island. Zang Tuum Tumbb didn't stay with Island, and essentially as

Keep On Running | 159

RELAX
FRANKIE GOES TO HOLLYWOOD
"relax don't do it when you want to go to it relax don't do it when you want to come!"

WELCOME TO THE PLEASUREDOME

Claudia Brücken of ZTT's Propaganda (above).

(Bottom right) One of the originators of speed and thrash metal, which they tempered with humour, New Jersey's Anthrax soon realized how a marriage of their own sound could merge with that of hip-hop. In 1991 they toured with Public Enemy, recording with the latter group a version of PE's classic 'Bring the Noise'.

(opposite) A frame-grab sequence from Nine Inch Nails' video for their 'Head like a Hole' tune.

soon as it left Island it was never the same thing. As far as I was concerned, as far as I hoped, ZTT was an Island act as much as Cat, Grace or U2, as much as anything on the *Nice Enough To Eat* sampler. It ridiculously succeeded, and gloriously failed, as part of the Island vision, as a mobile research and development unit feeding into the story Island were telling about themselves and their own ethics. Leaving Island, for all the usual damned near vicious legal, financial and emotional reasons, meant leaving where Zang Tuumb Tuumn belonged, where it could be potentially important and valuable because it was part of a story far more extraordinary and influential than its could ever be.

Just about the final constructive act of the doomed relationship between Zang Tomb Tomb and Island Records was to transform a Grace Jones song into a whole album, a musical biography of Grace, because the budget for the single in the end, once Trevor and company had connected all the necessary machines and got them to talk the same code-breaking language, was what you would usually spend on an album. Well, a few albums. I think the cost of organising the hi-hat sound alone could have bought an apartment overlooking Central Park. All things considered it was probably worth it: the view from the hi-hat is utterly extraordinary, let alone the view you get from the voice of Grace, and from the bass as it floats through outer space.

'Slave to the Rhythm' was a 1980s story in the way it generated and manipulated the image of Grace, and the song she was singing, and invited the listener to be a participant in the construction of meaning. It was a 1980s story in the way it symbolised how money was being turned into music and then, if you were lucky, back into money, more money than you started out with. 'Slave to the Rhythm' didn't turn back into more money, but it turned into one of those pieces of music that just had to exist, even if it doesn't sell as many copies as you think it might, or want it to.

Island were fantastic at making sure against all odds amidst whatever distracting trends were operating elsewhere that the best most exotic and uplifting music imaginable could exist even if it wasn't necessarily going to sell – or immediately sell. Somehow this approach meant that they found time, in their own oblique, strangely understated way, to rule the 1980s, pursuing their special understanding of why music is important, and why the selling of it does not have to be methodical and soul destroying and ruin the magic.

Grace Jones disguised cameo in 1985 as a Zang Tuumm Tomb artiste on the Trevor Horn-produced song 'Slave to the Rhythm' that became a whole biographical album was the ultimate sonic, conceptual and phantasmic completion of the soundtrack to the particular 1980s that Island owned. The decade Island owned because 'Slave to the Rhythm' sublimely voiced the carnal appetites, imperiled lust and underlying ache of the decade, because they released the song that launched MTV, because Kid Creole and Cristina freshly crashed through mundane everyday routine, because Julian Cope couldn't be tamed, because they released the hyperglam Frankie singles that provoked 80s-shaped Beatles hysteria, because they gracefully elevated the memory of Marley to a constantly higher level, because they released the record that led to the video where Robert Palmer was surrounded by sex, because they released Erik B and Rakim's *Paid in Full* where rhythm went deeper than ever because of attitude and language, because they encouraged U2 to administrate their own momentous musical territory, because they set up a series of dazzling climaxes to what we can now see was the vinyl age and their own spectacular independence, because they handed in their independence just as the compact disc, and further technological advancements, threatened the basic outline of what a record label actually is, as largely established by the likes of Island Records.

162 | Keep On Running

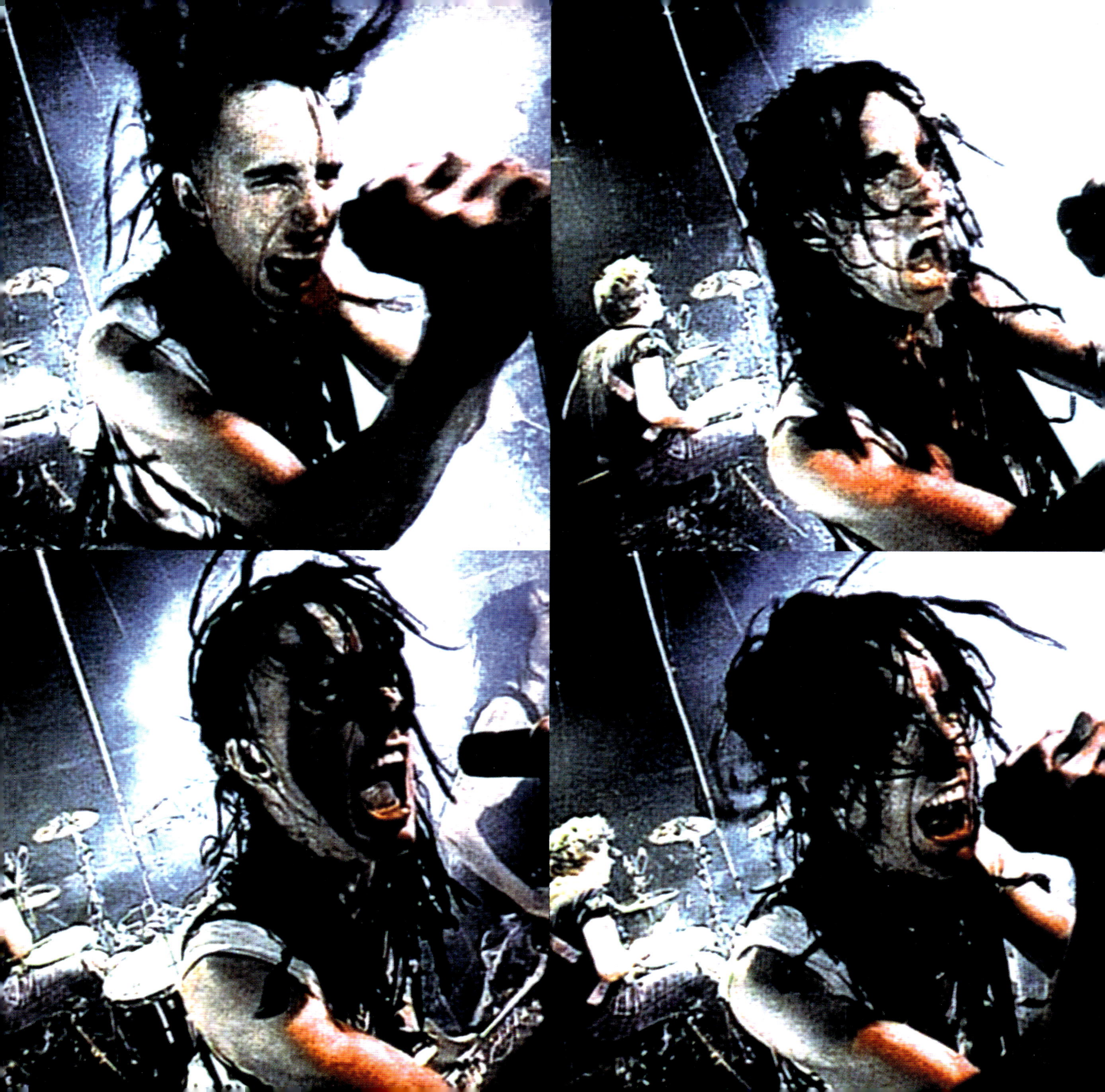

BAHIA BLACK

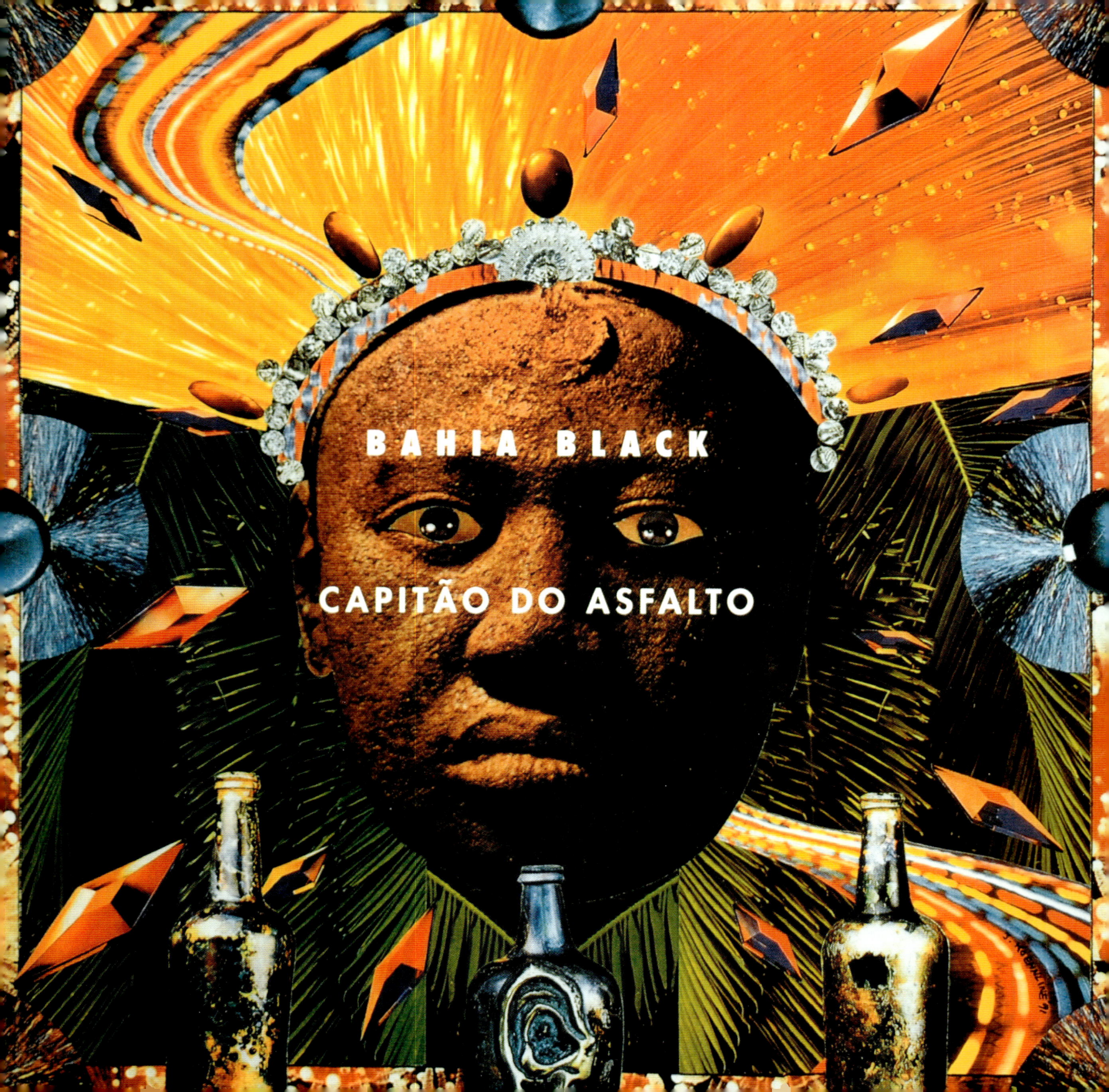

CAPITÃO DO ASFALTO

from africa and beyond

by Robin Denselow

Was Island Records the first successful 'world music' label? Almost certainly. After all, Island achieved impressive record sales with artists from the developing world, and those whose lyrics weren't in English, long before that rather vague term was invented in the upstairs room of a London pub in June 1987.

'World music' came into being after a meeting between the bosses of other British independent record labels (all far smaller than Island) who were interested in promoting new music from Africa or Eastern Europe, and were looking for ways to get their product better displayed in the racks of record stores. If the Bhundu Boys from Zimbabwe were racked under 'pop' next to David Bowie, they argued, the albums would be ignored, and what was needed was a new category. So a new musical genre, 'world music', was born. Was it necessary? Well, it's a term that has stuck and has been used in the promotion of hundreds of artists from around the world over the past two decades, but Island had managed to dominate the world music market even before it was invented.

It was thanks to Island that Bob Marley was hailed as the 'first Third World superstar', and that reggae became firmly established as the first globally-popular musical style from outside the UK or North America (though reggae was mysteriously not treated as a 'world music' style at first, because it was deemed to be already a successful genre of its own). And having shown that Jamaican ska and reggae styles should rightly be regarded as world-class popular music, it was only natural that Island would start to take an interest in Africa, the continent that is the obsession of so many great reggae songs. The process started with Manu Dibango, the saxophonist, composer, pianist and arranger from Cameroon, who can be regarded as the first great world music star from West Africa, thanks to his celebrated, sax-driven 1973 instrumental 'Soul Mokassa', a massive dance hit in the States and elsewhere. Dibango liked to experiment, mixing African themes with jazz and funk: Island helped the process by inviting him to record with the great Jamaican rhythm section of Sly Dunbar and Robbie Shakespeare, on his 1980 album *Gone Clear*, and on 1981's *Ambassador*.

Island's early connection with West Africa continued with a couple of brave and somewhat unlikely compilation sets, *Sound D'Afrique* (1981) and *Sound D'Afrique 2 – Soukous* (1982), put together by producer, musician and African music fan Ben Mandelson, featuring music from across Francophone Africa – Senegal, Cameroon, Ivory Coast, Upper Volta and Zaire. The first set included Youssou N'Dour's band Etoile de Dakar, while the second featured Moussa Doumbia from Mali, the country which within a decade would begin to dominate the African music scene.

There may have been no big name artists involved in these compilations, but it didn't matter. British audiences knew little about Africa in 1982, but it was a year of change, with punk and realism on the way out, and a bleak economic climate leading to a mood of escapism and search for new fashions. *Sound d'Afrique* notched up unexpectedly good sales, and showed Africa could be a source of great dance music – this in the year when the drummers of the tiny central African state of Burundi had influenced such post-punk bands as Adam and The Ants and Bow Wow Wow.

King Sunny Adé
And His African Beats

"Juju Music"

What Africa needed now was a new star performer, a figure who could match the massive popularity of Bob Marley, who had died tragically the previous year. An obvious contender was Fela Kuti, the highly controversial and political Nigerian star who had been involved in a serious confrontation with the country's then-military government: he had declared that his Lagos club, The Shrine, and its surrounding compound, was an independent state, the Kalakuta Republic. The soldiers were not amused, and in 1977 his mother was killed in a brutal full-scale assault. Fela was both a rebel and a brilliant musician; Island were interested in signing him, and contacted his French producer, Martin Messonier. But Fela was already under contract to Arista Records, who were finding him difficult to promote as a major star in the UK – his lengthy songs were at that stage not appreciated by British audiences, and he had a reputation for being difficult. 'He kept missing everything and was always late – it drove them crazy!' said Messonier.

So was there another potential international star on the Nigerian scene? One day in 1980 Messonier heard an 'extraordinary' track blasting out from a pirate cassette shop. There was, he remembers, 'a wild pedal steel guitar solo. It reminded me of Hendrix, with an incredibly powerful deep African beat behind.' Messonier bought the cassette, and found that he had been listening to King Sunny Ade, already a Lagos superstar. He eventually tracked Ade down: 'the Chairman', as he is known across Nigeria, owned several homes, constantly moving between them to get time to himself on those rare occasions when he wasn't working.

He was, after all, a very busy and successful man. King Sunny Ade, who really does come from a royal family, had already released an astonishing 50 albums in Nigeria, many of them for his own record label. Though he was bringing out new material every three months, each new album would sell at

> 'a wild pedal steel guitar solo. It reminded me of Hendrix, with an incredibly powerful deep African beat behind'. Messonnier stopped to buy the cassette, and found that he had been listening to King Sunny Ade.

least 100,000 copies on the local market. He also played regular live shows, often at the request of wealthy fans. In the early 80s, the military had briefly handed over to Shehu Shagari's oil-rich civilian government; as Messonier recalls, 'Lagos at this time was the promised land of music. Every night there were huge parties, taking place all night in the main roads of the city, and every night King Sunny and his band The African Beats would play for large crowds. The main guests would spray money on the band, and the backing singers would collect the money and put it in a cardboard box to be split 50-50 between King Sunny and the band. It was a happy time. King Sunny was making a fortune.'

When Messonnier suggested King Sunny might also enjoy an international career, the 'Chairman' was 'ready and excited'. The producer decided to work with King Sunny, and he was signed to Island; Messonier was in charge of a project that would transform attitudes towards African music in Europe and North America.

Part of the recording budget for the first album came from the Bob Marley royalties in Nigeria; Messonier was asked to collect the money from CBS Nigeria and presented with bags of cash. Like many African artists, King Sunny specialised in long songs, most lasting for at least fifteen minutes. But Chris Blackwell wanted 'at least ten songs on the album' (though in the end there were just seven). Messonier listened to King

Sunny's live shows and extensive recorded repertoire, selected 'twelve good songs', and rehearsed shorter versions of this chosen material at King Sunny's Lagos club, the Ariya.

Despite Nigeria's wealth of music and oil riches, in the early 80s there was no suitable recording studio in Lagos. Accordingly, King Sunny's album was recorded in Togo, to the west of Nigeria: the Otodi facility outside the capital Lome boasted 'a multi-track studio with good maintenance.' King Sunny arrived there with his full 19-piece band, with six guitarists, including himself on lead guitar and vocals and the great Demola Adepoju on steel guitar, eight percussionists, three talking drums, and six additional singers. The entire album was recorded in just two nights, with the whole band playing together at once, and Katrin Lesevre, Fela Kuti's live sound engineer, overseeing the recordings, and Messonier acting as producer. Hearing the tapes of the tracks, Chris Blackwell suggested the involvement of Godwin Logie, who had engineered numerous classic reggae albums: he was responsible for adding dub effects.

In June 1982 the first British release by King Sunny Ade and His African Beats hit the streets. The album was titled *Juju Music*, named after Ade's musical style, with its mixture of highlife, Yoruba traditional music and Western sounds. It really was special. When I reviewed it that month in *The Guardian* I described it like this: 'The songs all have light but complex percussion and chanting vocals, and against these the guitarists break through with anything from Hawaiian-style gentle slide solos to twanging Shadows-like sections. Then there are swirling passages where lead guitarists spar with each other in an elaborate tangle of solos against that insistent drum beat. African music has been taking note of what's been happening in the rest of the world, and it's time the rest of the world took some notice in Africa. This album could change a lot of misconceptions.'

Listening to it again today, *Juju Music* still sounds as fresh, subtle and distinctive as ever, thanks to those intertwining guitars and sophisticated dance beats. It was a hit album, both in the UK and the USA; King Sunny followed its release with the first high-profile concert in the UK by a West African artist, at the Lyceum in London in January 1983. King Sunny was rightly treated as a star, driven around in a Bentley by Blackwell's Rasta driver Satch, and he was playing in a hall where Marley had recorded a legendary live album. When it was suggested that there should be an opening act, he pointed out that it wasn't necessary. Unlike British bands he could play for far longer than one and a half hours 'for in Lagos we usually start about 10 pm and when we finish depends on the people's demands. It's usually about around 6 am.'

While in London, King Sunny and his band recorded a new album in Matrix studio off the Holloway Road, where the 'Chairman' could be found sporting short hair, a neat moustache and a camel-coloured coat, looking like the successful international musician he had become. When I visited the studio, there was a party atmosphere; Ade discussed the Western influences in his music: 'I'm a lover of Louis Armstrong and jazz but I also listen to people like the Everly Brothers, Jim Reeves and Don Williams.' Inevitably, he recorded far more than was needed for one album, with all the African Beats recording together at once; Messonier spent time on overdubs, adding Prophet 5 bass over the talking drums. This new style worked well in dance clubs: the title track from the 1983 album *Synchro System* became a Top Twenty hit in the UK. When the album was released in the States, King Sunny could boast two albums in the Billboard Top 50.

In two years King Sunny Ade had transformed the African music scene. Back in Lagos, The Chairman and his band recorded *Aura*, their third Island album, with Godwin Logie joining the production team from day one. Now the emphasis was on experimentation, King Sunny keen to enhance traditional Nigerian styles with the latest technology and new sounds, matching electronic percussion against talking drums. But in the middle of recording, there was a major disaster for the Nigerian music scene, and indeed for the entire country: President Shagari was overthrown in a military coup. The Lagos street parties stopped, the mood in the city changing dramatically. Recordings for *Aura* were switched to London. But even though it contained harmonica work from Stevie Wonder on the song 'Asem', the album was not quite the success of the earlier records. Shortly afterwards, King Sunny Ade and Island Records parted company.

In the USA, King Sunny Ade's albums had been released on the Island subsidiary label, Mango: in 1986 Mango was re-launched as the home for all of Island's world releases, including much of the reggae catalogue. In the UK the label was headed by a South African DJ and A&R man, D.A. 'Jumbo' Vanrenen, a

Ostracised as a youth by his family and community for his albinism, Salif Keita pursued a brave course to become one of Arica's most successful singers. In 1987 he broke through internationally with his *Soro* album. But still the egregious discrimination he had received as a youth not only rankled but desired that a statement be made regarding it. For his 1995 album *Folon*, therefore, he asked his niece, also an albino, to be the cover-image. In more recent years, being an albino in parts of Africa has become a life-threatening burden.

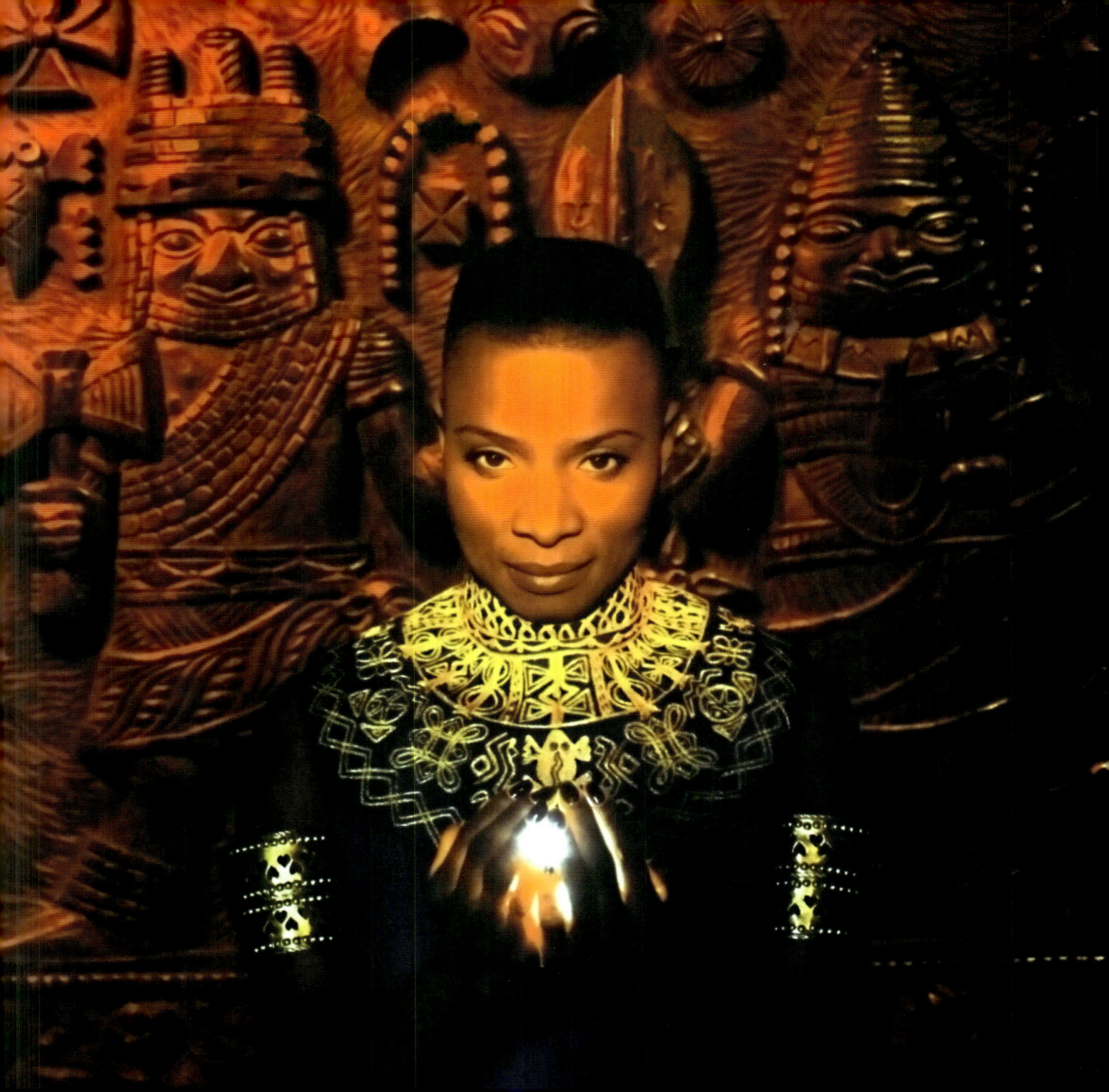

massive fan of African music. One of Jumbo's friends was Island engineer Paul 'Groucho' Smykle, who suggested Jumbo should be brought in to look after Mango's London office, specialising in African releases; in New York the office was headed up by Jerry Rappaport, who had worked for Tower Records in the States, looking after their Latin, reggae and African catalogue: he was mostly responsible for Mango's signings from across Latin America and the Caribbean, and 'knew his stuff', according to Jumbo.

Between them, they brought a massive array of different artists' styles to the label, with the London office specialising in African music. At that time the African music scene was dominated by a remarkable array of musicians from the poor, land-locked state of Mali, on the southern edge of the Sahara: the world's interest in Mali began with two extraordinary musicians both signed to Mango. Salif Keita, now recognised as one of the greatest singers in the world, had moved from Africa to Paris in the mid-80s; there he became fascinated with electronics and new music technology. This resulted in the 1987 album *Soro*, a brilliantly inventive work involving electronic drums and synthesizers, but which – says Jumbo – was posing a problem for Salif's label EMI: 'None of its European operations knew what to do with it.' Thanks to Groucho and Jumbo, Chris Blackwell got to hear a pre-release cassette of the album and was rightly impressed; Jumbo's first task for Mango was to secure Salif Keita. He succeeded. *Soro* was already distributed in the UK by the independent Stern label, but this seminal album was released by Mango in the States – and Salif became a Mango artist. The first album that he recorded for the label was *Ko-Yan* in 1989, which again broke from the African tradition with its use of electronic percussion and programming. The follow-up, *Amen* (1991) was even more adventurous, matching Salif's soaring vocals against saxophone work from Wayne Shorter and the guitar playing of Carlos Santana, with another American star Joe Zawinul playing keyboards, and acting as arranger and producer. Salif proved that Mali could produce a world-class singer, while his compatriot guitarist Ali Farka Toure emerged as one of West Africa's legendary instrumentals. In the UK, his albums were released on World Circuit, but in North America they could be found on Mango.

From Benin in West Africa, Angelique Kidjo relocated to Paris in 1983 (opposite page) fleeing political turbulence. Studying in Paris at the CIM jazz school she met and married producer Jean Hebrail, with whom she has subsequently co-written most of her music. With influences that encompass, among others, Afro-pop, Congolese rumba, Caribbean zouk, jazz, and Latin, as well as James Brown and Jimi Hendrix, she was well-placed to make her first solo album, *Parakou*, released by the Open Jazz label. She also became an exceptional live performer. When Chris Blackwell came across Kidjo in 1991, he immediately signed her. Angelique Kidjo recorded four albums for Mango - *Logozo*, *Aye*, *Fifa*, and *Oremi*.

(Left) Salif Keita

Jumbo's African connections extended to the north of the continent, and the Rai scene that had transformed the pop music of Algeria by mixing electronics and explicit lyrics with traditional dance music – to the fury of the country's Islamic fundamentalists. Jumbo had released a compilation of Rai stars on his Earthworks label, and several of them subsequently signed to Mango, including Chaba Fadela and her husband Cheb Sahraoui, who had been responsible for the biggest Rai hit of the 80s, 'N'Sel Fik'. It wasn't an easy project. The Rai stars came to London to discuss the recordings along with Rai's top producer Baba Rachid Ahmed, who went home 'with lots of new equipment' for his studio in Tlemcen. But when Mango arranged for journalists and TV crews to travel out to Tlemcen in 1988 to publicise the project, the Algerian authorities became nervous. An MTV film crew was detained, and photographer Adrian Boot remembers that 'the police raided the studio after we had left.' Writer Chris Salewicz considered Algeria 'the most sinister place I've been,' and subsequent events proved he had reason to be worried. Following the cancellation of elections in 1992, the Islamists declared war on the government, and instigated a terror campaign against those they regarded as their enemies – including Baba Rachid Ahmed, who was shot on his doorstep by fundamentalists in 1995.

By then, Rai had developed a massive following across Europe, thanks to the rasping, soulful singing of Khaled, who had joined the exodus of those fleeing from Algeria to France to escape the violent upheavals in his homeland. In 1992 he sold

THE ISLAND RECORDS AFRICAN SERIES.

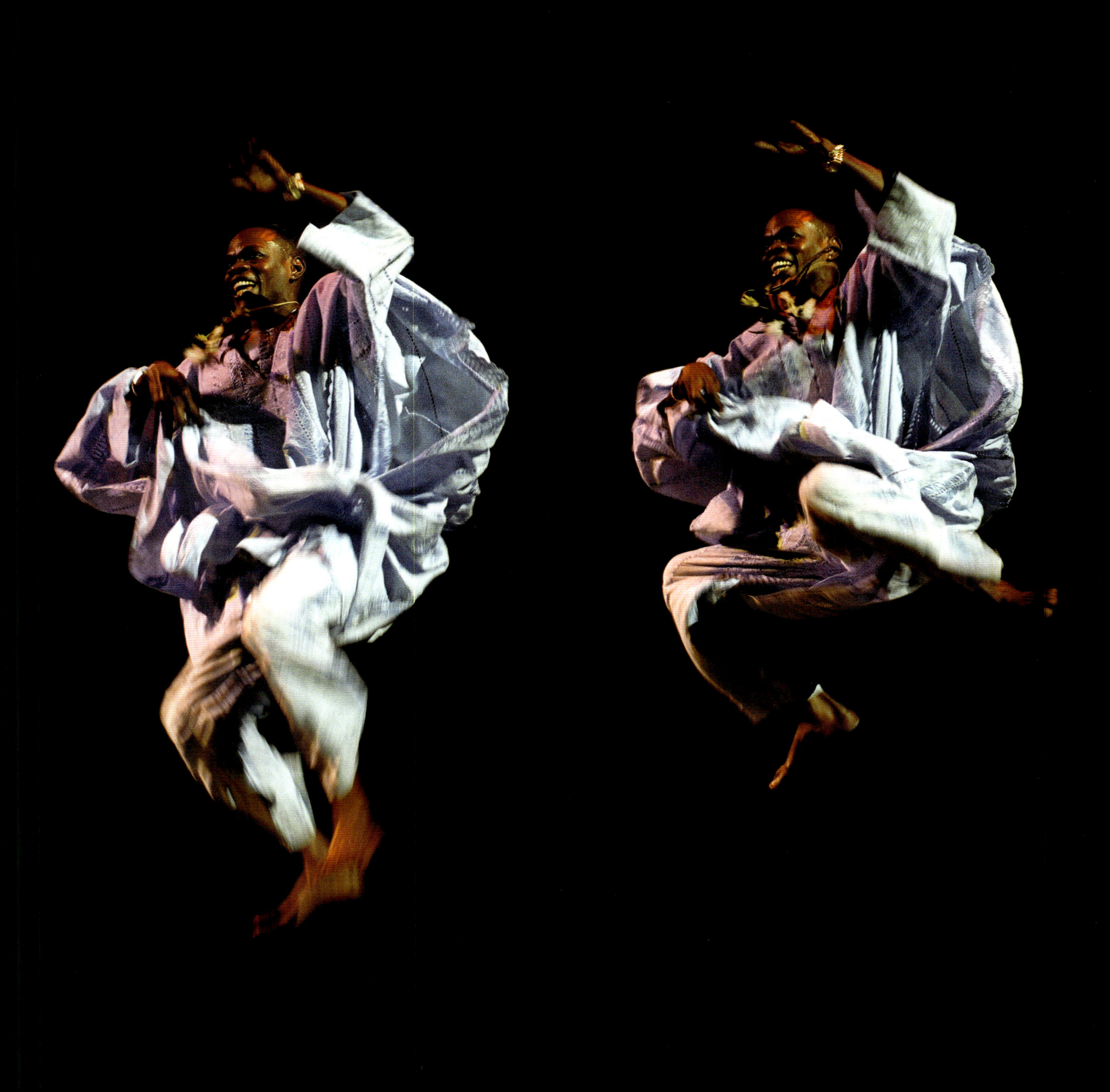

an astonishing million copies of his song 'Didi', which mixed Algerian dance styles with Western R&B, and was produced by Don Was, who had worked with the Rolling Stones. Khaled's 1993 album *N'ssi N'ssi* included more tracks produced by Don Was, and appeared on Mango.

As Algeria descended into chaos, there were thankfully more cheerful developments at the other end of the continent, as South Africa moved towards majority rule following the release of Nelson Mandela from prison. Here too, music reflected politics, and Mango was involved. The label released recordings by the ANC's exiled choir in London, and the ANC's official election album, *Sekunjalo*, which included songs by the likes of Hugh Masekela, encouraging black South Africans to vote for the first time. When the election was over, and President Mandela was invited on a state visit to the UK in July 1996, there was a concert in his honour in London's Royal Albert Hall, featuring Phil Collins, Hugh Masekela and Ladysmith Black Mambazo. Watching the show that night, I reported that the real stars were the Soweto band Bayete and their singer Jabu Khanyile, whose album *Mmalo-We* had been released on Mango three years earlier. Mandela obviously agreed, for during Bayete's set he stood up in the royal box, started dancing and waving his fists to urge them on, while the Queen, looking a little bemused, clapped along.

Over in the States, Jerry Rappaport found it was sometimes difficult promoting African artists 'because the US is provincial – but we sold a fair amount of records, and it was a great place to be.' Mango USA handled African bands, of course, as well as reggae artists, but concentrated on signing Latin artists who developed a following in the States, like the Brazilian axe and samba star Margareth Menezes. The label was also successful with a Caribbean signing, Arrow, the soca star from Montserrat famous for the dance anthem 'Hot Hot Hot'.

Even so, one major Latin American deal was handled in London by Jumbo, simply because he was a massive fan of the Colombian dance styles, Cumbia and Salsa and the recordings of the Discos Fuentes label. So he flew off to Medellin in Colombia but managed to survive any feuds between the city's notorious rival drugs gangs and returned with a stack of classic Cumbia recordings. A whole batch of classic Discos Fuentes records were now released through Mango from 1990 onwards, with impressive new artwork and sleeve notes, and these included albums by the likes of Joe Arroyo, Fruko or Alfredo De La Fe. Some of the tracks could also be heard on the 1991 Mango compilation *Big Cumbia*.

Mango covered the world, but in the end it was African music that defined the label, and two major African stars were launched, and developed, by the label. One was Angelique Kidjo, the fiery singer from Benin who mixed African influences and rock, and the other was one of Africa's greatest vocalists, Baaba Maal. Both were personal favourites of Chris Blackwell, and Jumbo remembers taking the tapes of Angelique's album out to Blackwell when he was in Nassau 'and he took me out to some far-flung island on jet-skis at night to listen to it in peace. It was one of the most terrifying and exhilarating times I've had. Thank God he liked it.'

The role of Baaba Maal is his native Senegal is like that of an alternative statesman. One of the most achieved musical artists in the whole of Africa, his music is imbued with both the purity of the African village and the thinking of the intellectual who studied his subject in the Senegalese capital of Dakar and at the Conservatoire in Paris. Baaba Maal's music combines the timeless Fulani musical traditions of the tiny northern Senegalese villages in which he grew up with the musical cutting edge of contemporary western music. It is music of high principles, the philosophy of an artist who is striving for global unity and an end to bigotry. His melancholy tone, elevating melodies and remarkable rhythms are only complemented by his extraordinary stage performances.

King Sunny Ade

Keep On Running | 175

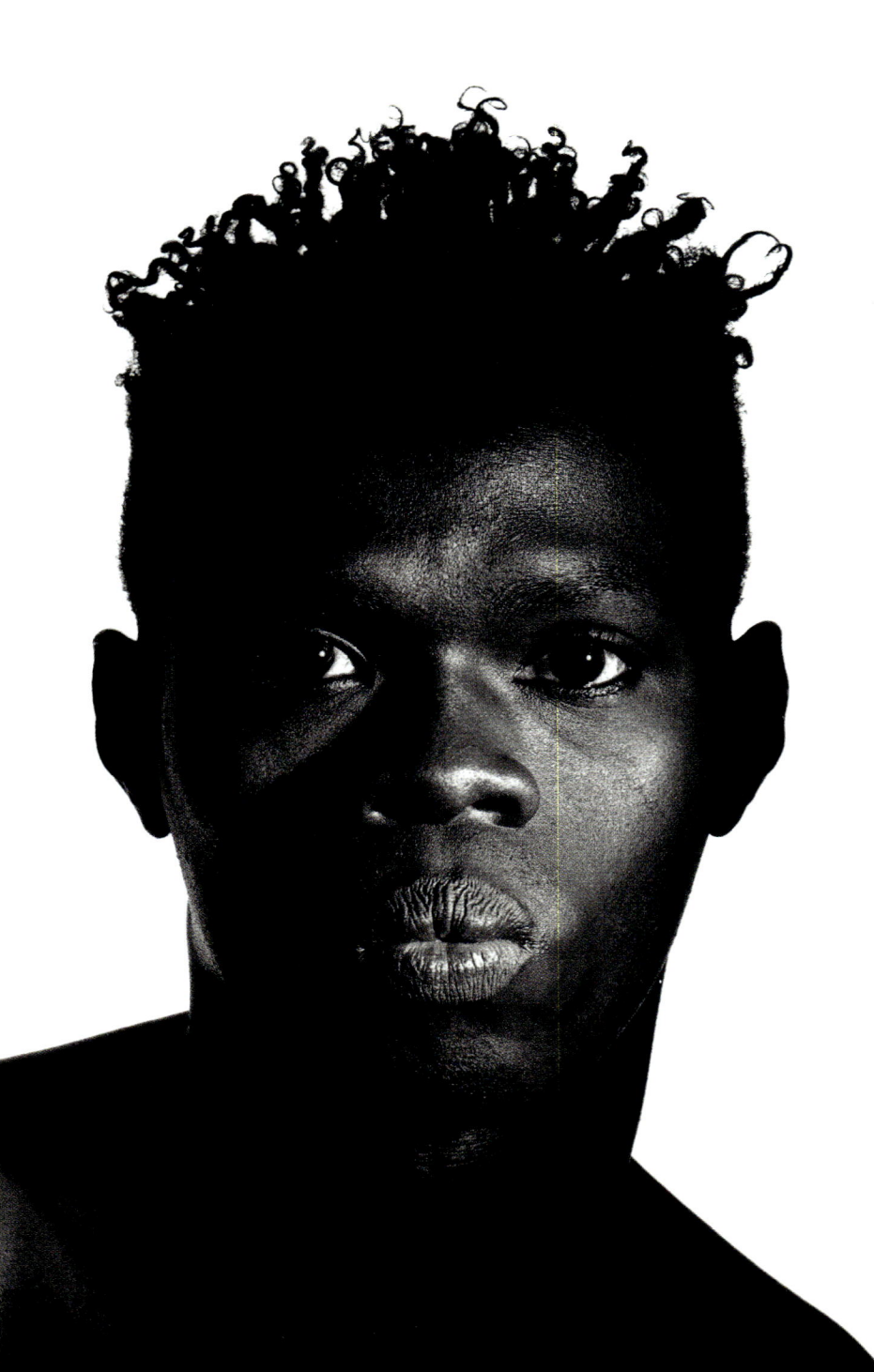

As for Baaba, Jumbo gave Chris Blackwell a cassette of his extraordinary singing on the first day that he worked for Mango, and this resulted in Mango US releasing Baaba's celebrated debut set *Djam Leeeleii*, recorded with his close friend the blind griot Mansour Seck and originally released as a cassette back in 1985. Baaba has one of the great voices of Africa and is one of the great innovators, capable of thrilling acoustic work and equally remarkable musical experiments with a full band. Both sides of his work can be heard on his Mango recordings, from the acoustic *Baayo* to the bravely modern *Lam Toro* and *Firin' In Fouta*, which included contributions from rappers Positive Black Soul. Even when Blackwell had severed his connections with Island, and Mango had ceased to trade after Island had been merged first with Polygram and then with Universal, Baaba retained his close links with Chris Blackwell and his aide Suzette Newman, by continuing to record for Blackwell's independent label Palm Pictures.

Island may be rightly famous for its rock acts and reggae, but Island and Mango also played a crucial role in developing and popularising music from right across the world. Looking through the CDs in my collection, it's remarkable to find how many of my favourites have the red, orange and green flash that became the trademark of a Mango recording. Like King Sunny's albums, many of them have become global classics.

> Baaba has one of the great voices of Africa and is one of the great innovators, capable of thrilling acoustic work and equally remarkable musical experiments with a full band.

AFRICA FÊTE

178 | Keep On Running

Deep in the background of assorted Island studios, but with his work always at the forefront, has been Paul 'Groucho' Smykle, a constant presence since the late 1970s.

After having overhauled and dubbed up sound system smashes in 1979 for Jah Shaka and Twinkle Brothers, Groucho gave a similarly tantalizing treatment to Island's important reggae acts: Bob Marley, Rico, Ijahman, Gregory Isaacs, Ini Kamoze and Aswad, among others. His stark, sparse work on Black Uhuru's Anthem earned him a Grammy.

But this dubmaster also introduced Island to a style of music it had not previously encountered. In 1987 Jumbo Van Rennen played Groucho Smykle a copy of *Soro*, a record made in France by the Malian master-singer Salif Keita. Not only did he introduce this stunning piece of music to Chris Blackwell, but he helped secure Jumbo a job as head of Island's Mango label; then Groucho Smykle proceeded to Paris. There he moved his work into a new phase; he produced records for numerous Paris-based African acts: these included two CDs for Ray Lema and further Salif Keita releases.

In the 1980s and 1990s Island Records continued its already established policy of distributing smaller creative labels. ZTT had already proved its worth. Meanwhile, with acts like The Ghettovettes, the visionary producer and musician Bill Laswell showed the worth of the Axiom label he started in 1990 with the backing of Island Records. A believer in 'collision music' – the bringing together of musicians from wildly divergent spheres – Laswell released records on which his protégées Material worked with – among others – Sly and Robbie and William Burroughs; but he also put out records he had produced by the likes of Roland Shannon Jackson, Umar Bin Hassan of The Last Poets, and Ginger Baker. He also delved seriously into world music, releasing recordings by The Master Musicians of Jajouka, as well as Fulani and Mandinka music, among many others.

Delicious Vinyl, distributed by Island, was formed by Matt Dike and Michael Ross in Los Angeles in 1987, and quickly became successful. Tone Loc's 'Wild Thing' single sold three million copies, Young MC shifted a million units of 'Bust a Move', and Def Jef had a pair of LPs considered the epitome of hiphop credibility. With its pizza-box artwork and vinyl-chewing logo, Delicious Vinyl exhibited a humour utterly in synch with the Island ethic.

Jon Baker's Gee Street was another label that specialized in hiphop but was always prepared to sneak out around the perimeter for other action. As well as acts like the Jungle Brothers, Doug E. Fresh, and Queen Latifah, Gee Street enjoyed sales of eight million albums for Stereo MCs' *Connected*. And with P.M. Dawn the label really moved on the cause of hiphop, releasing their profound debut album, *Of the Heart, of the Soul and of the Cross: The Utopian Experience* – though not before Gee Street, on the verge of bankruptcy, had been sold to Island.

Artwork for Buckwheat Zydeco, consummate practitioners of Louisiana Creole music.

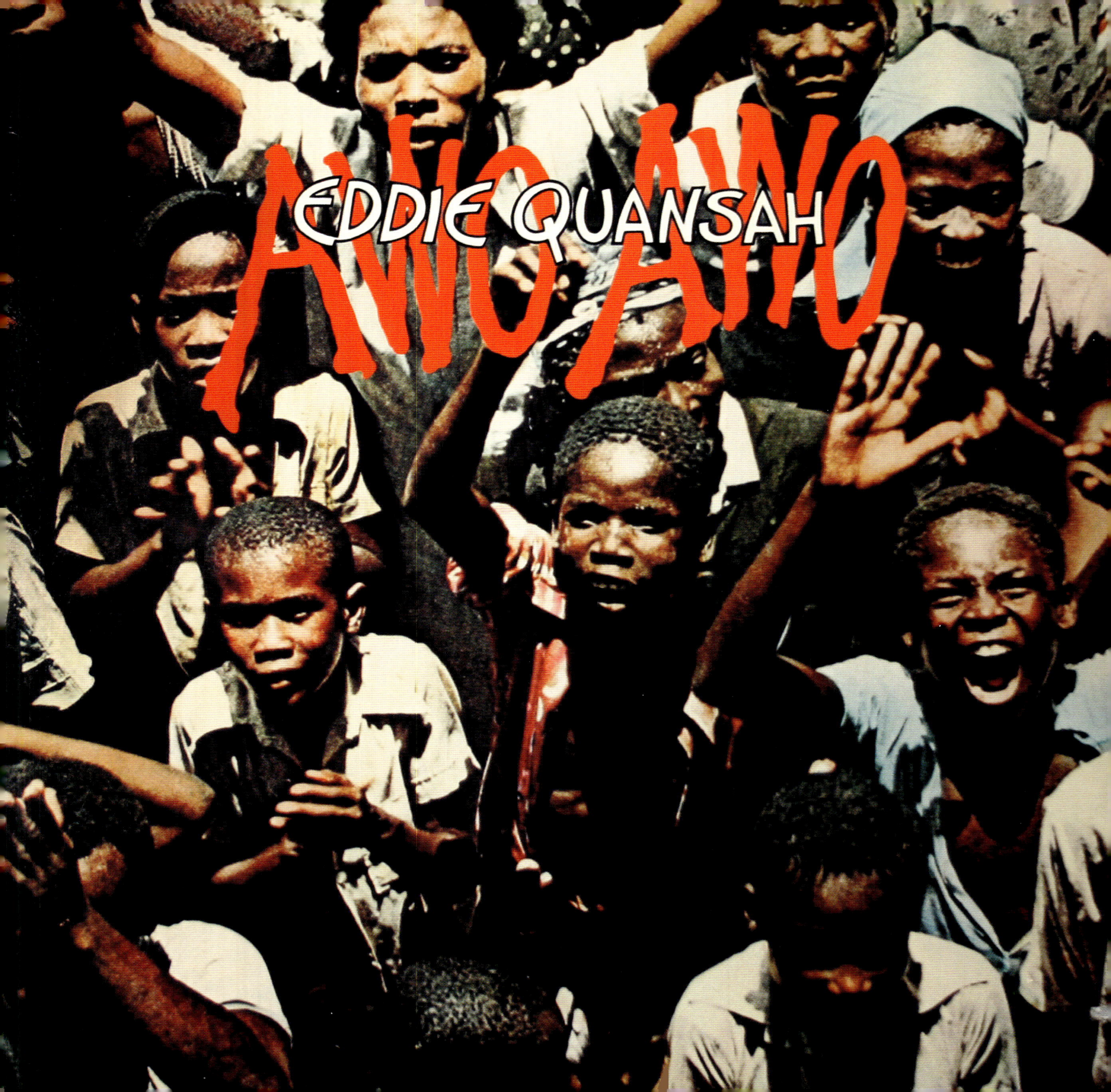
AWO AWO
EDDIE QUANSAH

Salif Keïta
"SORO"
MANU DIBANGO GONE CLEAR
YOMO TORO
G R A C I A S
THOMAS MAPFUMO
and the BLACKS UNLIMITED
CHAMUNORWA
WILD Tchoupitoulas
LOS VAN VAN
SONGO
Sanougue Kouyate
RAY LEMA
N'ANGADEEF
ZAHOUANIA
Nights Without Sleeping
3
LAM TORO
ZANI DIABATE & THE SUPER DJATA BAND
ARROW
SOCA DANCE PARTY
SOUND D'AFRIQUE II "SOUKOUS"
Salif Keita
angélique kidjo
fifa

re-birth of the cool

Go-Go music is the only musical form indigenous to Washington, D.C. The music sounds like the heart of the city, driven by a continuous African drumming groove from a variety of percussion instruments such as congos, cowbells, horns, timbales and drums. Go-Go gradually began to gain national American exposure following Chuck Brown's 1978 number one hit with 'Bustin' Loose'. Brown's sobriquet is 'the Godfather of Go-Go', and he is celebrated for his four-hour, half-sung, half-spoken shows. But he is by no means D.C.'s only Go-Go exponent. Experience Unlimited, Rare Essence, and Trouble Funk all own the groove and near big-band complement of musicians necessary to roam free within Go-Go's loose form.

In 1985 Island Records signed Trouble Funk, who were regarded by many as on an even higher Go-Go plane to Brown, with epic tunes like 'Pump Me Up'. The groove is the thing with Go-Go: set to a multi-rhythmic base, punctuated with Latin percussion, horns, keyboards and even rock-style guitar, with chanting-style vocals, the nine-piece Trouble Funk's music mesmerized Britain when they played the country early in 1986. It is impossible not to dance to Go-Go, as it proved at any Trouble Funk show.

To help popularize the musical movement, in 1986 Island Pictures produced *Good To Go*, the story of a D.C. journalist, struggling to clear his name after being framed for rape and murder. Set to a Go-Go soundtrack, the film is still a collector's item amongst fans of the music.

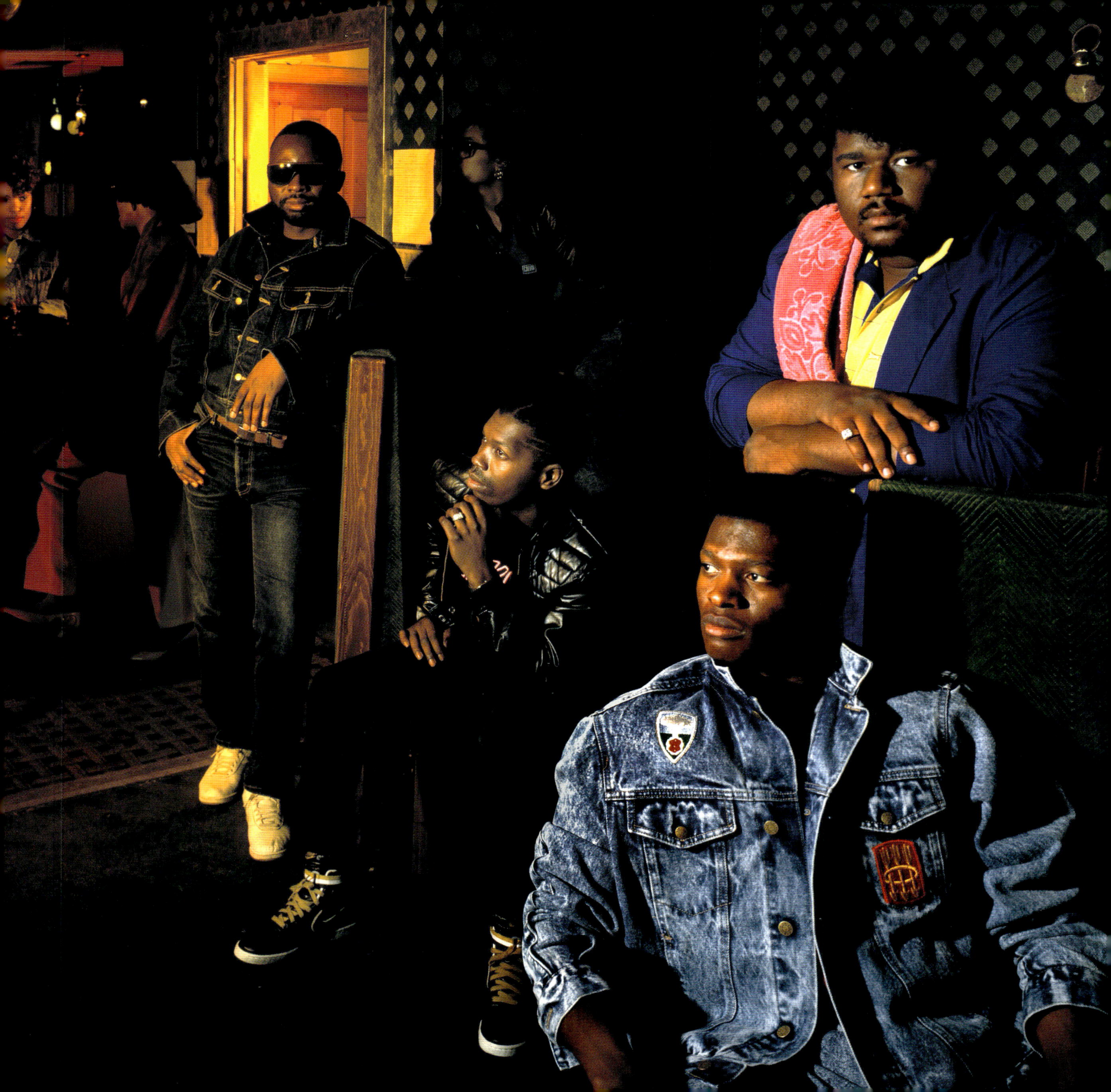

GO GO CRANKIN'

FEATURING ★ HOT COLD SWEAT ★ TROUBLE FUNK
CHUCK BROWN AND THE SOUL SEARCHERS ★ E.U. ★ SLIM.

WARNING
THIS IS **THE** D.C. SOUND ATTACK

DROP THE BOMB

PAINT THE WHITE HOUSE BLACK

4th B'WAY

ALBUM + CASSETTE AVAILABLE NOW. DC LP 100 + DC CA 100

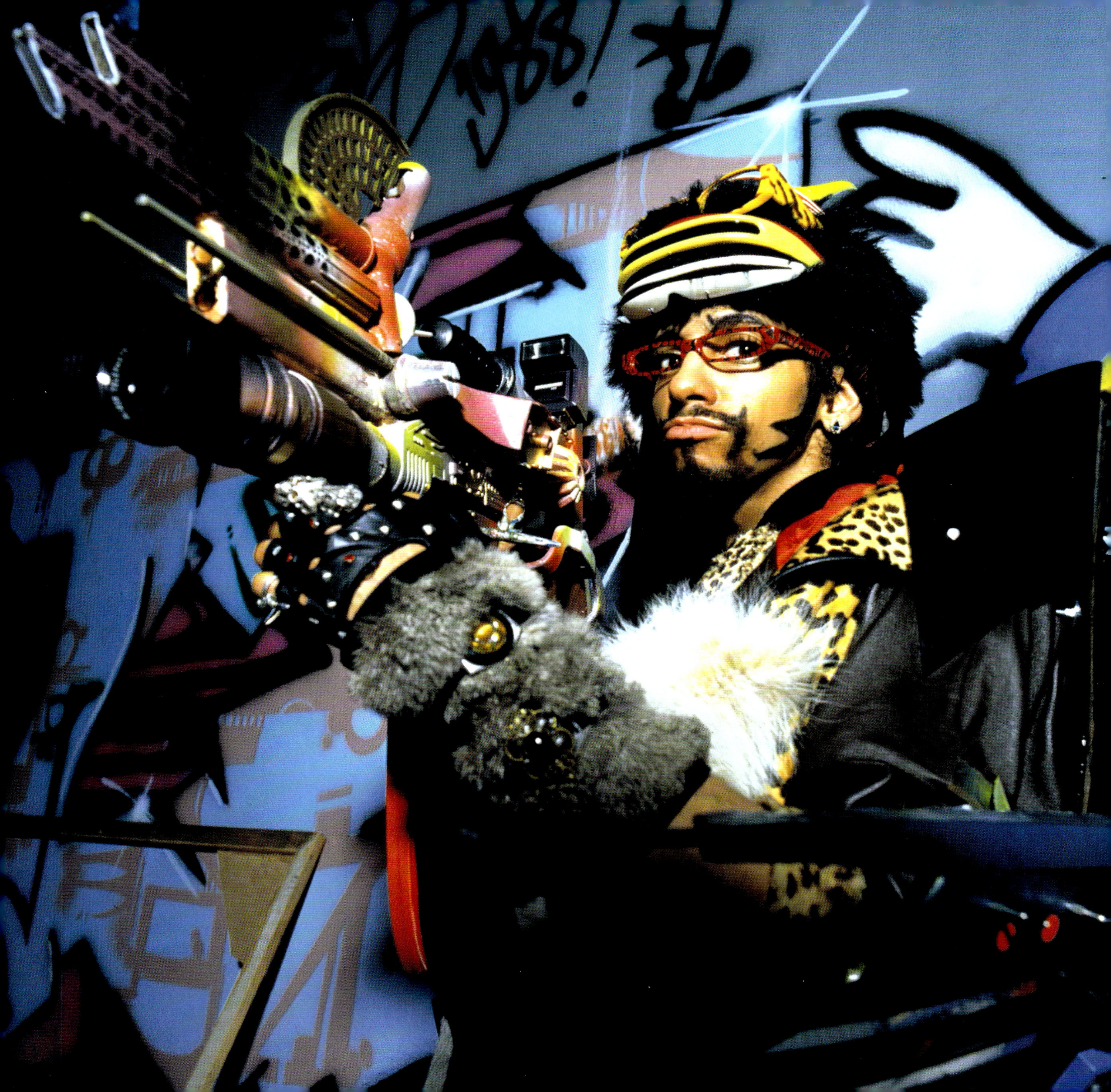

COURTNEY PINE *"Journey To The Urge Within"*

Sniffing the wind in 1986, Rob Partridge, the head of Island's public relations bureau, sensed the time was right for a big-selling indigenous jazz artist. By astutely manipulating the quality press, Rob Partridge watched the sales of UK saxophonist Courtney Pine's *Journey to the Urge Within* gradually escalate until the album was the number one record in the country, the only time this has happened for a jazz record. 'Many said it could not be done,' said Pine, 'but Rob's constant enthusiasm proved all those doubters wrong. Over the years his passion for jazz changed the way that the UK looked at the music.'

Meanwhile, Island's Antilles label also signed Andy Sheppard, another sterling saxophonist, releasing his self-titled debut album in 1987. Star trumpeter Randy Brecker featured on several tracks, and the record was produced by the great American bassist Steve Swallow – the beginning of a significant musical relationship. An immediate critical and popular success, the album was boosted by Andy winning the Best Newcomer at the British Jazz Awards. The follow-up album *Introductions In the Dark* featured a sophisticated mix of acoustic and electric sounds – the album immediately entered the British pop chart.

Having started off in business by releasing an LP by Lance Hayward, Island Records was no stranger to jazz music. In the early 1970s, for example, Island put out a pair of landmark recordings by another British sax maestro, John Surman: 1972's *Westering Home* and *Morning Glory* the following year.

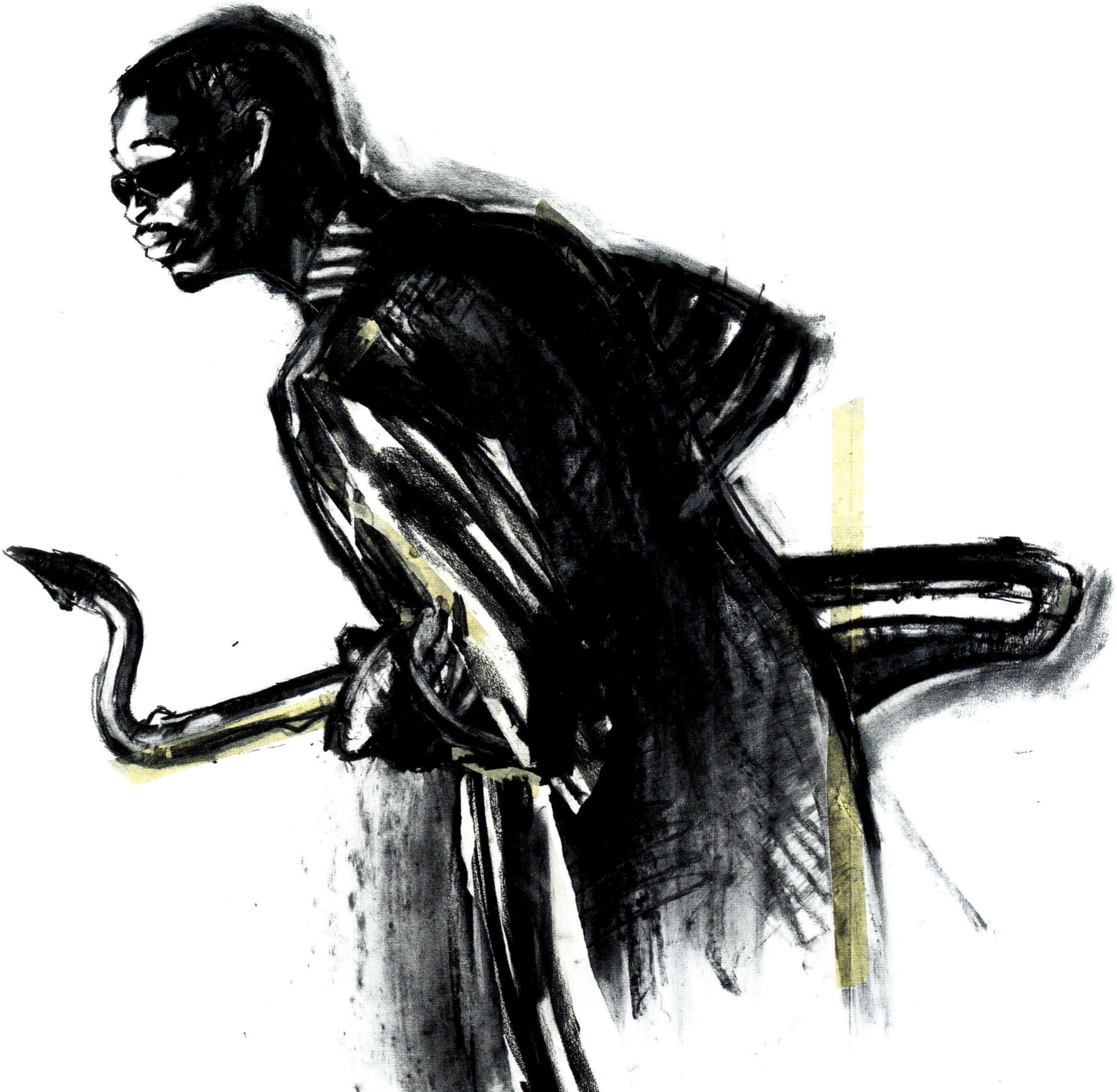

BEAUTY ✚ THE BEAT ➡ ON BROADWAY

With the 1980s just into their stride, it became apparent that a watershed had been reached and breached. In British clubs in major cities, a new style and culture had emerged from the efforts at breaking down musical racial divides in the last years of the previous decade. The idea of black music as the engine of dance had taken a quantum leap, breaking through barriers to a relatively large audience. Hip-hop was humming and house music was layering deep soul hooks with digitised funk grooves.

At Island Records in both the United States and Britain this new mood was expressed through the birth of the Fourth and Broadway label – known as 4th & B'way Records in the USA – in 1984. (Fourth and Broadway was the address of Island in New York City.) A hip, chic brand, whose singles were almost always released in a twelve inch form, it took Fourth and Broadway, and its parent Island, into a new era of fashionability, only enhanced by the graphically detailed artwork employed.

Early UK releases included Keith LeBlanc's militant 'No Sell Out', allegedly the first ever sampling record, M/A/R/R/S' 'Pump Up the Volume', and the *Paid in Full* album by Eric B and Rakim, rap's premier MC/DJ combo, one of the greatest hiphop acts of all time: the Coldcut remix of their 'Seven Minutes of Madness' hit tune off *Paid in Full* is considered a signpost in hip-hop. 'Coming into 4th & Broadway put us on notice that the game we'd been playing was real,' said Rakim. 'Tripping over to London, ya realized that if you brought the music, this was a group of dedicated people, talented individuals who were going to work day and night to make sure you got heard across the world, and work to make sure you got paid. It was the crossroads for me: seeing that this wasn't just a dream or a lifestyle, but also might actually be a career. I had my street soldiers for that swagger on the block and now here was this label, this additional army there to fight to bring us the whole world. You could taste the energy in those offices. There was fun to be had, but it was also serious business – and you knew these were the people to make sure everything that we did, we were supported 107%.' Tone Loc's 1988 mega-smash 'Wild Thing' and the next year's 'Funky Cold Medina' were both co-written with another Fourth and Broadway artist, Young MC, whose own hit was 1989's 'Bust A Move.'

The Fourth and Broadway mood was contagious. The legendary soul outfit Womack and Womack signed to Island, 1988's *Conscience* album one of the finest R&B records of the 1980s. Meanwhile, a 17-year-old south London girl called Mica Paris signed to Fourth and Broadway, releasing *So Good*, a stunning debut album in 1988. When *Contribution*, the album's successor, was released, it featured 'If I Love U 2 Nite', a track written for her by Prince, who had played with Paris at a London after-show performance.

With superb soul acts like Will Downing, and signings like The Disposable Heroes of HipHoprisy, Fourth and Broadway continued to lead the culture into the 1990s.

Vivien Goldman

ERIC B. & RAKIM

PAID IN FULL

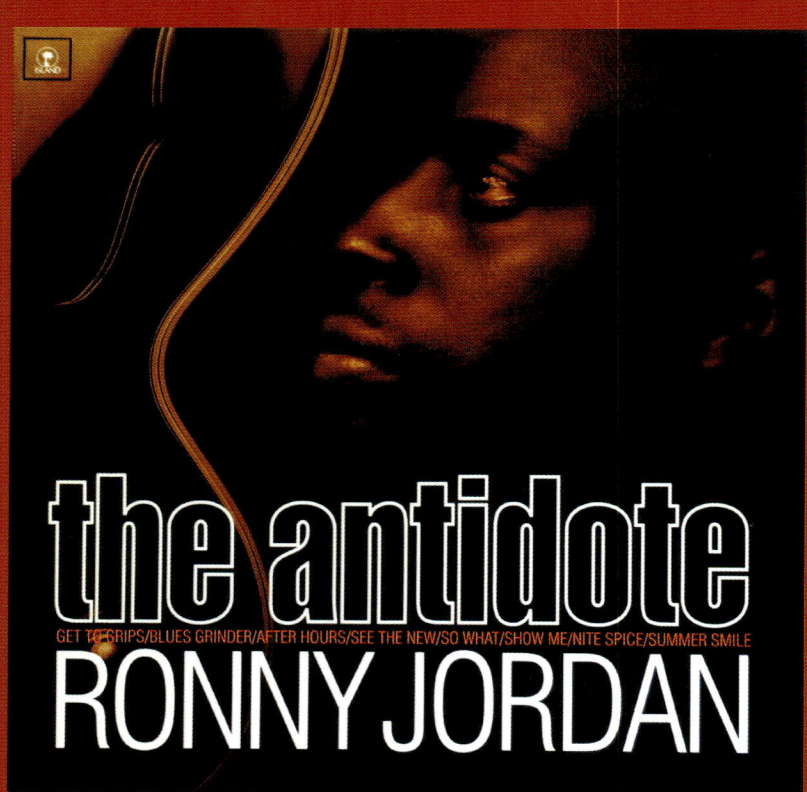

the antidote
GET TO GRIPS/BLUES GRINDER/AFTER HOURS/SEE THE NEW/SO WHAT/SHOW ME/NITE SPICE/SUMMER SMILE
RONNY JORDAN

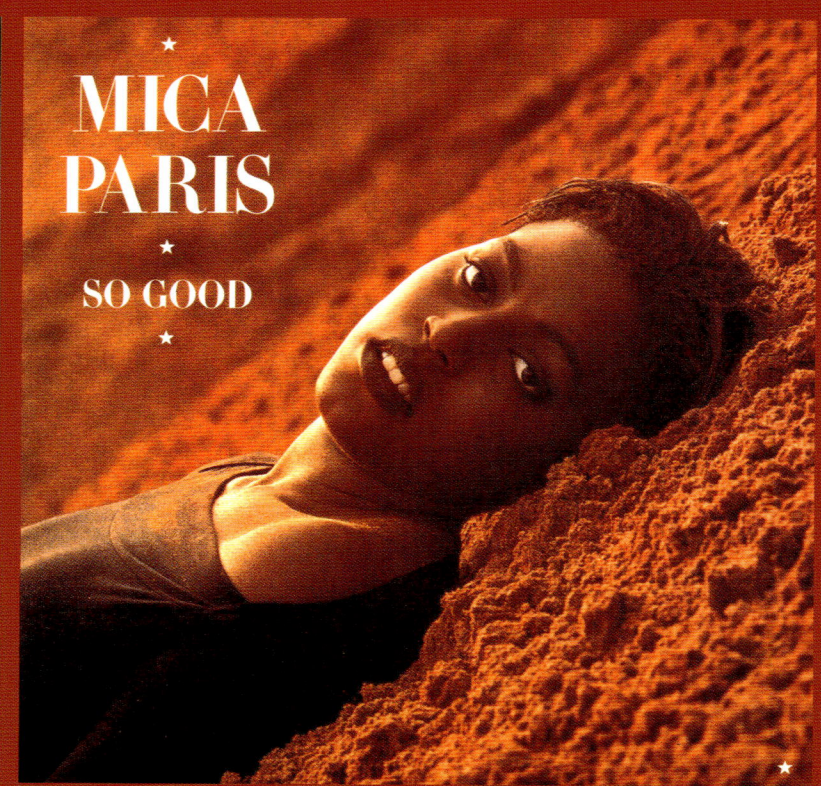

MICA PARIS
SO GOOD

CONSCIENCE
WOMACK & WOMACK

Gwen Guthrie

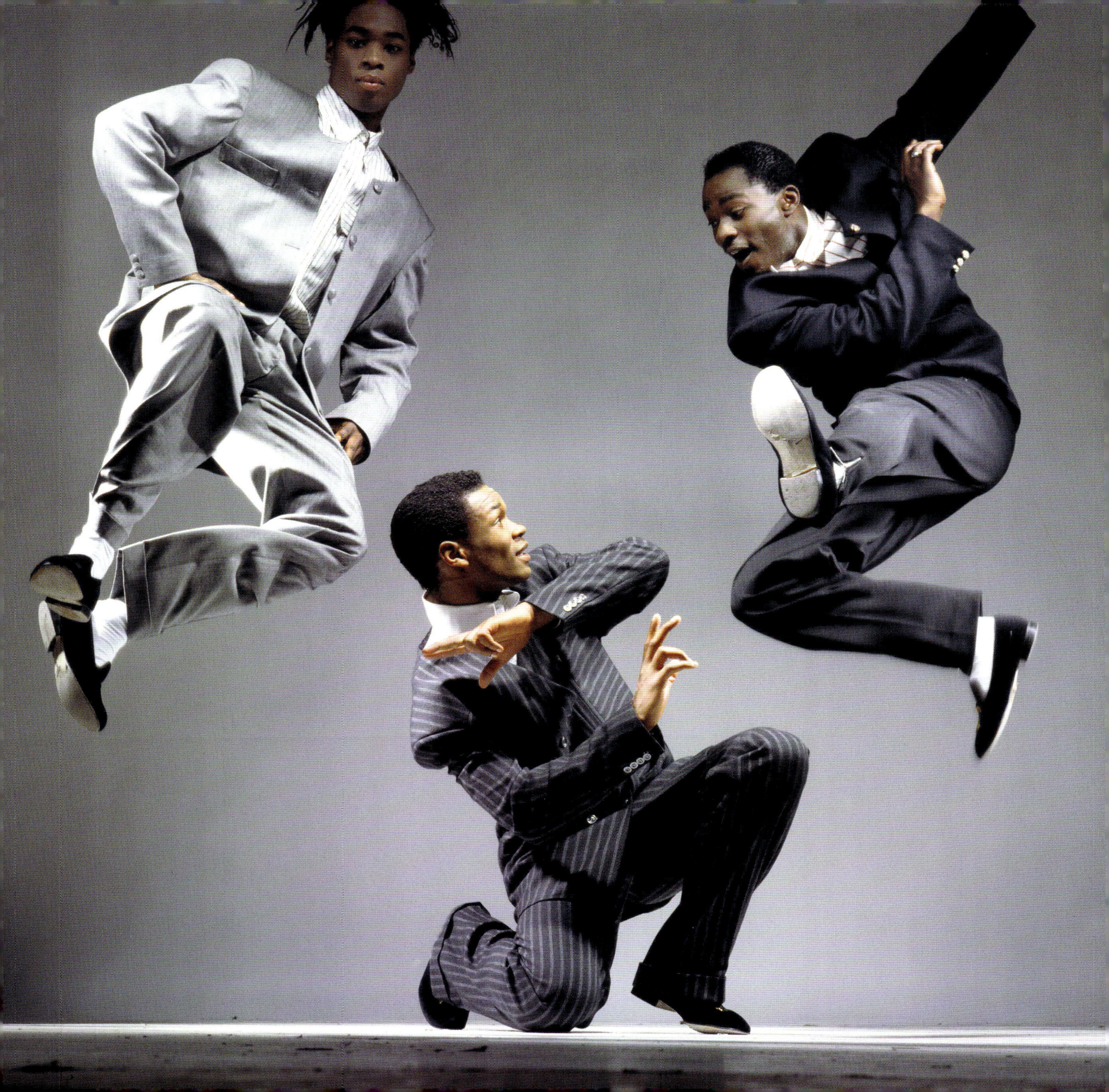

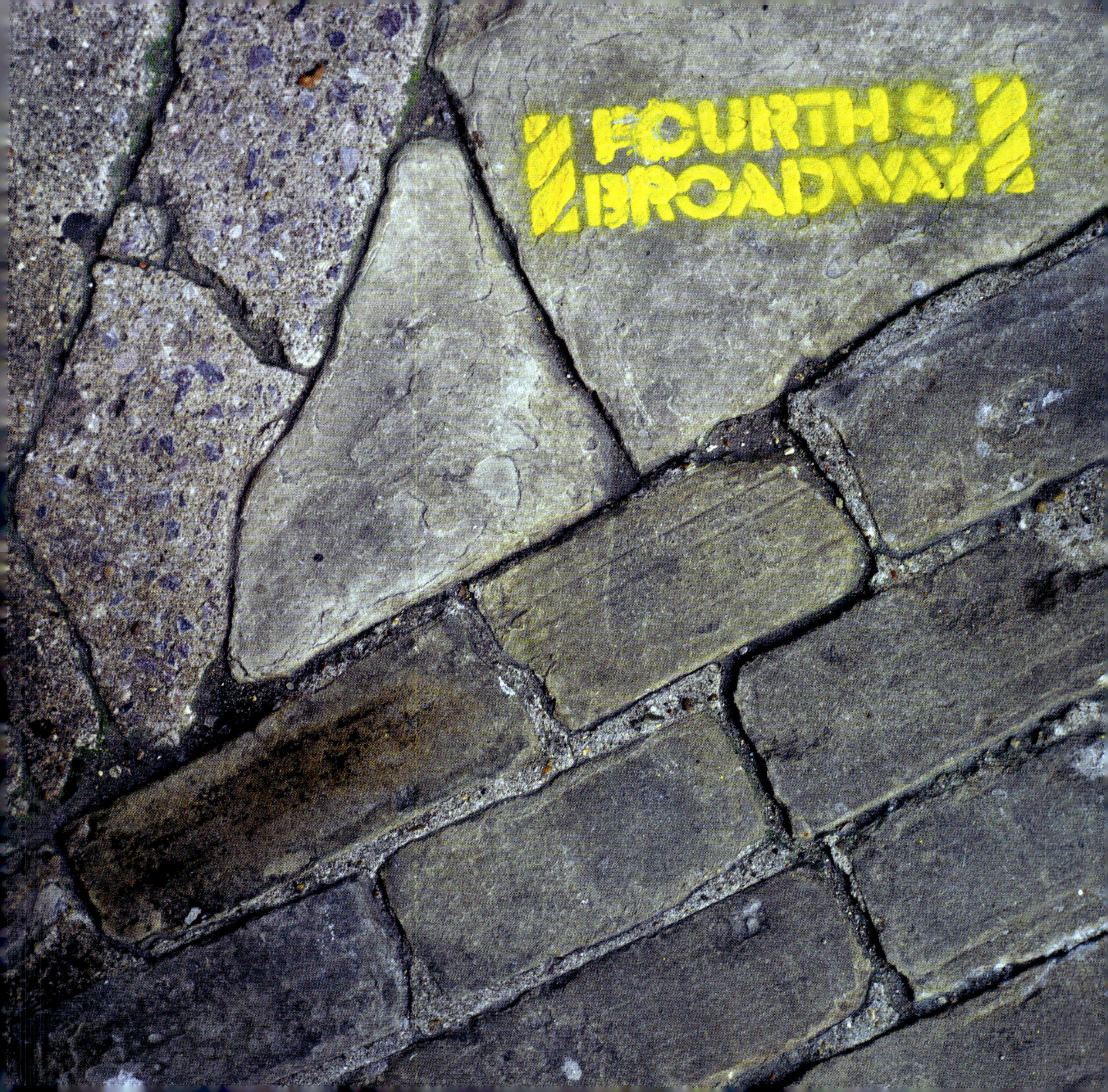
FOURTH &
BROADWAY

Delicious

"this is delicious – eat to the beat"

VINYL

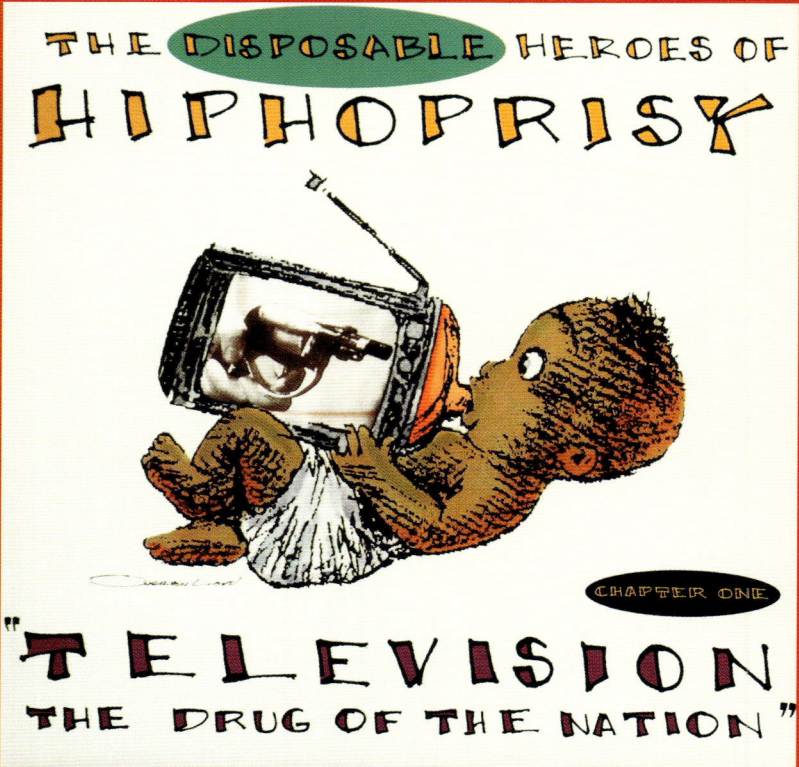

Dub poet Michael Smith's universal catchphrase (right) from his eponymously titled album; later, tragically, he was stoned to death in Kingston, Jamaica.

194 | Keep On Running

"Mi C-Yaăn beLiēVe iT"

PULP
DIFFERENT CLASS

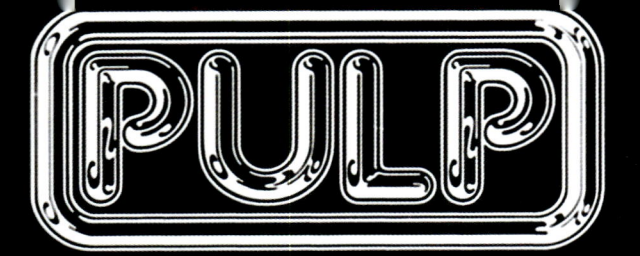

the new millennium

by Sylvia Patterson

In July 1989, Chris Blackwell sold Island Records and the Island Music Group to the Polygram UK Group for a reported $272 million and the biggest independent record label in history ceased, technically, to be an independent record label.

That summer, as Britain continued to boogie its soul asunder to the sounds of rave, a young man was losing an important part of his brain somewhere in a field in Hampshire – an episode he would later document in one of his best known songs. It was this individual who would continue to define Island's spirit of independence throughout the forthcoming 1990s. Back then, he had long hair which he wore in bunches, lovingly decorated with a pair of clear Perspex hair bobbles in the shape of teddy bears' heads. He was also wearing a Cagoule. 'So I looked,' mused Jarvis Cocker several years later, 'like some demented Girl Guide instructress.' Just the kind of person, then, to find himself signed to Island Records in 1993 as, ironically, the label's Corporate Years ushered in some of its most winningly idiosyncratic characters yet.

Into the gloomy landscape of the post-rave era, a glum-rock period dominated by American grunge, Pulp arrived like a glittering orange comet across an infinite foggy skyline, releasing *Intro* in 1993, their singles collection originally recorded on micro-label, Gift; their comically dazzling synth-led disco-pop was lit from within by the wryest observational lyrics since Morrissey at his 80s apex, ruminations on love, sex, drugs, Sheffield and, naturally, furtively hiding in wardrobes. Self-styled 'weirdo' Jarvis Cocker, the People's Poet in a fetching brown corduroy suit, stood as a minority of one in championing the sound, look and glittering angle-poise showmanship of the 1970s – at a time when his Britpop peers were simultaneously emerging in a black-and-white rerun of the 1960s. 1995 would be Pulp's creative zenith, the year they released their dancefloor-igniting and Mercury Award-winning *A Different Class*; this thundering, twinkling record included the mighty 'Common People', Single of the Year, sound of that year's Glastonbury Headline Moment and possibly the cleverest pop song of the decade, an exploding prism of class-war indignation. Jarvis Cocker may be, to this day, the most authentically eccentric English front-man ever to become The Most Famous Man In Britain – after he had waggled his backside at Michael Jackson during his preposterously pompous 'Earth Song' performance at the Brit Awards, 1996; later he moved to Paris to become a one-man National Institution of Multi-Fold Arts. Back in 1995, Jarvis

JB51

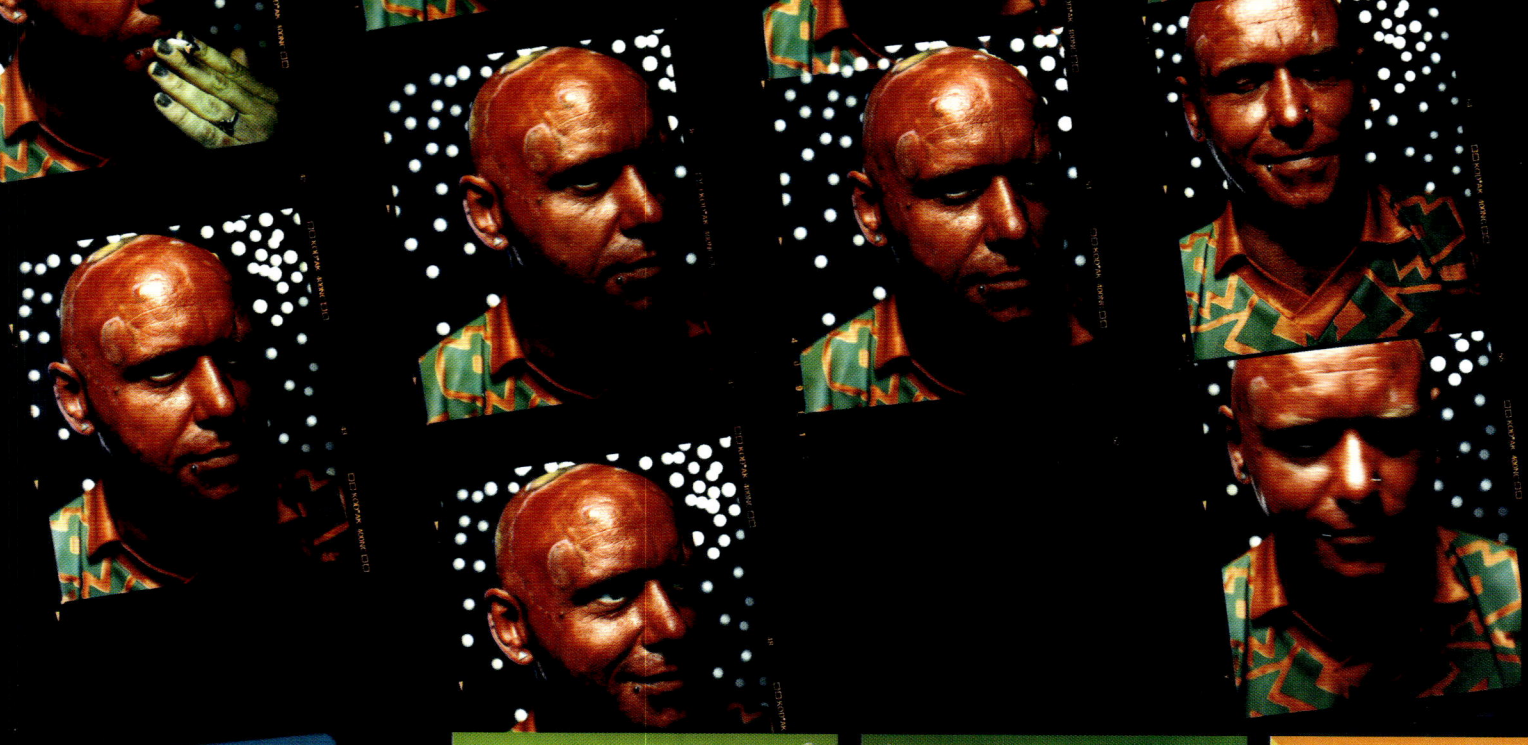

Led by Alex Paterson, The Orb first began DJ-ing and producing music in 1986, initially in collaboration with future KLF member Jimmy Cauty. After at first working with house music beats, the pair decided to remove the percussive sounds, pioneering the ambient 'chill-out' sound. Building up melodies using multitrack recordings linked to multiple record decks and a mixer ensured their pioneering reputation. But Paterson and Cauty ceased working together in 1990, the former taking The Orb name, and recruiting Kris 'Thrash' Weston, an inspirational recording engineer, and Steve Hillage, the former Gong guitarist. In 1992 their 40-minute-long 'Blue Room' tune made the UK Top 10 singles, the longest ever song in the singles chart. Signing with Island the next year, their first release was the *Live 93* set. But on The Orb's next release, the collective demonstrated one of their notable contributions to electronic music, the blurring of the distinction between sampling and remixing. Their next Island release, *Pomme Fritz*, which reached number 6, consisted largely of manipulated samples. However, the follow-up, 1995's *Orbus Terrarum*, featured more 'earthbound' and 'organic' sounds. Rolling Stone made it their album of the month, though it was less popular with UK fans. 1997's *Orblivion* marked a return to more spacey material. After *Cydonia*, released in 2001, The Orb left Island.

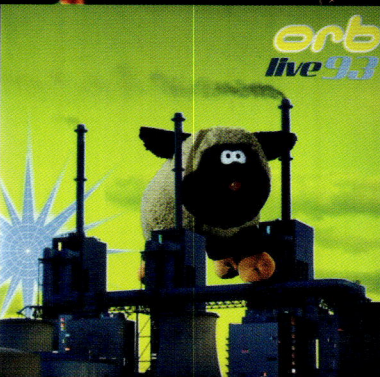

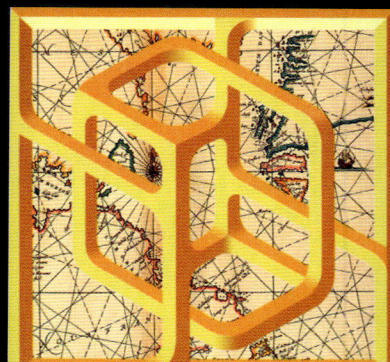

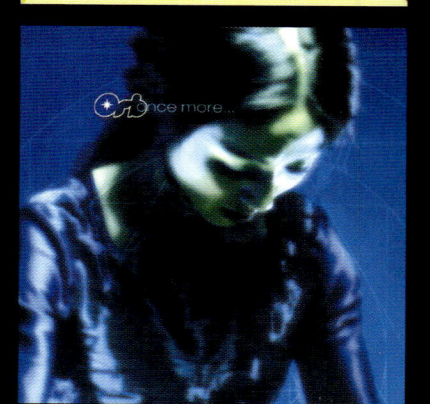

Orbivion

Tricky (on the right).

pondered which words he'd like carved on his gravestone. 'Here lies Jarvis Cocker,' he decided, with a smile, pushing back those enormous, unmistakable spectacles. 'Now thinner than ever.'

The pop-art cartoon personalities of the Britpop giants came in luminous contrast to the shadowy strobe-lit specters who flickered through the genre we knew as 'the faceless dance act'. Such figures were bad news for the character-led pop magazines, but excellent news for the clubbers as dance-floors (and fields) throbbed until dawn on a revolution in technology – and on Ecstasy. The Orb's dazzling, dubby debut album *U.F.Orb*, a UK No.1 in 1992, was as playful as it was prog, inspiring excitable rumours, sadly untrue, that chief Orb Dr. Paterson had found a way to make the summer festival stages actually physically levitate. Stereo MCs, meanwhile, saw the irresistible, bass-berserk 'Connected' single, from the *Connected* album, win them Best Group and Best Album at the 1994 Brit Awards, all of which failed to make any more of a household name of the willfully enigmatic Rob Birch, the Stereo's vocalist and permanently undulating flame-haired goblin.

> PM Dawn mainman Prince Be held a typically Buddhist view. 'It's a hip-hop Zen Koan,' he once observed, gently. 'If a sample falls in a forest but there are no lawyers...'

It took a pair of metaphysical brothers from New Jersey to redress the visibility balance: PM Dawn, the mellifluous, conscious-hip-hop duo who floated towards us in billowing purple kaftans as if buoyed on a marshmallow cloud, wafting in through the Daisy Age portal first created by New York's late-Eighties enigmas De La Soul. Their 1991 debut album, *Of the Heart, of the Soul, and of the Cross: the Utopian Experience* was a dreamscape classic, a beguiling mix of luscious harmonies, skittering beats and inspirational sampling; the record's globe-spanning hit single 'Set Adrift On Memory Bliss' was buoyed on a gossamer cloud of infinite charm by the sampling of Spandau Ballet's deathless ballad 'True' (alongside Eric B And Rakim's 'Paid In Full'). A master of the still-emerging art of the sample steal, PM Dawn mainman Prince Be held a typically Buddhist view. 'It's a hip-hop Zen Koan,' he once observed, gently. 'If a sample falls in a forest but there are no lawyers...'

Hip-hop in the 1990s would eventually challenge country music as the biggest-selling musical genre in America while holding on, occasionally, to some of its original political roots. Island's Disposable Heroes of Hiphoprisy not only supported U2 on their 'Zoo TV' colossus in 1992 but saw head Hero Michael Franti's old Beatnigs song, 'Television, the Drug of the Nation', become the early Nineties blistering anthem to 'the united states of unconsciousness', arguably the most pertinently powerful anthem ever written about the sinisterly manipulative powers of mainstream TV.

By the mid-90s UK hiphop was carving its own unique groove in the universal conscience, a sound as introspective and local as the Britpop titans were grandiose and global, the

Stereo MC's.

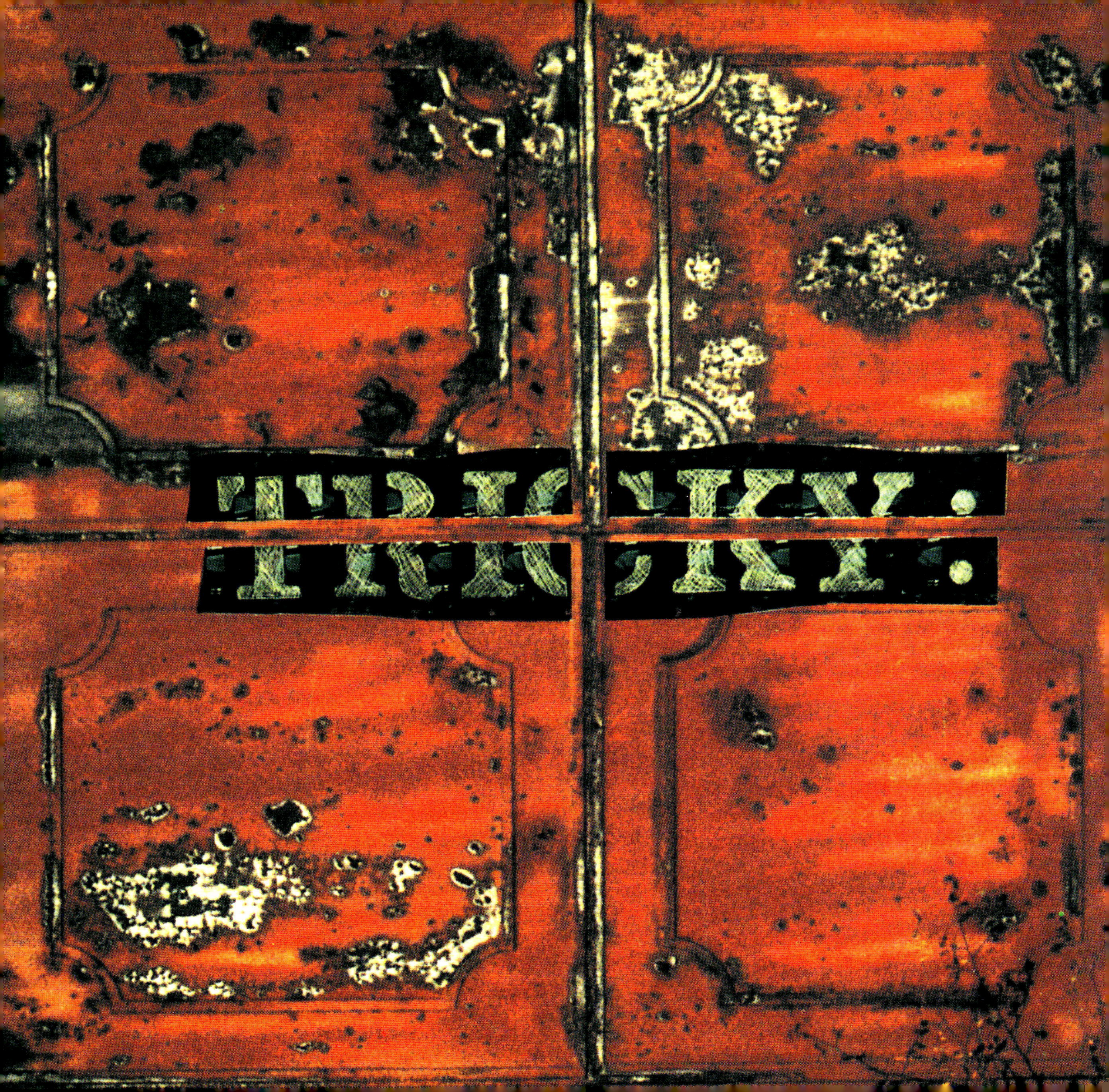
TRICKY:

Talvin Singh (left).
The Cranberries (right).

Artwork from the sleeve design of PM Dawn's *Of the Heart, of the Soul, and of the Cross: the Utopian Experience* (opposite).

other side of the 1990s party, distinctive enough to be given its own genre: trip-hop. Tricky emerged from Bristol, the sometime Massive Attack collaborator releasing his *Maxinquaye* debut in 1995, the murky, mesmerizing atmospheric he named after his mother who committed suicide when Tricky was four years old. Meanwhile, 1998 brought us yet more pioneering soundscapes in Talvin Singh, break-out artist of the so-called Asian Underground, a sometime classically-trained tabla player whose debut album, *OK*, won the Mercury Music Prize the next year. Over in Ireland, meanwhile, U2 looked up momentarily from their kitsch-pop 'Zoo TV' adventure to see a traditional, guitar-pop 'indie' band from Limerick, The Cranberries, sell 14.5 million albums throughout the 1990s in America alone after MTV's unexpected fixation on their re-released second single, the mellifluous 'Linger', back in 1993.

'Tease mi, tease mi, tease mi, tease mi bay-buh! (Eeow!)' trilled one of the biggest, greatest and most distinctive singles ever to emerge from Jamaica as the gloriously-titled Chaka Demus & Pliers became the first Jamaican act in history to score three consecutive top five hits in the UK; 1993's irresistibly chipper 'Tease Me', their cover of Curtis Mayfield's 'She Don't Let Nobody' and the Isley Brothers' 'Twist And Shout', the incorrigibly bootie-fixated dancehall doyens remaining, as far as we know, the only musical act in history to feature a man named after a tradesman's tool. (Apart from, as it happens, Pliers' brother, also a singer, called Spanner. And Shovell from M People.)

Island's Jamaican 90s also brought us Beenie Man's dancehall classic 'Blessed' in 1995; and conscious reggae returned with Luciano's profoundly moving 'It's Me Again Jah', even dancehall renegade Buju Banton substantially altering his colours with his groundbreaking *Til Shiloh*, with its lyrical shift from violence and discord to a new-found peace and redemption in the Rastafarian movement.

In the 90s, Island had its share of one-offs, 1997 seeing its first and only release from Morrissey, a life-long fanatic of the label who resurrected the Island 'Palm Tree' logo, obsolete since the 1970s, for his sixth solo album, *Maladjusted*. A Sparks, Roxy Music and Nico devotee, Morrissey's solo shows throughout the decade were prefaced with a quiver of Nico's 'Innocent And Vain' from her 1974 Island album *The End*, declaring that the song contained 'my youth in one piece of music'. Made in the wake of the fabled Smiths' court-case, *Maladjusted*, ultimately, was a creatively troubled affair, an album with alarmingly grey artwork, despite that burst of Island sun, featuring a photograph of Morrissey in a curious squat position inspiring him to observe, astutely, that he looked like 'a mushroom'.

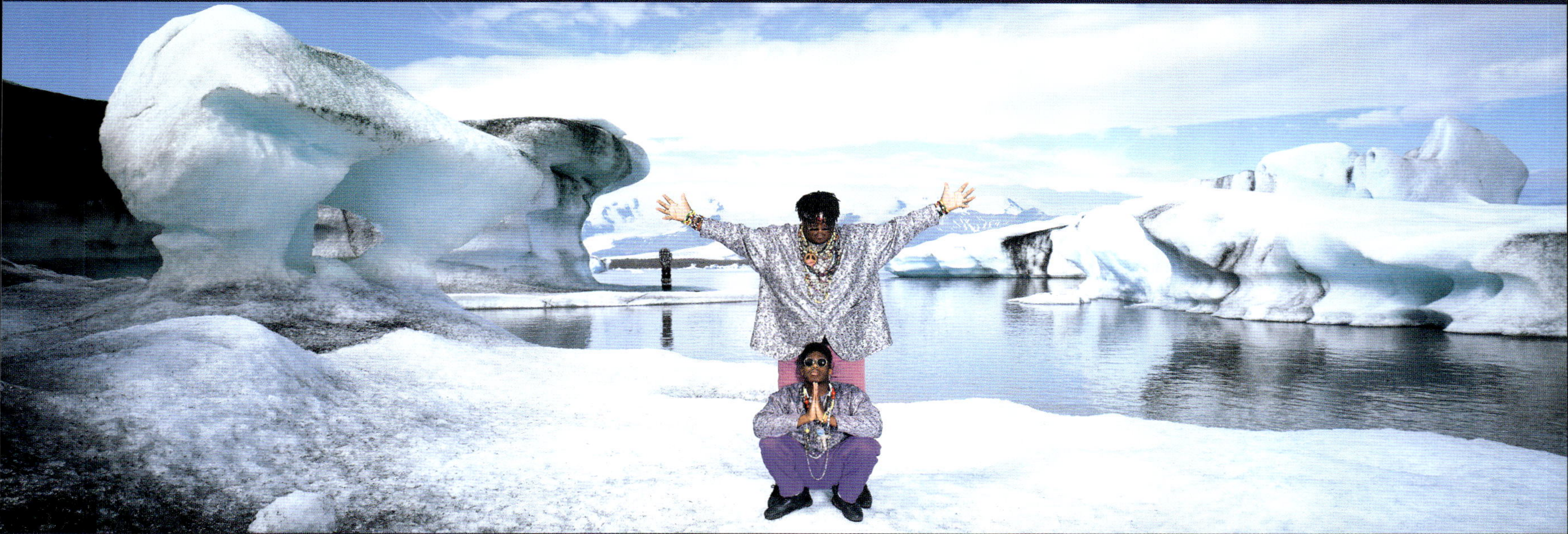

PJ HARVEY
STORIES FROM THE CITY, STORIES FROM THE SEA

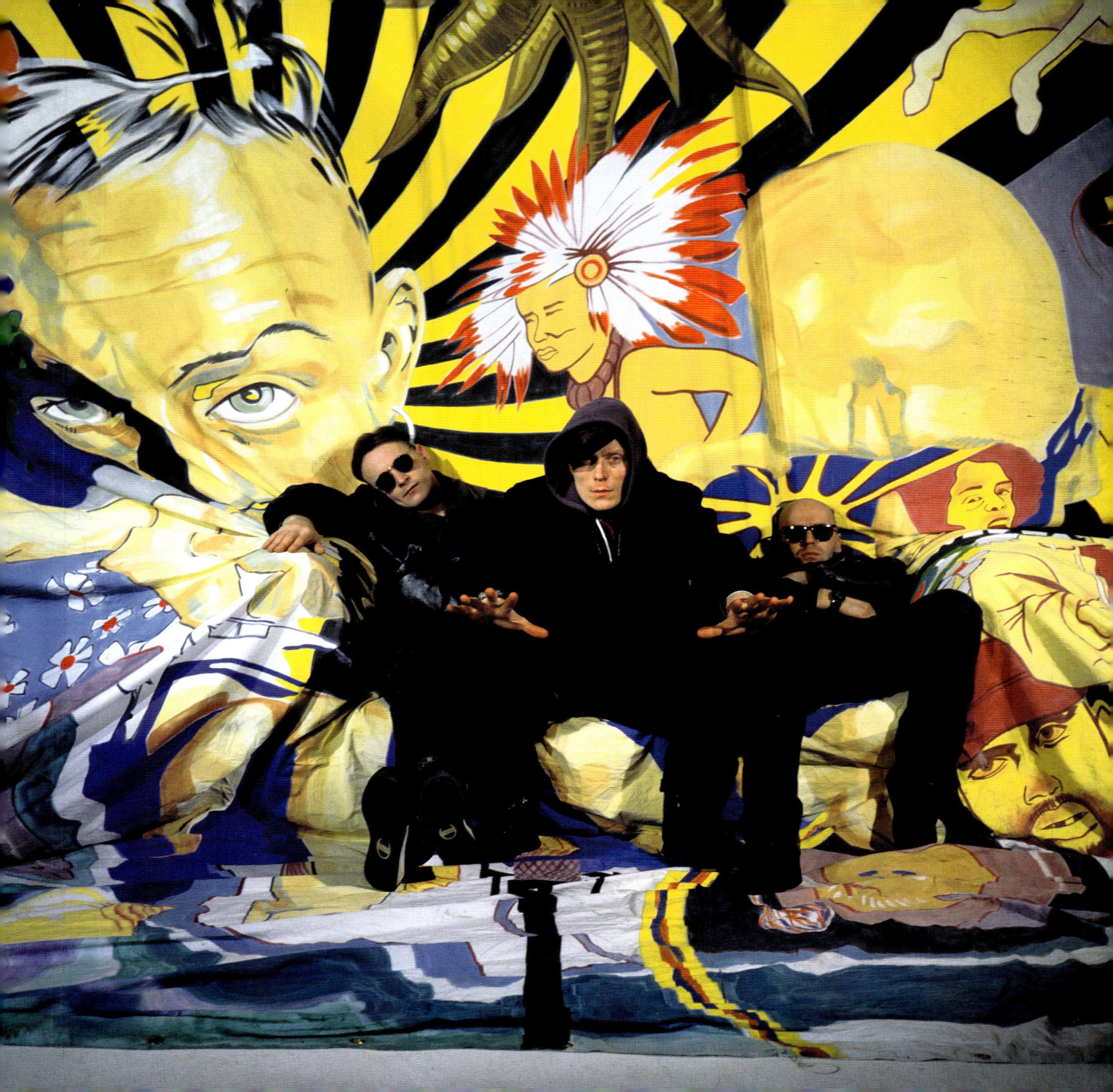

For all the dazzlingly eclectic sounds, visions and characters which illuminated Island like a moon-sized light-bulb throughout the 1990s, it took a shy, soft-spoken, tiny woman from Dorset to make, arguably, the most influential contribution of them all. An art-rock amalgam of blistering primal beats, alarmingly visceral lyrics and a compelling new version of beauty, PJ Harvey, 22-years-old as she released her *Dry* debut album on the Too Pure label in 1991. A move to Island, inspired by her life-long love of Tom Waits, gave us *Rid of Me* two years later, produced by Steve Albini, a Mercury-nominated art-rock blues-punk benchmark featuring furious guitars, a vocal howl the size of infinity and less a hold on female sexuality than a lyrical grip on a poetically poisonous barbed wire. The poster girl for zero-compromise, she dazzled and confounded through 1995's Mercury-nominated *To Bring You My Love*. Produced by Flood and John Parish, this million-selling terror-synth success was voted Album Of The Year across the worldwide critical spectrum. Simultaneously she became her very own art-rock construct, her live appearances increasingly flamboyant spectaculars featuring ball-gowns, pink cat-suits, glittering microphones, a broomstick and smeared make-up – like some demented vision, as she noted herself, of 'Joan Crawford on acid, my twisted sense of beauty.' Beyond the moody atmospherics of *Is This Desire?*, her 1998 tour de force and personal favourite, it would be the musically stark and vocally stunning *Stories From the City, Stories From the Sea*, released in October 2000, which saw her finally win the Mercury Music Prize, Island's fourth Mercury win since its inception eight years previously, official recognition of the label's position as the most creatively innovative of the 1990s. It would be September 11, 2001 when Polly heard of her win, while contemplating the view beyond her Washington DC hotel window of the newly-attacked Pentagon building. A brand new century had brought with it a brand new world.

'Celebrity,' announced Bono in a restaurant in Dublin sometime in the year 2000, 'is ugly. The thing about celebrity is, it belittles real life. Which is where actual heroism lies.'

The first decade of the twenty-first century will forever be synonymous with the invincible reign of Celebrity Culture: years when music was often viewed, more than heard, through the unforgiving, magnified lens of increasingly brutal tabloid gossip in the hyper-speed realm of the 24-hour global Media

(Previous spread, left) PJ Harvey's sixth album scooped the Mercury Prize in 2001; Polly accepted her award from a Washington hotel only yards from a still smoking Pentagon on 9.11. (Previous spread, right) Stereo MCs *Get Connected*.

PJ Harvey in repose (opposite, top).

The Modfather Paul Weller finally arrived at Island. (opposite, bottom).

Sugababes Mk II circa 2002 (left) – Mutya Buena, Keisha Buchanan and newcomer Heidi Range.

Sugababes Mk III circa 2006 (right) – Amelle Berrabah joins Heidi and 'Urbabe' Keisha.

From summer 2002 James Bourne, Charlie Simpson and Matt Willis of punk-pop teen sensations Busted (below) ruled the airwaves and broke many a teenage heart when they split at the height of their fame in January '05.

Age. If you were Paul Weller, there was surely only one thing for it. 'If you see me at a pub or bar,' he announced in 2000, 'it's pretty certain I'll be off my fucking bollocks.' This was Weller's decade as exuberant bon viveur, dues-paid elder statesman and caretaker of rock 'n' roll's most consistently fine-coiffed barnet. Arriving on Island in 2000, as his former label Go! Discs foundered, his fifth solo album, *Heliocentric* took the sometime frenetic teenage front-man into his 40s via profoundly affecting, emotionally searching guitar-rock; Nick Drake's sometime string arranger, Robert Kirby, was cleverly added to the general effect with a glimmering poignancy.

He would not make another record on Island for another eight years: *22 Dreams*, again for Island, was an exercise in creative audacity – flashes of cosmic jazz, piano ballads and a twist of folk-tinged tango – with chum Noel Gallagher on guitar, and vibes. The album was cited by many as the best solo record of Weller's career, his position in 2008 peerless as the nation's foremost 50-year-old invincible bar-fly in the world's most fabulous shoes.

Yet it would be the unpredictable youth who would dominate the decade for Island, the early 2000s seeing a pop world fracture along two opposing lines; invincible sheen-pop selling in multi-millions, from Britney to Kylie to Westlife, jousting alongside spiky, avant-garde art-rock guitar bands from The Strokes to The White Stripes to The Libertines. Island went along with neither, bringing us instead the cool-pop phenomenon of the Sugababes (picked up from London Records) whose second album, *Angels With Dirty Faces*, featured the pulsing electro-pop club classic 'Freak Like Me' and announced the 'Babes, alongside the Xenomania production house, as a bona-fide new force: unassailable pop-lab alchemists creating some of the most hypnotic, glittering and salaciously perverse class-pop singles of the decade.

Youthful pop, suddenly, was in renaissance, Island also bringing us Busted and McFly, the school kids' favourites, pioneers of the guitar-pop boy-band who — heck! — wrote their own music and everything, both bands finding their ferocious party-hard pogo-punk din consistently mistaken for parrot-haired US 'proper' punks, Green Day.

If the pop kids were ecstatic, the students were all of a quiver as an increasingly frenetic 21st Century was sonically assuaged by the sound of the sensitive man, on piano, illuminating the long-locked secret corridors of the vulnerable male soul. Coldplay, Snow Patrol and Island's own Keane wrapped their searching, euphoric, epic melancholia all around the decade like a planet-sized cashmere comfort blanket as these hitherto whimsical bands became the arena-tour giants of the era. Keane, three childhood friends from Hastings, saw their 2004 debut album, *Hopes And Fears*, sell 5 million copies worldwide led by 'Somewhere Only We Know', heralding in front-man Tom Chaplin a gifted vocalist of celestial dimensions.

Stratospheric fame, success and expectation would take their toll on these mellow-mannered romantics, seeing Chaplin endure a spell in rehab in 2006 as second album, *Under the Iron Sea*, documented personal inter-band tensions. Yet in 2008 they emerged intact to release their kaleidoscopic 80s-tinged optimism opus *Perfect Symmetry*, described by their novelist friend Brett Easton Ellis, a fellow shadowy-world forager, as 'a masterpiece'. (Keane also became innovators of the latest technology, in 2006 releasing a limited edition of 'Nothing In My Way', their third single taken from *Under The Iron Sea*, on a groundbreaking new format for a singles release, the USB memory stick.)

Through the mid- to late 2000s, intriguingly diverse new artists continued to emerge on Island; The Feeling, from Sussex, pioneers of the easy-listening, power-pop resurgence; Scott Matthews, whose exquisite vocals and acoustic reveries drew comparisons with Jeff Buckley; The Fratellis, from Glasgow, part of the post-Libertines frenetic guitar-pop uprising who gave us the chipper-rock classic 'Chelsea Dagger' with its ubiquitous terrace-chant refrain "Derer-eh! Derer-uh!"; DJ Shadow, whose award-winning instrumental hip-hop even included a Keane re-mix; Tom Vek's acclaimed release of the *We Have Sound* album, raw garage rock, driven by subtle electronic touches and a backbone of funk; Gabriella Cilmi, the teenage Australian grit-rock vocalist whose 2008 debut album, *Lessons to Be Learned*, won her six Australian ARIA Awards. Meanwhile, the outright fabulous Mika, the Beirut-born, London-based, classically-trained, operatic kitsch-pop showman, brought us his aptly-titled debut album *Life In Cartoon Motion*, announcing 'pop is about beauty, style and class' while wearing preposterous humbug pantaloons, as a proper pop star must.

As the first decade of the twenty-first century hit its stride, the

The Fratellis *Costello Music* cigarette cards. Island Records specially commissioned artist Sam Hadley to create a series of images in the style of 50's pin-up art for the release of the band's million selling debut album, *Costello Music*, with the three girls becoming the centre piece for the entire campaign. The set of illustrations morphed into a number of different images and sat nicely with the spiky pop rock of The Fratellis.

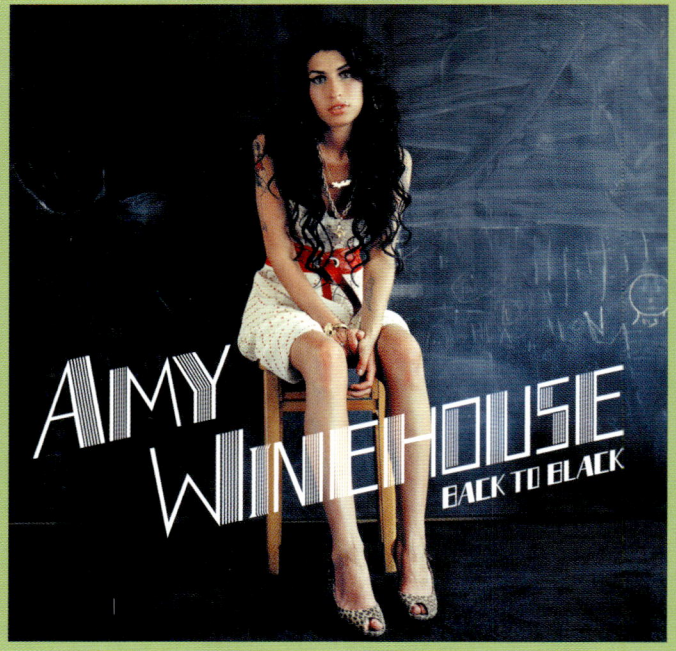

vaunted rise of the feminine principle was made manifest in popular music. Idiosyncratic pop now belonged to Lily Allen, Adele, Kate Nash, Duffy, the vocal phenomenon of Leona Lewis and – before any of them – the staggering force of nature we know as Amy Winehouse.

A London-born music obsessive versed in jazz, soul and hip-hop, in 2003 the then-glossy-haired ex-pupil of the Brits School of Performing Arts brought us her debut album *Frank*, an intriguing melange of jazz-soul beats, incorrigible rude-girl lyrics and a striking vocal inflection meandering through the grooves between Etta James and Erykah Badu. She was, already, a volatile personality, prone to food disorders, self-harm and a monumental weed habit. But by the time she got to New York in early 2006 to meet DJ, beat-smith and producer Mark Ronson, post break-up with her on-off boyfriend Blake Fielder-Civil, she was physically unrecognisable; heavily tattooed, toweringly bee-hived and considerably lighter, prone to minimal eating and maximum black-out boozing. She was also at her creative zenith, arriving at Ronson's studio with a selection of newly-discovered favourite records, mostly the Shangri La's as well as assorted Phil Spector classics. 'Those records blew me away,' remembered Mark Ronson in a bar in New York in January 2007. 'They were epic, beautiful, heartbreaking. She left the studio, I wrote the little piano riff from 'Back To Black', played a little kick-drum tambourine and that was all I really had. When she came back the next day I was kind of cringing, thinking, "If she doesn't like this, she's going back to England tomorrow and that'll be the end of it." And she said, "That's it. That's what I want my record to sound like." And then she wrote *Back To Black*.'

Back To Black, the album, released in October 2006, would be the decade's retro-soul masterpiece, steeped in the sounds of the 50s and 60s doo-wop era and yet unmistakably contemporary in its brutal emotional honesty and downright scandalous wit, a goth-black, poetic expose of a splintering broken heart, voice as emotive as a languid trumpet searching for answers through the too-late wisdoms of pain, regret and self-recrimination. *Back to Black* not only saw Amy realise her potential as the most naturally gifted vocalist of her generation but also as a lyrical force, the words filthy and illegal, full of dicks and drugs – and incomparably funny, 'Me And Mr Jones' housing, surely, the funniest one-liner of the modern lyrical age: 'What kind of…fuckery is this?' 'Love Is a Losing Game', meanwhile, is simply a timeless soul classic, a song Ronson played to his then-protégé Daniel Merriweather who

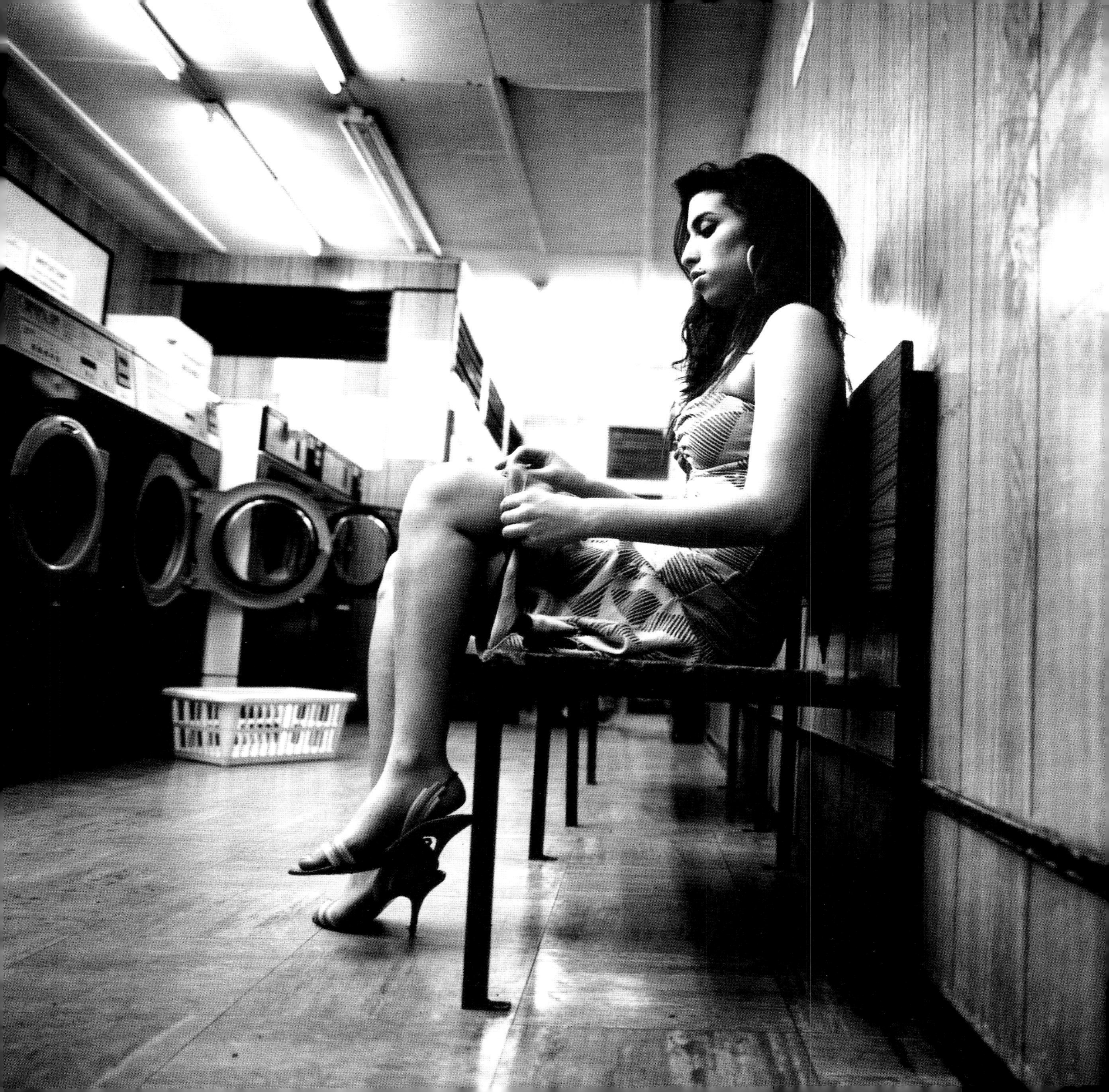

From Wellington in New Zealand, Ladyhawke (top left) cleverly interweaves electro-pop into her soft-rock sounds; but don't be deceived: the hooks may recall Fleetwood Mac, but the attitude is pure Chrissie Hynde.

Intelligent and entertaining, the classically-trained Northampton-born pop singer VV Brown (top right) defines her Spectorish sound as 'Indie-doowop, musical mashed potatoes.'

The Swedish singer Robyn (bottom right), who started out as something of a Scandinavian child-star, recalls Madonna when she was still a tough chick from the East Village. Like Madonna, Robyn already has her own record label, a vehicle for her ballistic electro-hyperpop, funny, hip, and sexually frank all at the same time.

From Melbourne in Australia, the home of her Italian parents, Gabriella Cilmi's (bottom left) huskily mature voice produced a sassy debut, Lessons To Be Learned, that soars those vocals into the stratosphere. The record earned her a multitude of awards in her native country. And she is still only 17.

immediately declared it, 'one of the best songs I've ever heard.' Back in 2007, Mark Ronson described Amy Winehouse, beyond her talent, as 'loud, brash, funny as shit, a true, modern-day pop star,' and mere weeks from then watched, like the rest of us, as she began her catastrophically true, modern-day trial through the vale of contemporary celebrity; her marriage to Blake Fielder-Civil, the sudden narcotic dependence, the overdoses, the fights, the rehab she said she would never go to, the paparazzi who manned her Camden doorway 24 hours a day as *Back To Black* became bigger and blacker, winning five Grammy Awards in February 2008. Spending time with Amy in the January of 2007, before the marriage, the drugs and the cataclysmic meltdown, was both hilarious and heartbreaking. She turned up to a photo shoot with her bare arm in criss-crossed shreds claiming she'd fallen over whilst drunk (it looked like frenzied self-harm), a bawdy personality by day who'd introduce herself on stage at night by hitching up her shimmering cocktail frock and saying, 'Allo, I'm Ad Rock from The Beastie Boys.' She knew she was an outlaw but she was no role model for anyone. 'I'm a spokesperson,' she announced, defiantly, 'for people who don't give a fuck, yeah?' Then 23 years old, she was about to be acknowledged as the most creatively exhilarating international female singing star in the world today – and also the most troubled. Back then, though, she had a vision of what she'd like from all this, in the end. 'I'd like to be… great,' she eventually decided. 'My actual goal, on paper, is to do another two albums. Do a bunch of EPs. Bunch of covers EPs. Go and have 20 kids. And then, when I'm about 60, The Las Vegas Tour. Can't wait! I'll have Elton's hair, yeah, like at his 50th birthday! And live at the top of some casino and just come down for the show every night and they wheel me on stage. It'll be great. And my kids will all be like, "Mum, you're so embarrassing." I can't wait!'

Exactly two spectacularly chaotic years later in January 2009, Amy Winehouse was to be found finally beginning work on her globally-anticipated third album, in St Lucia in the Caribbean. Not precisely where Chris Blackwell began his Island adventure, under the sun, exactly fifty years ago in Jamaica. But not that far off either.

Keep On Running | 213

KEANE
HOPES AND FEARS

MIKA

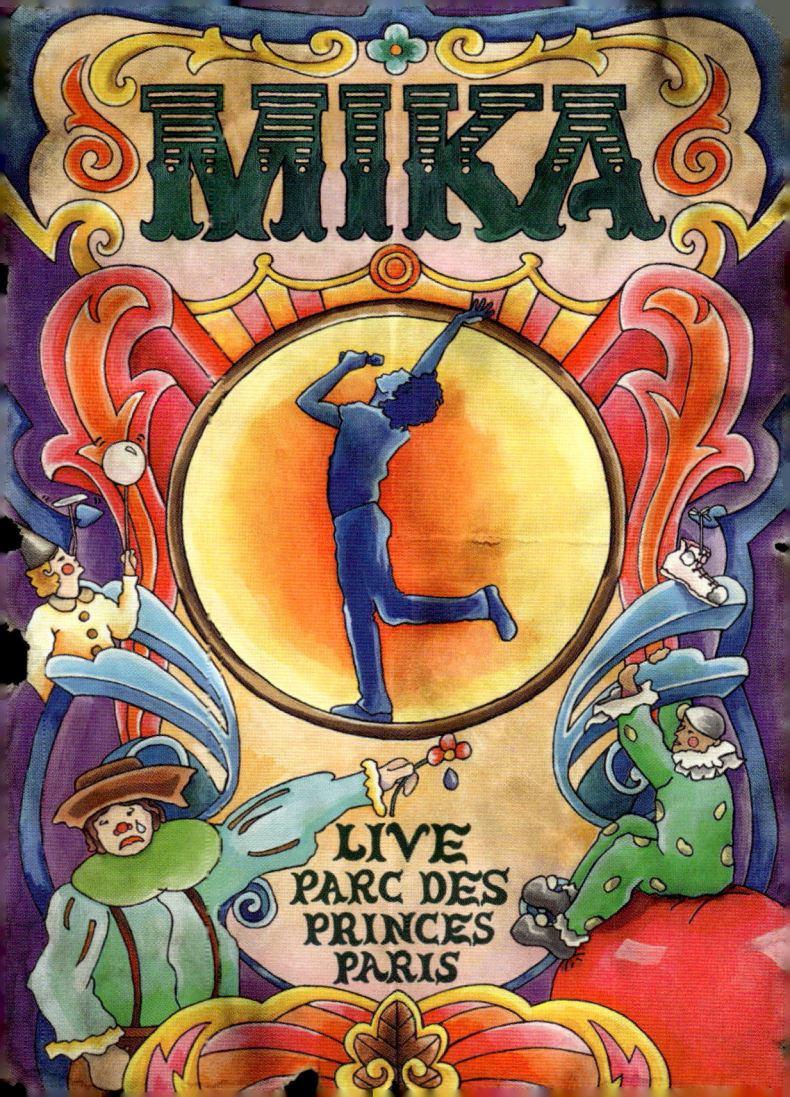

LIVE PARC DES PRINCES PARIS

PAUL WELLER 22 DREAMS

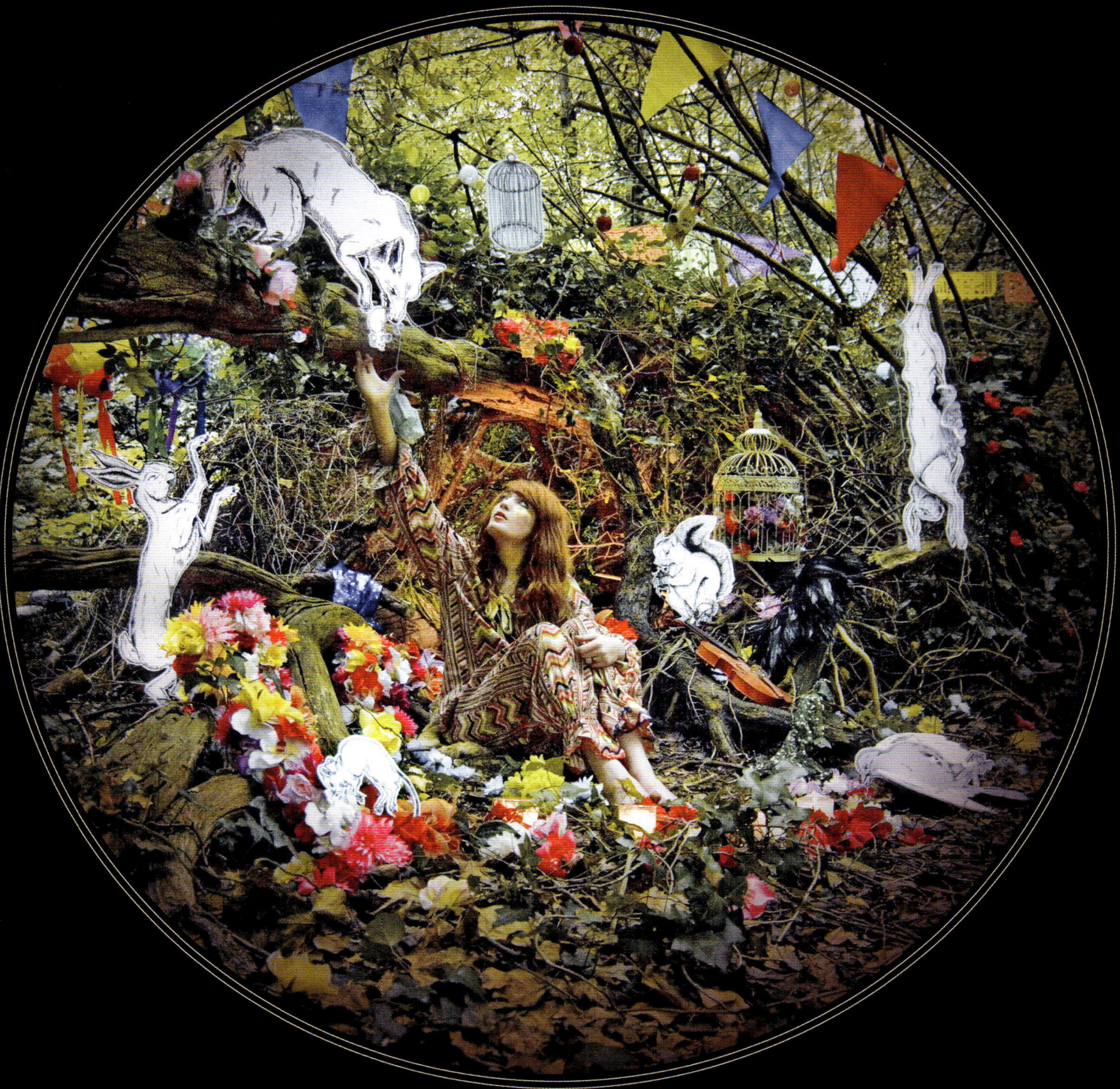

WE HAVE SOUND

Keep On Running | 219

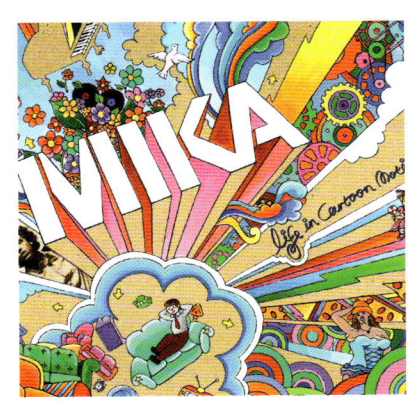

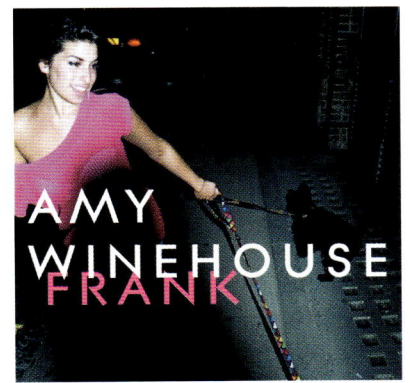

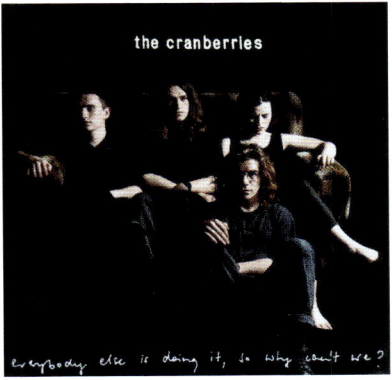

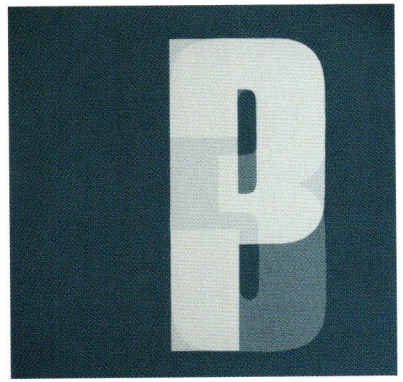

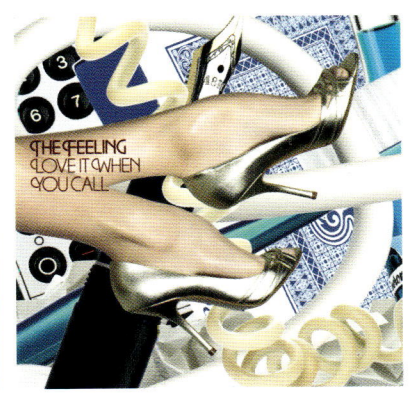

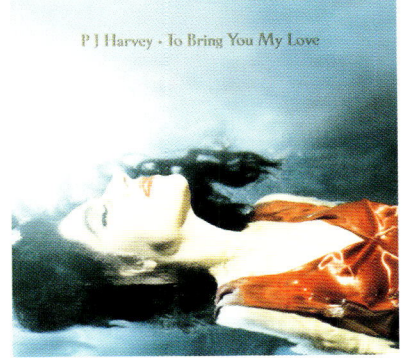

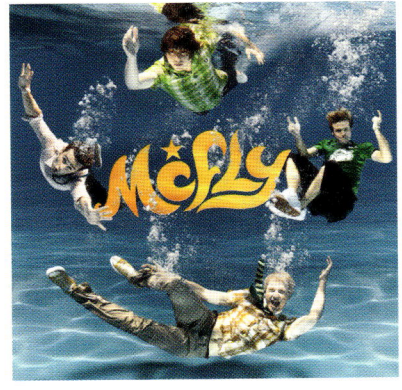

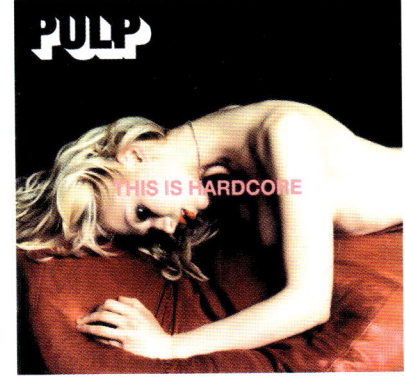

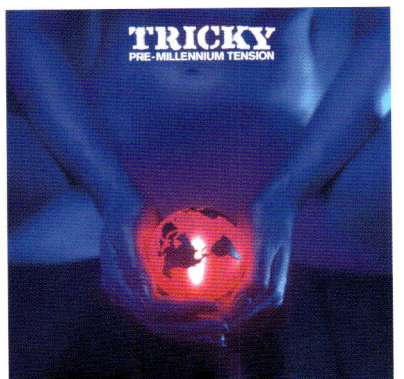

Joe Boyd is a record and film producer. Born in Boston in 1942, he graduated from Harvard in 1964. After university, he worked as a production and tour manager in Europe where he travelled with Muddy Waters, Coleman Hawkins, Stan Getz and others; and at Newport where he supervised Bob Dylan's electric debut. In 1966, he opened UFO, London's psychedelic ballroom. His first record production was four tracks by 'Eric Clapton and the Powerhouse' for Elektra in 1966. He went on to produce Pink Floyd, Nick Drake, The Incredible String Band, Fairport Convention, Sandy Denny, Richard & Linda Thompson, Maria Muldaur, Toots and the Maytals, REM, Kate & Anna McGarrigle, 10,000 Maniacs, Billy Bragg, Cubanismo, Taj Mahal and many others. As head of music for Warner Brothers Films, he organized the scoring of *Deliverance*, *Clockwork Orange* and *McCabe and Mrs Miller* and made *Jimi Hendrix*, a feature-length documentary. He later went into partnership with Don Simpson to develop film projects. He helped set up Lorne Michaels' Broadway Pictures in 1979, then started Hannibal Records, which he ran for 20 years. In 1988, he was Executive Producer of the feature film *Scandal*. He resides in London.

Lloyd Bradley is the author of several books, including the celebrated *Bass Culture: When Reggae was King*, the definitive history of the music. Associate producer on the BBC television series *Reggae: the Story of Jamaican Music*, he is a regular writer for *MOJO*. A classically trained chef, Lloyd Bradley is the former owner of the Dark Star sound system.

Robin Denselow is a TV and newspaper correspondent, producer and journalist who specialises in both politics and music. He has spent most of his career working for the BBC, travelling extensively in Africa and the Middle East. At the same time he has worked as a music writer for *The Guardian*, covering African and world music styles, and interviewing artists from Bob Marley to Fela Kuti. He is the author of *When The Music's Over, The Story of Political Pop*.

Vivien Goldman is a writer, broadcaster, educator and post-punk musician. As an Adjunct Professor at New York University's Clive Davis Dept. of Recorded Music she has created and taught courses on Punk, Reggae and Island Records. Three of her five books are Island-related, including two on Bob Marley and the Wailers, most recently *The Book of Exodus: the Making and Meaning of the Album of the Century*; *Indiscreet*, on Kid Creole and the Coconuts and *Pearl's Delicious Jamaican Dishes*, featuring the cuisine of Chris Blackwell's Jamaican chef, Pearl Bell. Island artists she has directed documentary and video for include Eric B and Rakim with 'I Ain't No Joke,' Chakademus & Pliers' 'Murder She Wrote' and *The Reggae Philharmonic Orchestra Go To Jamaica*. Virtually her first job was as PR for Island's reggae acts in the early 1970s.

Born in San Francisco but long resident in London, **David Katz** is author of *People Funny Boy: The Genius of Lee 'Scratch' Perry* and *Solid Foundation: An Oral History of Reggae*. His writing and photographs have appeared in many international periodicals and music books, and he has co-ordinated and annotated over 100 retrospective collections of Jamaican music. He has also co-hosted reggae radio programmes on three continents, released original records in the UK and France, and contributed to various radio and television documentaries and feature films, while his Dub Me Always deejay nights continue to be a regular feature of London's musical landscape.

Sean O'Hagan began writing for NME in the mid 1980s. He has worked for *The Guardian*, *The Times* and for various magazines. He currently works as a feature writer for *The Observer* and was named Interviewer of the Year in the 2003 Press Awards. He is also writing a memoir for Bloomsbury.

Sylvia Patterson is a freelance journalist who began work for *Smash Hits* pop gazette in 1986 and has been writing about pop ever since for publications such as *NME*, *Interview*, *The Guardian*, *The Word*, *The Sunday Times* and *Q*. She shares the same birthday as Gary Numan and Richard out of Living in a Box (a cardboard box).

Paul Morley wrote for the *New Musical Express* between 1977 and 1983 and formed Zang Truu/m Tum/b with Trevor Horn and Jill Sinclair in 1983. He currently writes about music and other matters for the *Sunday Telegraph* and *Arena Homme Plus*, is critic at large for *The Observer Music Magazine* and is a regular contributor to BBC 2's *Newsnight Review*. He has written books about suicide, Joy Division, the interview and Kylie Minogue. In 2009 he made a documentary series for Radio 2 about the history of the record label and studied composition at the Royal Academy of Music for his own state of mind and BBC 4.

Chris Salewicz has documented popular culture for over three decades, in print, on television and on radio. A features writer with the *NME* from 1974 to 1981, his writing, on a wide variety of subjects, has subsequently appeared in *The Sunday Times*, *The Independent*, *The Daily Telegraph*, London's *Evening Standard*, *Conde Nast Traveller*, *Q*, *MOJO*, *The Face*, *Time Out* and many other British newspapers and magazines, as well as countless publications worldwide. He is the author of more than a dozen books, including *Songs of Freedom*, the authorized biography of Bob Marley, the acclaimed *Rude Boy: Once Upon a Time in Jamaica*, and the best-selling *Redemption Song: the Definitive Biography of Joe Strummer*.

Jon Savage is the author of *England's Dreaming: Sex Pistols and Punk Rock* and *Teenage: The Creation of Youth, 1875 - 1945*. He has written sleeve-notes for Wire, St. Etienne and the Pet Shop Boys, among others, and his compilations include: Meridian 1970 (Heavenly/EMI 2005); Queer Noises: From the Closest to the Charts 1961 - 1976 (Trikont 2006); and Dreams Come True: Classic Electro 1982-87 (Domino 2008). His new book *The England's Dreaming Tapes* will be published in June 2009.

Stylorouge is an internationally renowned London-based creative consultancy specializing in the music and leisure industries founded in 1981 by Rob O'Connor. They have created memorable sleeve designs for Paul McCartney, Blur, Tears For Fears, Squeeze, Maxi Priest, Simple Minds, George Michael, Rolling Stones, Morrissey, and David Bowie. Work for the film industry includes poster campaigns for HBO in New York and their original poster for Danny Boyle's film *Trainspotting* which won them huge acclaim. Their collaboration with Island includes covers for Soul II Soul, Alexei Sayle, The Comic Strip, 1Giant Leap and Bob Marley.

Richard Williams took a break from a career in journalism to work for Island Records from 1973 to 1976, as head of A&R. Since then he has been on the staff of *Time Out*, *Melody Maker*, *The Times*, *The Independent* and, since 1995, *The Guardian*, where he is the chief sports writer.

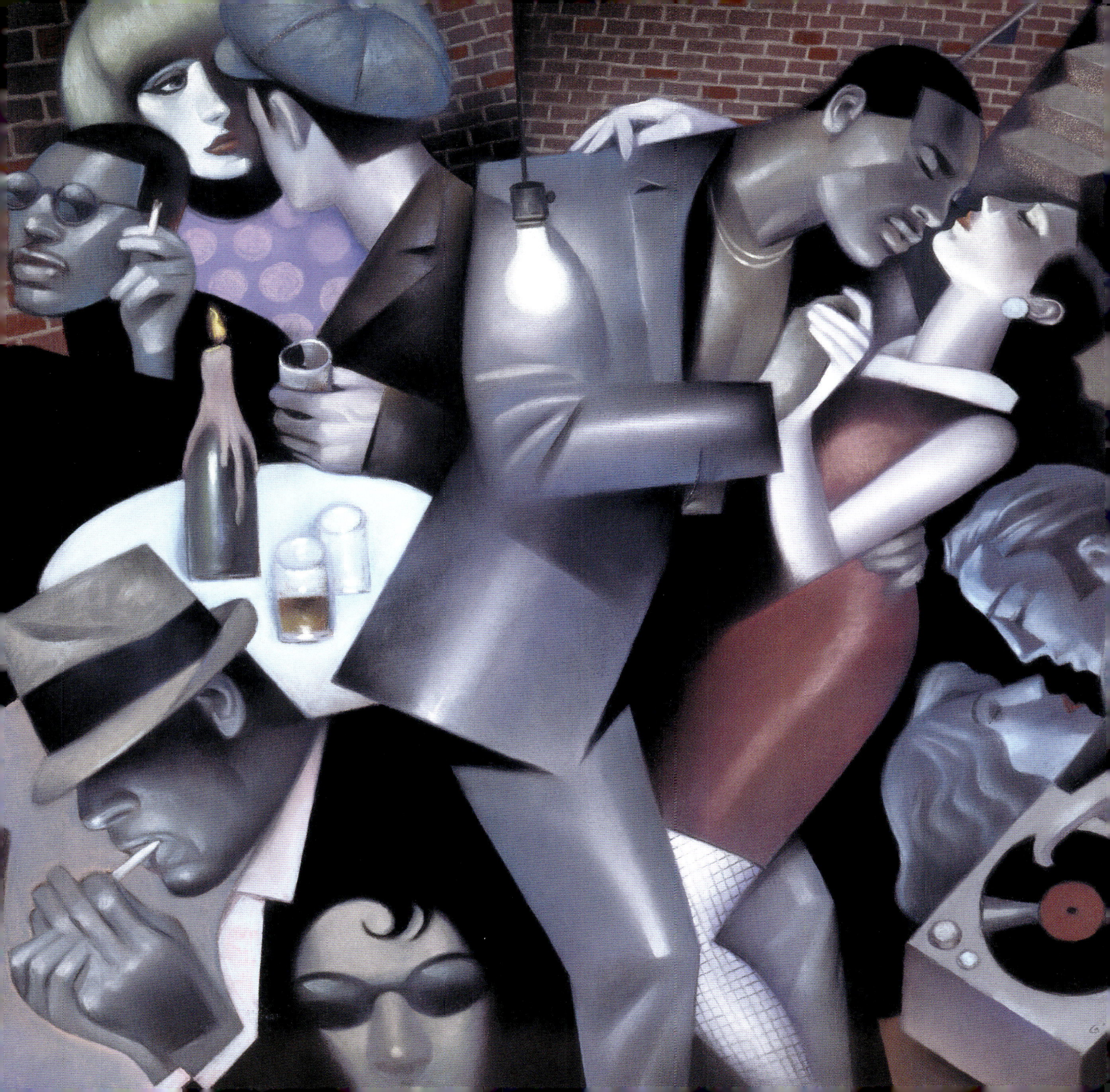

Book Credits

This book is produced by The Island Trading Company Ltd:

Suzette Newman

Adrian Boot

Edited by: Chris Salewicz

Contributing writers: Richard Williams, Jon Savage, Vivien Goldman, Lloyd Bradley, Sean O'Hagan, Robin Denselow, Paul Morley, Joe Boyd, David Katz, Sylvia Patterson and Chris Salewicz

Copy editor: Tadzio Koelb

Designed by: Stylorouge

Research & Production: Mark Painter

Co-ordinator: Cassie Wuta-Ofei

Archive Anorak: Ramus

Production: Christine Atkins - Universal

Special thanks to:

Tony Wright for his art and inspiration…always

Rob O'Connor & Mikkel Lundsager Hansen and all at Stylorouge, Jon Turner, Christine Atkins and Ted Cummings at Island Records.

Jean-Paul Goude for his Grace Jones layouts

Gered Mankowitz, Brian Cooke and James Grashow

All at Kensington Park Road who contributed tirelessly

To Rob Partridge who checked out early but inspired us all

Thank you to all the art directors, designers, photographers and artists who helped create all the sleeves in this book: especially Tim Clark, Stephanie Nash, Bruno Tilley, Cally Callomon plus too many more to mention.

Text copyright © The Island Trading Company Ltd.

Image and illustration copyrights as per photographic and illustration credit list.

Photo Credits:

All efforts have been made to try and contact all the copyright holders of all the photographs contained in this book. In certain cases the identity of the photographer was unknown or, when it was known, the photographer was uncontactable. We would appreciate any future credit and contact details for the few photographs that remain a mystery so that we may be able to rectify the situation in future editions. Please contact the publisher if you can help.

© Peter Ashworth: pages 138L, 148

© Johnny Black / www.urbanimage.tv: pages 92TL, 99

© Tim Blake: page 172

© Adrian Boot / www.urbanimage.tv: pages 10B, 15L, 91, 92BL, 92R, 95, 98, 114T, 114B, 126L, 126M, 127, 128, 135B, 156TL, 158TL, 171, 174, 175, 176, 182-183

© Adam Broomberg & Oliver Charnin: page 213

© Jake Chessum: pages 210L, 211

© Brian Cooke: pages 29, 38-39, 49, 64

© Corrine Day: page 207TL

© Nathalie Delon: pages 5, 6

© Matthew Donaldson: page 169

© Steve Double: pages 200BR, 205

© Andy Earl: page 203

© Julian Edelstein: page 162T

© Fifty-Six Hope Road Music Ltd. / Adrian Boot: pages 96T, 142, 143, 145

© Jean-Paul Goude: pages 121, 122, 123, 124, 125

© Karl Grant: page 170

© Sam Hadley: page 209

© Alice Hawkins: page 212TL

© Katie Kaars: page 212BL

© Alex Lake: page 212TR

© P. Lerichomme: page 135TL

© Gered Mankowitz: pages 15R, 19T, 20, 42, 76B

© Maria Mochnacz: page 139

© Keith Morris: pages 44, 58

© Ellis Parrinder: page 207B

© Jean-Paul Pietrus: page 207TR

© Valerie Phillips: pages 138R, 206T

© Guiseppe Pino: page 136

© Dickie Polak: page 28

© Mike Prior: page 96B

© Samantha Rapp: page 212RB

© Lawrence Watson: page 206B

© Nick White: page 191

© U2 Limited (Anton Corbijn): pages 156TR, 158M, 158TR, 159T, 159B

Island Records Archive: pages 47, 50TR, 63, 96M, 96B, 104, 130, 135TR, 147, 162B, 185, 198T, 202L, 202R,

Joe Boyd Collection: page 55

Illustration and Artwork Credits

Island Records Archive: pages 8; 18, 100, 160, 178, 187

Neville Garrick: page 144

Stephanie Nash: pages 192, 193, 195

Paul 'Groucho' Smykle: page 111

Tony Wright: pages 2, 11, 34, 51, 69, 77, 80, 81, 82, 97, 102, 103, 105, 106, 107, 108, 109, 113, 141, 177

Paul Waring: page 101

Gary Kelley: page 221

Sam Hadley: page 209

Da Wack/Mika/Richard Hogg: page 215

Tom Beard: page 217

Map

A Voyage to the Islands Madera, Barbados, Nieves, S. Christophers and Jamaica, with the Natural History of the Herbs and Trees, Four-footed Beasts, Fishes … London: by Sir Hans Sloane (1660–1753) © The LuEsther T. Mertz Library of The New York Botanical Garden, Bronx, New York.

Front cover credits.

© Adrian Boot / www.urbanimage.tv (Grace Jones, Tom Waits)

© Fifty-Six Hope Road Music Ltd. / Adrian Boot (Bob Marley)

© Ross Halfin (Amy Winehouse)

© U2 Limited (Andrew Macpherson)(U2)

Island Records Archive (Cat Stevens, Brian Ferry, Nick Drake)

Distributed by: PGUK – Stephen Ellcock

℗ & © 2009 Universal-Island Records & The Island Trading Co. Ltd. All rights reserved. No part of this publication may be reproduced, stored in a retrieval system, or transmitted, in any form or by any means, electronic, mechanical, photocopying, recording or otherwise, without the prior permission of both the copyright owners and the above publishers. The right of the copyright holders to be identified as the authors of this work has been asserted in accordance with the Copyright, Designs and Patents act 1988.

ISBN: 978-0-9561914-0-3

First published in Great Britain in 2009 by Universal-Island Records & The Island Trading Company Ltd.

www.islandrecords.co.uk

THIS BOOK IS DEDICATED TO THE MEMORY OF THOSE WHO WERE PART OF THE ISLAND FAMILY, ARTISTS AND STAFF, WHOSE COLLECTIVE SPIRIT LIVES ON